CHEAP AMUSEMENTS

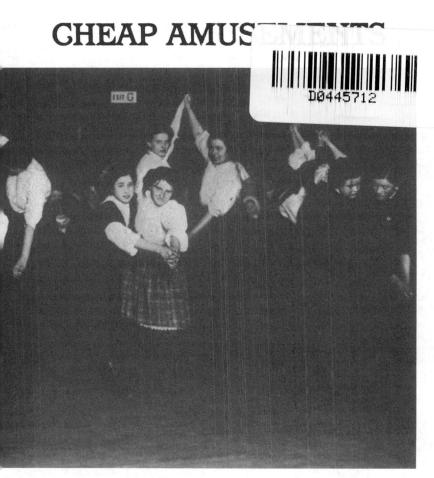

LEISURE IN TURN-OF-THE-CENTURY NEW YORK

KATHY PEISS

 TEMPLE UNIVERSITY PRESS
PHILADELPHIA

Temple University Press, Philadelphia 19122
© 1986 by Temple University. All rights reserved
Published 1986
Printed in the United States of America

This publication has been supported by the National
Endowment for the Humanities, a federal agency which
supports the study of such fields as history, philosophy,
literature, and languages.

ACKNOWLEDGMENTS:

Jacket: International Museum of Photography at George Eastman House

Frontispiece: U.S. History, Local History & Genealogy Division, The New York
Public Library, Astor, Lenox and Tilden Foundations

Grateful acknowledgment is made for permission to reprint "Dance Madness: New
York City Dance Halls and Working Class Sexuality, 1900–1920," an earlier version
of Chapter 4, which was printed in *Life and Labor: Dimensions of American
Working-Class History,* edited by Charles Stephenson and Robert Asher by
permission of the State University of New York Press. © 1985 by State University of
New York.

Library of Congress Cataloging-in-Publication Data

Peiss, Kathy Lee.
    Cheap amusements.

    Bibliography: p.
    Includes index.
    1. New York (N.Y.)—Social life and customs.
2. Amusements—New York (N.Y.)—History.
3. Women—New York (N.Y.)—History.
I. Title.
F124.P38   1985   974.7'1041   85-14783
ISBN 0-87722-389-0 (cloth : alk. paper)--
ISBN 0-87722-500-1 (pbk. : alk.paper)
ISBN 13: 978-0-87722-500-3

CHEAP AMUSEMENTS

WORKING WOMEN AND

FOR MY MOTHER AND FATHER, WITH LOVE

CONTENTS

ACKNOWLEDGMENTS

Anyone who writes about the history of New York City feels a kinship with the immigrant at Ellis Island, faced with a bewildering array of information, impressions, and leads, grateful for the help of colleagues, friends and passers-by. It is a pleasure to thank those who have aided me in the long project of researching, writing and producing this book.

My oldest debt is to Mari Jo Buhle, who guided this research as a dissertation; the conceptualization of the book, its organization and prose have benefited immeasurably from her careful readings of drafts and meaningful suggestions, while her friendship and belief in my work have sustained me for a number of years. I am obliged as well to another graduate school mentor, Howard Chudacoff, for his useful questions, intelligent criticisms, and unwavering support. Susan Porter Benson and Roy Rosenzweig read this manuscript in painstaking detail, and incalculably helped me to chart revisions. I am very grateful to Linda Shopes, for her insightful advice on several chapters; Judith Gerson, who sharpened my thinking about gender; David Green, who thoughtfully commented on many drafts; and Robert Earickson, for his help on countless details. These friends have also suffered through this work with me at various times, and offered their comradeship and good humor in what has often been a lonely task.

My work has benefited significantly from discussions with various scholars at different conferences and seminars; while our meetings have often been brief, they have given me much to ponder. Lewis Erenberg, Stephen Hardy, Daniel Horowitz, Dale Light, and Priscilla Murolo in particular made very helpful comments on various parts of this work. Lois Banner and her NEH Summer Seminar for

College Teachers in 1984 offered many useful suggestions, as did participants in my women's history study group, JoAnn Argersinger, Toby Ditz, Elizabeth Ermarth, Jenny Jochens, Marylynn Salmon, Linda Shopes, and Karen Whitman.

I could not have undertaken this project without the superb collections of the New York Public Library. The staff of the Rare Books and Manuscript Division, especially Richard Salvato, gave me creative advice on sources and extensive help in a project whose boundaries were broadly defined. I am particularly grateful to William Joyce and Robert Giroux for granting me permission to examine the papers of the National Board of Review of Motion Pictures. The New York Public Library's staff in the Local History and Genealogy Division, and the Theater and Dance Collections at the Lincoln Center Library of the Performing Arts were unfailingly helpful. I am also indebted to librarians and archivists at the following libraries: Tamiment Institute Library, New York University; the Rare Book and Manuscript Library, Columbia University; the Archives of the National Board of the Young Women's Christian Association of the U.S.A.; Laura Parsons Pratt Research Center of the YWCA of the City of New York; U.S. National Archives; City University of New York; Brown University; and University of Maryland Baltimore County. At UMBC, Tom Beck gave me expert help in finding photographs, and Cartographic Services skillfully and quickly drew the maps.

I have been fortunate to receive several research grants which allowed me time for uninterrupted work. A National Endowment for the Humanities Summer Stipend, Woodrow Wilson Foundation Predoctoral Fellowship in Women's Studies, and two University of Maryland Baltimore County Summer Faculty Fellowships have given me much needed support. My colleagues in the American Studies Department and the Dean of the Faculty at UMBC graciously gave me released time in order to complete the book.

The professionalism and enthusiasm of the staff at Temple University Press have enhanced the process of turning the manuscript into a book. I have been most fortunate to work with Janet Francendese, an editor whose infectious cheer and clear-headed advice have brought me out of writer's doldrums on several occasions. I am obliged as well to Candice Hawley, the production editor, and the many individuals who contributed to the production and distribution of the book.

Finally, thanks go to my parents, Clarence and Evelyn Peiss, whose wit, curiosity and passion for knowledge have irresistibly marked their daughter's life and work. This book is dedicated to them.

CHEAP AMUSEMENTS

INTRODUCTION

Just now her search is translated very lightly and gaily into the demand for "a good time" and a keen interest in the other sex.[1]

I was a lively girl, a devil, I was healthy, young and all that, and they used to say I was very pretty also, and I was all over, you know, I wasn't sleeping like other girls.[2]

This book is a study of young working women's culture in turn-of-the-century New York City—the customs, values, public styles, and ritualized interactions—expressed in leisure time. Wandering through the dance halls, streets, nickelodeons, and amusement parks of the metropolis, I explore the trivia of social experience for clues to the ways working women constructed and gave meaning to their lives in the period from 1880 to 1920. Until recently, the historical record silenced those who left few written accounts and committed no "great" deeds. The flowering of feminist scholarship has at last begun to restore working-class women to history, establishing the significance of their activities in the household, workplace, and political arena. But leisure?—a minor pursuit, if not an outright contradiction; as one Polish immigrant remarked, "Who had leisure time?"[3]

Nonetheless, many working women carved out of daily life a sphere of pleasure that belied the harsh realities of the shop floor and tenement. Their activities, moreover, offer a window into social practices often obscured in other areas of human experience, opening to view the central concern of this book, the cultural handling of gender among working-class people. Public halls, picnic grounds, pleasure clubs, and street corners were social spaces in which gender relations were "played out," where notions of sexuality, courtship, male power, female dependency, and autonomy were expressed and legitimated.

At the same time, leisure is not simply a vessel whose contents reveal a unified culture, nor is its relationship to other spheres of life such as work and family one-dimensional. Leisure activities may affirm the cultural patterns embedded in other institutions, but they may also offer an arena for the articulation of different values and behaviors. The working-class construction of gender was influenced by the changing organization and meaning of leisure itself, particularly the effects of ongoing capitalist development on the organization of work and time, and the intensive commercialization of leisure in the late nineteenth and early twentieth centuries.

Under industrial capitalism, leisure has come to be perceived as a realm of autonomy and choice, a sphere of life separate from the obligations of the workplace. As E. P. Thompson and others have argued, the development of wage labor, imposition of time discipline by employers, and rationalization of the work process resulted in a new sense of the rhythms of time and cognitively sundered "work" from "life."[4] Workers who sold their time and labor and submitted to the bosses' control could daily assert a sense of independence in the public spaces of the saloon or lodge. This was linked to the notion of reciprocity among one's working-class peers, both institutionally, in such organizations as mutual aid societies, and interpersonally, in such common practices as treating rounds of beer. Working-class leisure thus offered a refuge from the dominant value system of competitive individualism, as Roy Rosenzweig has argued, and provided an arena in which class consciousness and conflict could be articulated, along with ethnic, religious, and other divisions.[5]

Yet this conception of leisure did not develop historically in the same way for both sexes. Women's leisure does not fit neatly into a framework that ignores the ways patriarchal relations within the working class divided women and men's lives and consciousness.

The public culture of workingmen was not only a potential bulwark of solidarity against the ravages of capitalism; it was also a system of male privilege in which workers' self-determination, solidarity, and mutual assistance were understood as "manliness." Shaped by the sexual divisions that structured work, access to resources, and participation in public life, women's time differed from men's. Their leisure—at least that of married women—tended to be segregated from the public realm and was not sharply differentiated from work, but was sinuously intertwined with the rhythms of household labor and the relations of kinship.

Women's life cycle and the family economy, however, shaped the ways different women experienced the sexual division of leisure. During this period, the working-class family's strategy for survival in an industrial, waged-based economy commonly meant sending daughters and sons into the labor force to supplement the earnings of the father, while the mother cooked, cleaned, cared for children, and often manufactured goods in the home. Consequently, although there were many exceptions to this model, the typical wage-earning woman of 1900 (outside home production) was young and single.

For them, leisure as a separate sphere of autonomy was problematic. Cultural ideologies about women's roles and the material conditions of daily life did not readily support this conception of leisure. In the immigrant cultures that dominated the urban working class at this time, young women were to be dutiful daughters who helped with the housework after their day of wage labor, turned over their pay envelopes unopened, and followed Old World traditions about women's social participation that, in some cases, were highly restrictive. At the same time, other dynamics in young women's lives encouraged an orientation toward leisure. As wage-earners, they experienced rhythms of time and labor more similar to men's than married women's, and shopfloor cultures reinforced the notion that leisure was a distinct realm of activity to which working women could demand access. However, young women's pursuit of pleasure did not lead them to the traditional domain of workingmen, but to emergent forms of commercialized recreation, such as dance halls, amusement parks, and movie theaters.

The rapid expansion and commercialization of leisure in the late nineteenth and early twentieth centuries altered the traditional

structure of such popular working-class activities as dancing and ex-
cursion-going. Loosening the ties between leisure, mutual aid, and
male culture, commercialized recreation fostered a youth-oriented,
mixed-sex world of pleasure, where female participation was profitable and encouraged. Many young women, particularly the daughters of immigrants, came to identify "cheap amusements" as the embodiment of American urban culture, particularly its individualism,
ideology of consumption, and affirmation of dating and courtship
outside parental control.

In these commercial amusement places, as the following chapters
explore in detail, young women experimented with new cultural
forms that articulated gender in terms of sexual expressiveness and
social interaction with men, linking heterosocial culture to a sense of
modernity, individuality, and personal style. Creating this style was
an assertion of self, a working-class variant of the "New Woman."
This is not to claim that the social and sexual freedom expressed in
working women's leisure constituted a form of liberation; as Leslie
Tentler and others have observed, without economic independence,
such freedoms were ultimately hollow.[6] Indeed, one could argue
that this culture was primarily a product of the leisure industry's
efforts to market entertainment and consumption to working-class
women, who were lulled into a state of false consciousness. Without
denying the importance of these points, I think it is necessary to
understand how women pushed at the boundaries of constrained
lives and shaped cultural forms for their own purposes. In essence,
understanding working women's culture calls for a doubled vision,
to see that women's embrace of style, fashion, romance, and mixed-
sex fun could be a source of autonomy and pleasure as well as a cause
of their continuing oppression.

Delineating young working women's leisure not only opens to view
the dynamics of gender and generation within working-class life; it
illuminates aspects of a larger cultural process, what John Higham
calls the "reorientation of American culture" in the late nineteenth
and early twentieth centuries.[7] The complex passage from Victorian
culture to modernism involved, among many other changes, a redefinition of gender relations, what might be termed the shift from
homosocial to heterosocial culture. This book examines this cultural

transformation from a new standpoint, focusing on the role of young white working women in fostering these changes.

Scholars of women's history have documented the cultural elaboration of "women's sphere" in the nineteenth century, as an emergent market economy and industrialization heightened the sexual division of labor. Affirming segregated spatial and social worlds for bourgeois women and men, the ideology of true womanhood, with its precepts of domesticity, moral guardianship, and sexual purity, made a moral and social duty out of the traditional tasks of housework and child care. Historians have examined the multidimensional power of this ideology both to enforce women's subordination and to open possibilities for female influence and assertion in and out of the home. Moreover, it enhanced a rich female culture that engendered passionate same-sex friendships, female self-awareness, and activism. As middle-class women internalized this homosocial ordering of their world, defining their status and character in terms of it, they also sought to spread these ideals, particularly domesticity, to women of the laboring classes. [8]

By the end of the century, this dominant cultural construct was under strain, buffeted by the changing realities of women's lives. Women's movement into employment, higher education, and political activism expanded the notion of women's place. While few were ready to abandon the notion of sexual difference, the force of feminist demands for greater political rights and economic opportunities challenged the division of power in American society. In popular culture, the emergent ideal of the "New Woman" imbued women's activity in the public domain with a new sense of female self, a woman who was independent, athletic, sexual, and modern. [9]

In contrast to the Victorian ideology of spatial and psychological separation, a cultural preoccupation with the emotional and sexual bonds between women and men developed in the early decades of the twentieth century. From New York City to Middletown, the affirmation of heterosociality was pervasive, particularly in new forms of commercial entertainment. Urban nightclubs and amusement parks legitimated interaction between the sexes in such practices as dating and close dancing, while films in the teens and twenties offered visual models of heterosocial modernity. Social scientists, advertisers, and journalists too promoted the importance of mutual attraction, good sexual relations, and friendship in matrimony. Yet the public discourse affirming enlightened companionship between modern women and men obscured the ways in which the new culture reformulated women's subordination. Women's self-definition remained bound up in heterosexual and marital relationships; close friendships and intimacy between women were increasingly labelled deviant; and women's sexuality, freed from the strictures of passionlessness, became increasingly commodified, an instrument of a nascent consumer culture.[10]

In seeking to explain this transformation in the construction of gender, historians have looked at groups within the middle and upper classes as the catalysts of cultural change. Generally, a "trickle down" model is assumed in these interpretations: bohemian intellectuals, college students, or an elite urban vanguard develop new social forms, which are then diffused downward, via institutions of mass culture, to the broader middle class and, ultimately, to the working class. Models of cultural hegemony and social control often reinforce this view of the working class as passive recipients of cultural messages, whether these come from factory owners and reformers seeking to create a disciplined labor force or from mass entertainment moguls coopting the traditional pursuits of the masses.[11] Recently scholars have come to question this view, offering a much richer and more complex picture of cultural change as a multidimensional set of interactions, in which hegemonic intentions are accommodated, resisted, and reshaped in a variety of ways.[12]

In line with this approach, this book argues that, to explain changes in the construction of gender in these years fully, it is necessary to understand that in many ways, rather than being bystanders in the process of cultural change, working women pioneered new manners and mores. Some groups within the middle class, notably reformers, sought to repress or at least contain the heterosocial, sexually expressive culture of these working women, but they met with limited success. In contrast, an emergent group of leisure entrepreneurs encouraged that culture, played with its forms, and ultimately popularized it for a broad mass audience. I am not arguing for a "trickle up" theory, but rather suggesting that the lines of cultural transmission travel in both directions.

The exploration of gender relations and cultural change in this book is based upon research into the experiences of white working-class women in Manhattan. Of all the large industrial cities in the United States, New York—particularly Manhattan Island—seemed the most likely foundry of an emergent culture, given its cosmopolitan character and expansive leisure and entertainment industries. Moreover, sources on working-class life in New York are rich and extensive, ranging from the records of a virtual army of reformers to the oral testimony of immigrant women. As is the case today, turn-of-the-century New Yorkers were remarkably self-conscious about their city's life, to the delight of historians.

In determining who fell into the category of "working-class women," I have considered an individual's structural relationship to the means of production as the primary determinant of class, but not the only one. As feminist scholars have observed, women's class position is often problematic under this traditional Marxist definition, and like other social historians, I have paid attention to the larger web of social relationships within which women labored and lived. The working-class women discussed in the following pages typically were immigrants or daughters of immigrants, lived in well-defined tenement districts, and labored for wages while unmarried, usually in factories, homes, and sales and service jobs. This description of working-class women is, of course, historically circumscribed, emerging out of a specific social and economic context in the late nineteenth and early twentieth centuries.

The first three chapters of the book place young women's leisure in the larger milieu of working-class social life. The sexual division of leisure for married men and women is examined in Chapter One, which considers the segregated pattern of social participation in terms of differing work rhythms, access to income, and organizational life. Chapter Two explores the relationship between young women's wage-earning and their definition of leisure as mixed-sex fun and freedom; it focuses not only upon the material conditions of the workplace, such as wages, hours, and work processes, but also upon the work cultures young women created on the shop floor. The "style" young women created in clubs and the streets is discussed in Chapter Three, in terms of the conflicts between family and autonomy. The next three chapters are case studies of dance halls, excursions and amusement parks, and the movies. These examine in detail the commercialization of working-class amusements and how they articulated and popularized working-class youth's cultural practices. These studies suggest that working women had an impact on the evolution of popular amusements toward "mass leisure" and the new cultural attitudes toward gender and sexuality embedded in them. Finally, Chapter Seven looks at cultural transmission in the other direction, examining the efforts by middle-class reformers to impose their Victorian notions of wholesome leisure on working girls and their failure to forestall the commercial and heterosocial culture.

CHAPTER ONE

THE HOMOSOCIAL WORLD OF WORKING-CLASS AMUSEMENTS

Americans in the late nineteenth century perceived New York City's population as split into two classes, typified by the ostentatious mansions of Fifth Avenue and the squalid tenement slums of Mulberry Bend. Images of the elite "400" and the impoverished "other half," created by photographers and poets, cartoonists and crusaders, indelibly shape our understanding of the metropolis. Yet this picture oversimplifies the complex texture of Manhattan's culture, particularly that of its working-class inhabitants. The social worlds of the poverty-stricken day laborer, unionized craftsman, stylish young saleswoman, and boardinghouse keeper were often dissimilar, and diverged further according to ethnic and religious background. Patterns of working-class leisure were likewise kaleidoscopic: a neighborhood's facilities for recreation ranged from sparse to numerous; Old World celebrations and home-centered conviviality competed with commercial amusements; long hours of arduous labor left many without leisure, while others enjoyed the city's variegated nightlife.

As Jacob Riis graphically demonstrated, poverty was a pervasive fact of working-class life in turn-of-the-century New York, whose population was heavily dominated by immigrants and their children. In the 1880's, a majority of Manhattanites lived at the subsistence level, and the depression of the 1890's brought further hardship to the laboring poor. Already overcrowded working-class districts in lower Manhattan swelled with a massive influx of eastern and southern Europeans. Although living standards rose after 1900, many barely survived, uncertain of employment, scrambling to make ends meet.[1]

The income of laboring families varied considerably. Two extensive budget studies covering the period from 1903 to 1909 indicate that the typical working-class family, comprised of four to six members, earned on average eight hundred dollars a year, or fifteen dollars a week. In fewer than 50 percent of the households was the father the sole means of support. "An income of above $700 or $800 is obtainable as a rule only by taking lodgers or by putting mother and children to work," observed Robert Coit Chapin in his investigation of working-class expenditures. Unusually high rents, resulting from urban density, consumed the wages of the poor. Food was usually purchased daily, at higher cost than buying in bulk, and diets were often limited in variety and nutrition.[2]

Nevertheless, working-class standards of living clearly improved in the period from 1880 to 1920, particularly after 1900. A British study in 1911 warned not to confuse the lower East Side's density with squalor: "Poverty is not much in evidence; shops are bright; there is no lack of places of amusement; restaurants of some pretension are not hard to find."[3] Many were able to move out of the crowded slums of lower Manhattan to uptown addresses and newly built tenement apartments. The death rate dropped 30 percent in this period, a sign of improved sanitation and health conditions. Skilled workers in particular made important gains in wages and hours of labor, having organized many of New York's major industries, including the engine-operating, printing, building, and metalworking trades. The American-born children of Irish and German immigrants who had poured into Manhattan in the nineteenth century were coming of age and gaining a modicum of social mobility. Even the migrants from eastern Europe and Italy had established their communities on a firmer footing by 1900, the Russian Jews in particular organizing an extensive cultural and political apparatus.[4]

FAMILY ENTERTAINMENT

Since housing, food, fuel, and clothing consumed most of their income, the working-class family as a unit could afford only the cheapest of amusements. Chapin's budget study indicates careful and limited outlays for entertainment and relaxation, particularly among low-income families. For the laboring poor, leisure activity was brief, casual, and noncommercial. "In the evening they sit in front of the house," Chapin observed of one family, while the members of another "never go any place at all except to the woman's parents, who live across the way." Even among families earning more than seventeen dollars a week, inexpensive excursions and theater trips were the rule. These were more often occasional treats than regular events; a family might visit the amusement resorts at Coney Island or Fort George once or twice a summer.[5] Among the Greenwich Villagers whom Louise Bolard More studied in 1907, the poorest families spent nothing for recreation; even more prosperous households averaged only thirty-five cents a week for entertainment.[6] Similarly, a 1914 investigation of West Side families found that "amusement cost them very, very little and was extremely circumscribed," consisting primarily of walks, visiting friends, and reading the penny press. When these families did spend money on recreation, typically they attended moving picture shows or rode the trolleys for a nickel or, more infrequently, went to a dance or theater. As late as the First World War, working-class families spent only 2.4 percent of their earnings on amusements.[7]

The most common forms of recreation, especially among families living on the margins of self-sufficiency, were free. Streets served as the center of social life in the working-class districts, where laboring people clustered on street corners, on stoops, and in doorways of tenements, relaxing and socializing after their day's work. Lower East Side streets teemed with sights of interest and penny pleasures: organ grinders and buskers played favorite airs, itinerant acrobats performed tricks, and baked-potato vendors, hot-corn stands, and soda dispensers vied for customers. In the Italian community clustered in the upper East Side, street musicians and organ grinders made their melodies heard above the clatter of elevated trains and shouting pushcart vendors, collecting nickels from appreciative passers-by. Maureen Connelly, an Irish immigrant, remembered listening to the German bands that played in Yorkville and the men who would sing for pennies in the tenement yards. "Something was always happening," recalled Samuel Chotzinoff of his boyhood among lower East Side Jews, "and our attention was continually being shifted from one excitement to another."[3]

This multilayered world allowed different groups to construct their own amusements. For many, the after-dinner stroll to a park or window-shopping on Grand Street or the Bowery became a ritual. "Every night the brightly lighted main thoroughfares, with their gleaming store-windows and their lines of trucks in the gutters, provide a promenade for thousands who find in walk and talk along the pavement a cheap form of social entertainment." Sunday diversions might even include visits to tenement construction sites, "to wonder at and admire the light rooms, the bath tubs, and the other improvements."[9]

Parks, too, were a popular form of entertainment for working-class families, particularly among the average wage-earners, who could ill afford excursions or theater trips. An outing to Central Park on a Sunday was considered a special family treat, while the neighborhood parks, squares, and playgrounds were places for daily relaxation. On hot summer nights in Jackson Park, close to the East River, "the men were in their undershirts. The women, more fully dressed, carried newspapers for fans. Hordes of barefoot children played games, weaving in and out of the always thick mass of promenaders."[10]

Although working-class tenements were usually cramped and dark, the home also served as an important social center for family recreation. In the lower East Side, Jewish kinfolk and neighbors gathered together in tenement kitchens for everyday socializing and observance of religious holidays. Christian families likewise celebrated yearly festivals, decorating their rooms according to the traditions of their homelands at Christmas and Easter. Neighbors from the Old Country joined together for regular social evenings in the home, as in this typical Hungarian gathering:

> In the Grubinsky kitchen they sit in a circle, husbands and wives together. Martin Grubinsky and his wife are each at work on cane weaving. The babies play on the floor in the middle of the circle. Perhaps a pail of mild beer is handed around once or twice, but not too often.[11]

Italian friends often met in the home to drink homemade wine, play cards, and socialize. House parties for birthdays or other occasions were also popular. In the West Side Irish districts, revellers enjoyed popular songs, fancy dance steps, masquerading, minstrelsy, and alcohol at the typical house party. Similarly, high spirits in one East Side tenement caused a neighbor to complain, "They all had a jollification together in the upper rooms, drinking, music and dancing about till late."[12]

The close quarters of the tenement house engendered particular forms of sociability. Immigrant neighbors who had not learned—or could not afford—the American notion of privacy congregated in the hallways, left their doors open to talk between apartments, and used the airshaft to facilitate conversation. For Italian women, settlement worker Lillian Betts observed, a "tenement house hall in New York is the substitute for the road of her village."[13] The tenement yard was often a focal point of neighborhood interaction, particularly when catalyzed by singers and musicians, as one East Sider observed:

> After they had practised a time they would play dance music, and all the girls and boys in the flats would go in the yards and dance. How the people did enjoy that music! Every one would be at their windows listening. Sometimes they would play old song tunes, so soft and so beautiful. Then the people would clap their hands; it was inspiring in a neighborhood like that.[14]

As a recreational space, the home often brought together working-class wives and husbands. George Bevan's extensive 1913 study of male recreation indicates that married men spent about half their leisure time with their families. Men who labored long hours tended to pass their evenings at home recuperating from toil, while those who worked an eight-hour day spent Saturday afternoons at home. Indeed, two-thirds of the skilled workers reported that they took their recreation with their families, either at home or on outings. The behavior of these craftsmen and mechanics may well have been influenced by the popularization of domestic ideals in the labor press, which not only affirmed women's place in the home but advocated a close family life.[15]

Although this evidence suggests that informal, everyday leisure often was enjoyed within a familial context, closer examination indicates that much working-class social life was divided by gender. Highly skilled workers may have accepted the canons of domesticity, but other men frequently took their recreation apart from wives and children. Investigators of Italian children's home life, for example, found that their fathers were rarely at home during the caseworkers' evening and weekend visits, except during the dinner hour. In the households of the West Side, an area dominated by American, German, and Irish families, "the husband comes home at night, has his dinner, and goes out with the 'men,' or sits at home to read his paper."[16] Even when unemployed, one immigrant woman observed, Rumanian men never stayed at home but went to play cards at the union hall.[17]

A detailed 1914 study of thirty-four families indicates more specifically the differential and segregated quality of leisure for women and men. On Sundays, men would attend baseball games, go fishing, or take outings, while their wives stayed at home or took the children on walks or to local parks. In one Irish American family, for example, the wife sat on her front steps, gossiped with neighbors, and took her children to the park and to free movies at the local settlement house. In contrast, her husband on Saturday night went out "for a shave and afterward treat[ed] his friend at one of the saloons," while on Sunday he went out for a meal. A native-born couple with two young children spent about three dollars a year on theater trips and a nickel a month on streetcar rides, but their regular recreation was segregated: "On Sunday the husband goes to Rockaway beach for an outing. The mother and children take walks as a rule." While many of the wives surveyed went to church or did housework, "a great many of the men spend Sunday morning reading the Sunday papers."[18]

WORKINGMEN'S LEISURE

Workingmen could turn to a highly visible and extensive network of leisure institutions to which women had marginal or problematic access. Many of these forms of amusement were commercial ventures and included poolrooms and billiard halls, bowling alleys, shooting galleries, and gymnasia. Others were organized by working-class men themselves. Baseball teams, for example, were formed by workingmen's clubs, factory employees, and street gangs throughout the tenement districts. Urban spaces such as cigar stores, barber shops, and street corners were colonized by men as hangouts for socializing and relaxing. The most popular forms of workingmen's recreation, however, were the saloon, lodge, and club, places in which male camaraderie resonated with working–class economic and social concerns.[19]

Dominating the physical space of most tenement neighborhoods, the saloon exemplifies workingmen's public culture. Over ten thousand saloons were in business throughout greater New York in 1900. Saloons tended to be spread out along the wide avenues that ran the length of Manhattan, as well as such commercial downtown streets as the Bowery. The mixed land use in most working-class neighborhoods ensured that saloons, located on the ground floor of tenements and close to factories and businesses, would be central meeting places for men. Most street corners had at least one bar catering to local patrons. In the 15th Assembly District, for example, an area bounded by 43rd Street, 53rd Street, Eighth Avenue, and the Hudson River, almost one-half of the ninety-two street corners were occupied by saloons, and sixty-six taprooms were scattered along the blocks.[20]

Alcohol obviously provided a major attraction for working-class customers who sought to forget tedium, toil, and poverty. George Bevans found that men who labored the longest hours, and thus had the least leisure time, paid the most visits to saloons. Similarly, men who earned low wages disproportionately attended saloons. Noted one mechanic: "Men who get small wages and are in uncertain employment become easily discouraged when they think of the needs at home. . . . They go to the saloon to drown their despondency and trouble."[21]

More important, the saloon united sociability, psychological support, and economic services for workingmen. Their bright lights, etched glass, and polished fixtures, their friendly atmosphere, appearance of abundance, and informal conviviality marked a sharp contrast to crowded tenements and exploitative workplaces. Workers packed saloons on the Bowery and Division Streets on their way home from the factory, seeking "a 'half-way' stopping place where, over a schooner of beer, the men talk over their work of the day and

plan for the evening. . . . At nightfall these places are thronged four
or five deep about the bar."[22] A man could get a free lunch with a
five-cent beer and enjoy the good fellowship of the barkeep and
patrons in the bargain. If he wanted a job, a loan, or simply the
news, the workingman headed for the saloon. Italian men, for example, met in waterfront cafes on President Street to drink wine and
play cards as they waited for information about incoming ships and
day labor jobs on the docks. One regular informed Lillian Wald that
"the fellows just kind of talk about jobs when they're sitting 'round
in the saloons, and sometimes you pick something up."[23]

For newly arrived immigrants, saloons offered a wealth of important services to help in the adjustment to the New World. One saloon, for instance, advertised that it supplied Serbians, Croatians,
and Hungarians with a large meeting room, money barter, steamship tickets, employment, board, and lodging. In another advertisement, the owner of a hall and bar assured his countrymen of a well-
organized social life:

> Popular wine-beer hall and coffee house.
> The well liked meeting place of Hungarians. . . .
> Comfortably arranged furnished rooms.
> First class Hungarian kitchen.
> Billiard, also dance hall, comfortable
> for meetings further for weddings and
> balls. Those from the country receive
> proper elucidation.[24]

Although the saloon was often termed the "poor man's club," most
workingmen also frequented a fraternal society, mutual benefit association, or lodge. Such voluntary organizations combined recreation
and camaraderie with economic services, including protection
against sickness, disability, and financial emergencies. These forms of
working-class self-activity were necessary adaptations to an industrial
society that had few social welfare provisions. Some of these were
church-sponsored associations, such as the Workingmen's Club of the
Church of the Holy Communion. Founded in 1873, this club sought
"to promote social intercourse and brotherly regard among its members," while offering medical treatment, monetary assistance in times
of illness, free library facilities, and a proper burial.[25]

Even more common were the mutual benefit societies and lodges organized by immigrants. Insurance was considered a primary obligation of the breadwinner, and contributions to mutual aid associations were often heavy.[26] German immigrants formed Unterstutzung Vereinen, sickness and death benefit societies, which were organized by occupation or place of origin. Numerous Italian societies, estimated at from two to three thousand, thrived in greater New York, each composed of immigrants from a single town or island. The Societá di Mutuo-Soccorso Isola Salina, a typical benevolent order, limited its membership to those born on the island and required an initiation fee based on age. For monthly dues of one dollar, the member would receive a physician's attention, a steamship ticket to Italy for medical reasons, a funeral, and death benefits paid to his widow.[27]

The Jewish East Side was similarly "honey-combed with Clubs and Societies," ranging from national organizations and large Hebrew orders to numerous small societies consisting of emigres from a particular locality. The Kehillah, or governing structure of New York's Jewish community, estimated in 1918 that over one million Jews were involved in fraternal orders. While the "ancient form" of organization, the burial club, was still common, it observed, a number of societies had developed into "Vereinen" or "Friendly Societies," which not only buried the dead but provided sick benefits and loans: "This form of mutual aid received *in this world* by the members themselves has become extremely popular among the immigrant Jews, many of them belonging to two and more societies."[28] These immigrant voluntary societies not only addressed serious needs but also provided an outlet for sociability and entertainment. The yearly lodge balls and picnics, organized to raise money for charitable purposes, were often the central social events of working-class community life.

The activities of workingmen's voluntary organizations intertwined with the world of the saloon. Fraternal lodges and clubs regularly used the second-story halls and back rooms of saloons for meetings and entertainments. In Magyar Hall, a saloon patronized by Hungarians and Czechs, the "upper floors are occupied for meeting rooms, where different societys [sic] and workmen circles meet."[29] A survey of 702 clubs found that almost 70 percent met in saloons or neighborhood halls that sold liquor. Such clubs and other organizations paid a nominal rental fee to the saloon owner, but their members were expected to frequent the bar. Trade unions followed a similar practice in their meetings: "It is understood and expected that the members of the union will patronize the bar and will 'take it out in trade.' "[30] The close relationship between the commercial interests of the saloon and the voluntary associations of workingmen provided a foundation for the public social life of working-class communities.

At the same time, the interlocking network of leisure activities strengthened an ethos of masculinity among workingmen. This male culture is most clearly revealed in the social practices of the saloon. With the exception of German beer halls, saloons were defined primarily as homosocial worlds where men gathered to debate politics, commiserate over work and family obligations, and wrangle over sports. At one saloon, for example, a chalkboard prominently displayed baseball scores, and a "half dozen men [were] in here talking baseball."[31] Bars often encouraged rowdy behavior and vulgar language less acceptable in other areas of social life. At the Odd Fellow's Hall in St. Mark's Place, "one of the saloonkeepers . . . entertained us with disorderly songs and poems in [the] German language," observed a vice investigator from the Committee of Fourteen.[32] At another saloon, the behavior of the bartender and patrons rivalled a vaudeville turn:

> [The bartender] is a hot headed Irishman. He took a seltzer bottel and sqwoiter it on th[e] sleeping fellow the latter got up and went to the bar and filled his mouth with beer from one of the [glasses] and spewed it at [the bartender] dousing him about the face. [He] swor[e] at him and the fellow took the whole [glass] and doueused him with it. It was but low comedy with t[h]em the [re] was no ill feeling. It was their gentle way of supplementing words with action without getti[n]g real mad about it. This is about the way [the bartender] runs the place. Very disorderly I should say.[33]

Mutuality among workingmen was affirmed by the custom of treating rounds of beer or games of billiards to one's mates. Treating was considered a courtesy between men and a symbol of respectability. As one reformer recalled of the pre-Prohibition days, "A kind of obligation of honor was created which required the individual to continue drinking until everyone in the group he was part of had the opportunity to treat everybody else."[34] Barkeepers encouraged this practice by offering drinks on the house and herding men into large groups in order to swell the size of the rounds.

Gambling often played an important role in the social life of the saloon. At the Sport Cafe, a "resort for respectable Italian workingmen" near Pennsylvania Station, men shot pool and played cards for drinks. The stimulus of high stakes drew men to the back room of another saloon:

> The room was filled and at every table 3 or 4 men were playing cards and were stand[ing] up in [the] centre of room and around the tables watching them, they must have been playing for pretty big stakes, there was a lot of excitement here[;] some of the players almost got into a fight.[35]

Within this homosocial world, rituals of aggression and competition became important mechanisms for male bonding.

The presence of widespread prostitution also defined saloons as male worlds. Vice investigations of the day provide ample evidence that respectable working-class drinking coexisted with soliciting in the back room. George Kneeland's extensive study of prostitution found that in one-seventh of the 765 bars studied, streetwalkers met customers in the back rooms. The majority of these places were located along Third and Eighth Avenues from 14th Street to 125th Street, both major commercial arteries in working-class districts.[36] At Staunton and Dunleary's saloon, on the corner of Eighth Avenue and 17th Street, workingmen quietly nursed their beers and played cards, while the back room "appear[ed] to be a hangout for street walkers."[37]

WORKING-CLASS WIVES' RECREATION

In contrast to this male public culture, the leisure activities of married women were more limited and confined. While workingmen had a broad network of ethnic, class, and commercial institutions available to them, their wives often experienced a dearth of pleasure in their lives. Louise Bolard More's study of Greenwich Village is typical of investigators' observations: "The men have the saloons, political clubs, trade-unions or lodges for their recreation, . . . while the mothers have almost no recreation, only a dreary round of work, day after day, with occasionally a door-step gossip to vary the monotomy of their lives."[38] One of the few detailed descriptions of married women's leisure reveals its ephemeral quality, orientation to the home, and reliance on informal kin and friendship networks for sociability:

> Many women spend their leisure sitting on the steps of their tenement gossiping; some lean out of the window with a pillow to keep their elbows from being scraped by the stone sills; others take walks to the parks; some occasionally visit relatives or friends; and there is, once in a while, a dinner party; but, on the whole, except for the men, there is little conscious recreation.[39]

The constraints on married women's leisure time were in large part shaped by the work rhythms of the home. The scheduling of household chores, of cleaning, cooking, and child care, did not permit the clear differentiation between work and leisure experienced by most workingmen, whose labor was timed to the factory clock and the bosses' commands.[40] These scheduling problems were compounded by inadequate plumbing in the tenements, poor municipal sanitation, and the inability to afford simple labor-saving technology. When asked by an interviewer if her mother had worked for a living, Maria Cichetti's reply catalogued the non-waged labor of working-class wives: she had used a coal fire to heat her irons, handled big iron pots in cooking, chopped wood in the cellar, baked her own bread, and borne thirteen babies.[41] Many women also took in boarders to make ends meet, multiplying their household burdens.

Women's work continued long after men's had ceased. In a typical evening scene in an East Side home, while "the mother is attending to her household work, the father is reading a paper, or he may be watching the children at play."[42] A common form of working-class recreation involved reading and discussing the news, particularly the Sunday editions of the New York *Journal* and the *World*, but "the women have no time to read the papers, except the fashion or society notes, or some famous scandal or murder case."[43] Women had to fit their entertainment into their work, rather than around it. Washing the laundry, supervising children at play, or shopping at the local market, women might find a few moments to socialize with neighbors. "Many women do their washing in this yard," noted a middle-class tenement inspector. "Besides being the playground of children, it is the gathering vestibule for gossip and exchange for profanity."[44] Given the task-oriented nature of their work, married women's leisure was intermittent, snatched between household chores.

Indeed, a family's leisure often *became* work for women. Between child care and food preparation, outings, picnics, and parties were hardly relaxed times for mothers. Maria Cichetti, for example, recalls that when her mother took the children to Central Park for a "treat," she was occupied with making certain they looked presentable and would not disgrace the family in their adopted country by picking the flowers or walking on the grass.[45]

The distribution of resources among family members also restricted women's participation in recreation. As we have seen, household budgets allowed only small sums for family recreation, but a substantial portion of the breadwinner's income was allocated as spending money for personal use. Husbands retained the right to remove whatever spending money they desired before contributing the rest to the household. Workingmen spent about 10 percent of their weekly income on personal expenses, the bulk of it on beer and liquor, tobacco, and movie and theater tickets. While some husbands removed only transportation and lunch money from their pay envelopes, others abused their privilege: "The husband brings his wages to his wife at the end of the week or fortnight. He gives her the whole amount and receives back carfare and 'beer' money; or he gives her as much as 'he feels like' or 'as much as he has left after Saturday night.'"[46]

The issue of spending money was a constant source of tension within the working-class family. Wives voiced opposition to men's drinking up their wages in saloons, rather than committing their earnings to the household. Women in Greenwich Village agreed that "a good husband should turn over to his wife all his wages,

receiving one or two dollars a week for his personal use."[47] Whatever the outcome of this weekly negotiation, the designation of the
breadwinner's spending money as *personal* allowed men to pursue a
social life based upon access to commercial, public recreation. Married women, however, received no spending money of their own.
Although they controlled the household's purse strings, this power
was mitigated by the constant pressure to make ends meet, and
family needs usually governed their expenditures. Even a married
woman's own income, earned by keeping boarders or taking in laundry, was usually spent on the home and family, on clothing for the
children or better-quality food, rather than personal recreation.
"The usual attitude toward any expenditure for pleasure," Louise
Bolard More noted, "is that it is a luxury which cannot be afforded."
Only after 1905, with the rise of the nickelodeon, did large numbers
of working-class wives regularly enjoy commercialized forms of leisure (see Chapter VI).[48]

The grinding rhythms of household labor and limited access to
financial resources closely circumscribed many women's social participation. "The lives of the women are very narrow," noted one
observer, "and they have few interests outside their homes."[49] Indeed, many women sought to make the home into a center for recreation, an alternative to the saloons and streets. Working-class
wives carefully decorated their small tenement quarters, even des-
ignating one of the multipurpose rooms the "parlor." Surprised observers discovered that "the comforts of life are found in the vilest
tenements." Heavy overstuffed furniture, cheap lace curtains, car-
pets, and bric-a-brac crowded the more prosperous working-class
home.[50] Respectability was denoted by one's furnishings, even
when purchased on the installment plan. Families would get themselves into such debt that, for some, "the only recreation [was] the
display of their furniture." Having a piano or organ in the front
room, and lessons for the children twice a week, fulfilled the dreams
of many proud mothers.[51] Poorer women spruced up their tenement quarters with a variety of room decorations paid for in grocer's
coupons and trading stamps. Gaudily colored religious prints, portraits of Lincoln and Washington, and advertising posters mingled
indiscriminately in the tenement parlor: "Pictures of every kind are
prized, cheap lithographs, bill-posters, portraits of circus perform-

ers and cigaret girls, which are companioned by bleeding hearts, saints, angels and heads of Christ."[52]

Some women hardly left their tenement houses. In trying to attract married women to its programs, the College Settlement found it difficult to dislodge the "habit of staying indoors," a tendency fixed by the burdens of child care and housework and exacerbated by lack of money. Henry Moscowitz, a lower East Side resident and civic leader, reported that many mothers went out no more than twice a week: "Complaints, serious complaints are made, 'Why don't you come to visit me?' and they say 'We live so high up we seldom come.'"[53] This pattern seems to have been especially prevalent among Italian women, reinforced by the strong tradition of the sheltered female. While Andrea Bocci's father went out to a Prince Street saloon every night, her mother never went out: "If one of her friends would be sick, she would go and help them out, but otherwise she would stay at home."[54]

This comment reflects the tradition of mutuality and reciprocity prevalent within immigrant working-class communities, a tradition that was shared by men and women but whose expression took different cultural forms. For men, public institutions such as the saloon and fraternal lodge affirmed these values through such customary practices as treating rounds and the organization of mutual aid. These cultural forms were directly or indirectly related to workingmen's experience of industrial labor and comprised an alternative culture to competitive individualism and the values of the marketplace.[55] Mutuality among women was likewise expressed in ways central to their own experience, primarily through an interdependent network of kin and neighbors. Assistance in periods of need, or simply "helping out" in daily labor, was often the context for female sociability, although this was not strictly time for "leisure." The contrast between women and men may be seen in the intertwined lives of two Irish families in an upper East Side tenement: "Mrs. H. is very often in the house of Mrs. C. and they exchange many favors in the course of a day, while at night their husbands play cards and share their beer." Such cooperative housekeeping arrangements and joint social evenings were apparently quite common among families with kin ties.[56]

Elsa Herzfeld, in her ethnographic descriptions of West Side families, noted the reciprocal expectations of mutual aid and sociability among female kinfolk—offering assistance during illness and pregnancies, attending funerals, celebrating weddings and christenings, exchanging Christmas and Easter gifts, organizing family dinners during the holidays, and visiting for extended periods among relatives. The intensity of these obligations was such that failure to follow social forms could cause ruptures in kinship ties. "One woman gave up visiting her only sister because the latter had failed to congratulate her when her baby was born," noted Herzfeld, although later "when the sister died she did her utmost for the bereaved children."[57]

MARRIED WOMEN AND THE PUBLIC SPHERE

While women's sociability was centered in the network of kin and neighbors, there was no simple or rigid gender-based dichotomy between public and private realms of leisure. The Catholic Church, which dominated the religious landscape of New York, was one public institution figuring heavily in the social lives of many women, who attended services and participated in church organizations and celebrations. The point at which church functions, usually seen as "obligatory time," shade into leisure time is arguable; when questioned by interviewers, Italian women, for example, recalled that their churches sponsored few social activities. Still, such events as the saint's day festivals were public occasions for Italian women to parade the streets in colorful processions, set up shrines on the sidewalks and tenement house windows, wear elaborate dress, and eat picnic luncheons in the local parks.[58] Investigators did find that working-class women tended to go to church more often than men, although in many cases their attendance was hampered by child care and household chores.[59]

Some working-class wives also participated in the formal organizational life of their communities, although not to the same extent as middle-class women. Jewish women organized their own mutual aid societies, often as ladies' auxiliaries to fraternal orders, as well as philanthropic, economic, and cultural agencies. The Kehillah discovered fifty-five benefit societies, nine lodges, and forty-eight other organizations run by women in 1918. Some of these, particularly the philanthropic societies, were organized by middle-class Jews. Most of the mutual aid societies, however, met in the lower East Side and were led by women who lived either there or in uptown and Brooklyn working-class neighborhoods. Other Jewish women joined mixed-sex *landsmanschaft* organizations and attended their biweekly meetings.[60] While not all immigrant wives enjoyed such extensive participation, most were invited to attend the annual balls, picnics, and entertainments sponsored by their husbands' fraternal organizations.[61]

Despite this level of involvement, most women held a marginal position in the public institutions that organized much working-class leisure. The social patterns surrounding drinking were particularly problematic for women. While the saloon may have affirmed reciprocity and class-based sociability for its male patrons, this favorable view was not shared by their wives. The area around saloons could be hazardous spaces where women were subjected to harassment by drunks and loafers: "Women therefore zigzagged from one side of the street to another, even on short walks, to avoid passing bar rooms."[62] Many women never even entered a saloon. Sophia Margolis, struggling to describe the cafes where Italian men met and drank, said finally, "I don't know much about these cafes because I never went in one."[63]

For wives and mothers concerned with making ends meet, the lure of the saloon posed a threat to their families' survival. They particularly decried the customary practice of treating rounds: "The married man who can 'treat,' it is generally conceded, is not fair to his family; he keeps his wages at their expense." One settlement worker even recalled that working-class wives approached the staff for "the name of some kind of 'dope' which they could put into the husband's food or drink for the purpose of making alcohol unpalatable."[64] Working-class wives clearly differentiated a public and private sphere for drinking, favoring men who imbibed at home and censuring the husband who drank in saloons, away from his family. Many men went to beer saloons, observed Elsa Marek, "and they started yelling there and getting drunk and come home and the children cry, there was no money, then they start fighting." When her husband wanted beer, however, "he went with the pail and he brings the beer home . . . so he has everything home."[65]

Women who liked to drink penetrated the male sphere of the saloon in ways that were carefully delineated. Saloons were customarily divided into two sections—the barroom, with its long counter and stools, and the back room, containing tables and chairs and occasionally a music box or dance floor. It was unacceptable for respectable women to stand at the bar, and those who went unescorted into the back room ran the risk of being labelled prostitutes. By the 1910's, however, women increasingly frequented saloons, particularly if they purveyed food as well as drink. Women's labor leader Margaret Dreier Robins observed in 1913, "I know girls who have entered a saloon because they could there get a bowl of soup as well as a glass of beer for five cents, receiving in that bowl of soup better nourishment than any other expenditure of such five cents could bring them."[66] This growing tendency is confirmed by the Committee of Fourteen's investigation of saloons and vice. While there were prostitutes soliciting in Jack's Cafe, a middle West Side restaurant and saloon, an investigator nonetheless observed that "2 of the women that were here seemed to be respectable, they had been out marketing and had their market bags with them." A few blocks away at Ihrig's Cafe, the back room contained four respectable German couples.[67] Still, the presence of women remained controversial. In order to ensure their good reputations, many saloon keepers only served couples in the back room and barred unaccompanied women or men. One vice investigator recounts the story of his sitting down at a table in the back room and the boss asking him what he wanted: "I ordered a drink, he said this is no whore house, you'll have to come out to the bar."[68] The saloon was thus acknowledged to be a dangerous environment for women, who were "fair game" unless protected by an escort.

Given the persistence of this male culture, working-class women usually chose not to seat themselves in the saloon, but more commonly "rushed the growler," buying a bucket's worth of beer to be drunk at home. Except for one prostitute, the only women observed at The Pippin, an upper East Side bar, were a few "that came in for pints, none of them remained here or sat down at the tables or consumed any liquor on the premises." Tenement "beer parties" were a frequent occurrence, and some neighbors complained that "with the women it was a constant parade of beer kettles from early morning until late at night."[69]

Working-class women also gambled, but the context in which they did so differed significantly from the male rituals of shooting pool, rolling dice, and betting on cards. Gambling in direct competition reinforced notions of masculine skill and aggression, of winning at another's expense, while at the same time it strengthened male solidarity. Women's betting took place, not against a face-to-face opponent, but in an impersonal and abstract system of chance. Women typically played "policy," a daily lottery based on picking combinations of numbers. As one newspaper account observed, "many of the players are women who live in the tenement districts and spend almost every cent they earn in playing 'gigs,' 'horses,' and 'saddles.' "[70]

IMMIGRANT TRADITIONS AND THE "AMERICAN STANDARD"

Sexual divisions in work, income distribution, and organizational life contributed to the differing uses of leisure time by working-class women and men. Married women remained marginal to the vigorous public culture expressed in saloons and voluntary societies. It is important to acknowledge, however, that this pattern of segregated, homosocial leisure varied among working-class immigrants and their American-born offspring. In succession, different Old World cultures took root in New York's neighborhoods and confronted new ways of organizing leisure time. The cultural patterns of working-class recreation at any given moment of New York's history were extremely complex. Some immigrants rejected the modern culture, seeing a threat to age-old customs, while their children anxiously converted to the American standard, revelling in commercial entertainment. Others accepted certain types of urban recreation, such as the saloon, or adapted traditional forms of pleasure to new conditions. Cultural exchange—food, fads, and forms of amusement—also took place among the different immigrant groups, who often lived in close proximity.[71]

As many recent historians have argued, cultural traditions and "ways of seeing" indigenous to particular national groups were the lenses through which immigrant working-class families responded to a new industrial and urban environment. Familial values, attitudes toward women's roles, and resistance and adaptation to the workplace were all filtered through such traditions.[72] These also shaped working-class patterns of recreation. Germans, for example, encouraged mixed-sex participation in an amusement usually considered a bastion of male prerogative by taking family groups to huge beer gardens. Such beer halls, where all indulged in drink, song, and socializing, catered to respectable and well-behaved crowds of women and men.[73] Italian men, in contrast, took their everyday recreation apart from the family, but joined their wives and children to commemorate saints' days. The festival tradition remained an important part of Italian life in New York, an opportunity to honor the patron saint of their Old World home with parades and fireworks.[74]

Native-born and "Americanized" immigrant groups tended to frequent commercial amusements and spend the most money on recreation. George Bevans, for example, traced workingmen's leisure activities by national origin and found distinctive differences. German men took their leisure most often with their families. The British-born worker could usually be found in the saloon or union hall. Russian Jews were most likely to spend their evenings in didactic pursuits, at public lectures, libraries, and night schools. In contrast, American-born workingmen, who were most often sons of immigrants, used their leisure time in clubs and lodges, movies, theaters, dance halls, and poolrooms.[75] Budget studies reveal similar trends. Native-born Greenwich Villagers tended to allocate more of their income for commercial forms of recreation and personal spending than did foreign-born families, who supported the traditional network of home, neighbors, and church by spending their money on household goods and furniture, religious contributions, education, drink, and gifts to friends. Robert Chapin likewise found that "a larger expenditure for amusement and recreation prevails among the nationalities that have adopted most completely the American standard."[76]

To some extent, this "American standard" simply reflected the tendency of families with higher incomes to have larger outlays for recreation and the likelihood that recent immigrants were on the lowest rungs of the economic ladder. For many immigrants, however, participation in urban recreation was part of the broader experience of Americanization. Even though immigrants tended to segregate themselves by national origin, the *forms* of amusement in tenement districts crossed ethnic lines: saloons, lodges, socials, dances, and excursions were common in all working-class neighborhoods.[77]

Forged in an urban and industrial society, these American amusements offered a novel conception of leisure to the newly arrived immigrant—the idea of segmenting and organizing leisure into a distinct sphere of activity. David Blaustein, the head of the East Side's Educational Alliance, suggested the difference between the Old World and the New:

> Now to-day the immigrant becomes bewildered when he first comes here to America. As a further illustration, take organized amusement. I call it organized amusement, the way we have picnics, balls, assemblies. The people who come here mostly from eastern Europe are not accustomed to such life. If they have any amusement or gathering it is a birthday party, it is a wedding party, and a funeral; it always centers around the family. But this large scale of amusement, taking out people on excursions by the thousand—when he comes here he becomes bewildered.[78]

For the immigrant, traditional celebrations and everyday pleasures now took place in an unfamiliar context. On the lower East Side, weddings that had once been family affairs were held in rented halls, with dances and entertainment after the marriage ceremony. Five hundred people came to Rose Pasternak's wedding, which was held in the Grand Lyceum Hall. Observed the head worker at College Settlement, "The most sacred ceremony, the wedding, is performed in a public hall to which anyone is admitted on payment of the hatcheck."[79]

Americanized leisure activities did not entirely supplant traditional cultural forms, but coexisted with them uneasily, providing a range of alternatives for first- and second-generation families. "The social life of the Tenth Ward is divided somewhat sharply by a line of cleavage," explained a University Settlement reformer. "On one side is the theater, the lodge, the saloon, the dance hall, and the club; and on the other, the synagogue." Even on a religious holiday like Passover, traditional celebrations at home or in the synagogue competed with special matinee theatrical performances.[80] Moreover, the different cultural institutions of East Side social life often met in the same saloon or tenement house. In one Essex Street tenement, David Blaustein found dancing schools giving lessons during the day, lodges meeting at night, and religious services on Saturdays: "In other words, in the same place they worship and they dance and they meet and wrangle; and all this in one tenement house."[81]

Similar cultural conflicts surrounded the leisure activities of the city's other immigrant groups. Italians in New York celebrated the saints' days with enthusiasm, noted one priest, but "in the summer time they like excursions to Coney Island, Staten Island and Little Italy, and it comes hard for them to give generously to the church."[82] The pull of alternative cultures could be felt within families as well. In a Hungarian household where traditional Easter and Christmas customs were lovingly maintained, "Mrs. Grubinsky, true to her more American tastes, would like to go to a moving picture show occasionally with the children; but Grubinsky will not hear of that, and so she doesn't go."[83]

A vibrant mixture of Americanized working-class, commercial, and Old World forms of leisure could be found in most immigrant neighborhoods, offering myriad options for pleasure-seekers—and complicating the picture of sex-segregated recreation drawn here. Nevertheless, working-class men of whatever background enjoyed greater opportunities for leisure than their wives. The patterns of men's work, their rights to spending money, and their role in the political and economic life of working-class communities allowed them access to a public world of pleasure and relaxation. In addition, the association of "Americanism" with commercialized recreation and consumption may have heightened the sexual division of leisure in these years; Bevans found that American-born men spent the smallest percentage of their leisure hours with the family than any of the immigrant groups he studied.[84] Women's participation in public and commercial forms of leisure was narrowly defined, their activities located instead in the home, streets, parks, and churches. The modern notion of leisure as a segmented part of social life may have been alien to them. However, one group of working-class women—single, adolescent, and usually earning wages—form an exception to the homosocial patterning of recreation in this period. Unlike their mothers, young women gained access to new forms of social life in the public arena, an experience structured and informed by their entrance into the labor force.

CHAPTER TWO

LEISURE AND LABOR

After ten or twelve hours a day bending over a sewing machine, standing at a sales counter, or waiting on tables, what energy could a turn-of-the-century working woman muster to attend a dance hall or amusement park? Quite a lot, according to the testimony of employers, journalists, and the wage-earners themselves. "Blue Monday" plagued employers. The head of a dressmaking shop, for example, observed that her employees "all took Sunday for a gala day and not as a day of rest. They worked so hard having a good time all day, and late into the evening, that they were 'worn to a frazzle' when Monday morning came." On week nights, working women hurriedly changed from work clothes to evening finery. Said one saleswoman, "You see some of those who have complained about standing spend most of the evening in dancing." The training supervisor at Macy's agreed, noting in exasperation, "We see that all the time in New York—many of the employees having recreation at night that unfits them for work the next day."[1]

Young, unmarried working-class women, foreign-born or daughters of immigrant parents, dominated the female labor force in the period from 1880 to 1920. In 1900, four-fifths of the 343,000 wage-earning women in New York were single, and almost one-third were aged sixteen to twenty. Whether supporting themselves or, more usually, contributing to the family economy, most girls expected to work at some time in their teens. Nearly 60 percent of all women in New York aged sixteen to twenty worked in the early 1900's. For many young women, wage-earning became an integral part of the transition from school to marriage.[2]

Women labored for wages throughout the nineteenth century, but by the 1890's, the context in which they worked differed from that of the Victorian era. New jobs in department stores, large factories, and offices provided alternatives to domestic service, household production, and sweated labor in small shops, which had dominated women's work earlier. These employment opportunities, the changing organization of work, and the declining hours of labor altered the relationship between work and leisure, shaping the way in which leisure time was structured and experienced. The perception of leisure as a separate sphere of independence, youthful pleasure, and mixed-sex fun, in opposition to the world of obligation and toil, was supported by women's experiences in the workplace. Far from inculcating good business habits, discipline, and a desire for quiet evenings at home, the workplace reinforced the wage-earner's interest in having a good time. Earning a living, an economic necessity for most young working-class women, was also a cultural experience organizing and defining their leisure activities.

WOMEN'S WORK IN THE VICTORIAN CITY

In the late nineteenth century, New York's economic landscape was crowded with flourishing commercial enterprises, a thriving port, manufacturing lofts, and workshops. New York achieved prominence early in the century as the leading mercantile city in the United States, ensuring its primacy in commerce, shipping, and finance by dominating the Atlantic trade and developing transportation links to the hinterlands. By the Civil War, New York led the country in manufacturing, its strength lying in the garment trades, tobacco-processing and cigar-making, printing and publishing, metal-working, and furniture- and piano-making. Manufacturing was spurred by commercial trade, with merchant capitalists developing products such as ready-made clothing for the national market. Other types of business were developed to answer the clamor for goods and services arising from the city's burgeoning population. Unlike many American cities, where the age of industry was characterized by huge, mechanized factories, the city's high rental costs, cheap immigrant labor supply, and lack of a good energy source led to a myriad of small, highly specialized shops.[3]

This expanding mercantile and manufacturing economy brought many young women into the labor force after 1840, but not primarily as "mill girls" or factory hands, as was the case in cities where capital-intensive industries flourished. The majority of women workers in Victorian New York labored as domestic servants, needlewomen, laundresses, and in other employments seemingly marginal to an industrial economy.[4] As late as 1880, 40 percent of all New York working women were in domestic service, an experience particularly common among adolescent Irish and German girls. Home-based occupations and street trades, such as keeping boarders, washing laundry, cleaning, ragpicking, and peddling, provided necessary income for poor working-class wives and widows. In manufacturing, New York women were concentrated in the needle trades, with over one-fifth working as dressmakers, tailors, and milliners in 1880. In these years, garments were produced in small workshops or in the home. Even after the introduction of the sewing machine, much of the clothing trade was contracted to tenement sweatshops, often conducted as a family-based enterprise. A similar scale of production characterized cigar-making, a common employment among women.[5] Relatively few women, married or single, were engaged in the type of large-scale, mechanized factory production considered the vanguard of an industrial society.

Much of women's wage work was centered in the home and followed household routines, or fitted into them without serious difficulty. This was especially true for married women, whose productive labor was often ignored by census enumerators. Keeping boarders, for example, a common occupation of working-class wives, involved the same tasks of cooking, washing, and cleaning that women performed for their families. Sewing and other forms of industrial homework, which endured among southern and eastern European immigrants well into the twentieth century, filled the days of mothers already occupied with child care and housework. As the daughter of an Italian homeworker observed in 1913, "My mother works all the time—all day, Sundays and holidays, except when she is cooking or washing. She never has time to go out or she would get behind in her work."[6] The task-oriented rhythms of such work, its lack of clear-cut boundaries, and the sheer burden of the "double day" left little time for leisure.

With greater job opportunities and limited household concerns, single women had fewer restrictions on their time than did working mothers. Indeed, by the mid-nineteenth century, some young working girls achieved notoriety in the city as pleasure seekers. While their mothers turned increasingly toward domestic pursuits, young factory hands, domestic servants, and prostitutes sought a life of finery, frolics, and entertainment. Industrial workers in particular found possibilities for leisure, sociability, and fun affirmed in the workplace. These Victorian "rowdy girls"—controversial figures within working-class communities—prefigure the broader trend toward a pleasure-oriented culture that swept working women's lives at the turn of the century.[7]

At the same time, women's access to a world of leisure at mid-century was limited by their work situations, as well as by poverty and social disapprobation. Single women who labored as domestic servants found that middle-class mistresses encroached upon their opportunities for leisure. Servants' desire to wear fine clothes and attend entertainments collided with employers' edicts limiting their time off. Maids were often on call twelve or thirteen hours a day and generally had only one afternoon and evening a week free.[8] Similarly, the exploitative conditions in the dominant manufacturing industries often permitted little free time. Grueling hours of labor for small wages in sweatshops and tenements characterized the work of seamstresses and needlewomen, cigar-makers, and others. Many of them labored fifteen to eighteen hours daily, working by gaslight late into the evening to earn enough for food and rent. Fatigue and poor health were more often their lot than finery and entertainments.[9]

Periods of sociability and amusement were often snatched within the rhythms of work. Domestic servants, for example, would meet together in the street or park to gossip and socialize while tending their mistresses' children. Yet for many, the relatively isolated nature of their labor, its long hours, and task-oriented rhythms did not reinforce a concept of leisure as a separate sphere of social life. One important exception to this pattern lay in the experience of female factory workers, whose work involved the segmentation of time and sociability among peers. By the end of the century, the distinction between household-based work and new forms of labor located in centralized production widened. While married women continued to do home-based work, single women increasingly entered an array of jobs not only in factories but in department stores, restaurants, and offices.

CHANGES IN WOMEN'S LABOR

By 1900, important changes in the social organization of labor and expanding job opportunities in New York created new work experiences for women. Small shops, lofts, and trading companies still crowded lower Manhattan, but the city's economic landscape was rapidly changing. The wards at the southern tip of Manhattan were increasingly given over to corporate headquarters, banking and investment firms, and specialized business offices. Towering skyscrapers and the canyons of Wall Street symbolized New York's transformation from a mercantile city to the nation's center for corporate industry. This expanding office complex created a demand for workers increasingly filled by female clerks, "typewriters," secretaries, and telephone operators. The explosive growth of the white-collar sector in the twentieth century, and women's participation in it, was anticipated in New York a decade before it affected the rest of the country. A negligible number of New York's clerks, typists, and bookkeepers were female in 1880; in 1900, 7 percent of all New York working women were filling such positions; and by 1920, this number had increased to 22 percent. These were native-born women who had received a public school education, primarily daughters of American, German, and Irish parents.[10]

Women's opportunities for jobs in trade and services expanded as consumers, travellers, and businesses demanded a range of urban amenities. Retail trade grew substantially, symbolized by the emergence of such large department stores as Macy's, Bloomingdale's, and Lord and Taylor's. The center for retail business moved uptown, near Fifth Avenue, Broadway, and 34th Street, close to an emerging commercial center, railroad connections, and middle-class residents. This expansion coincided with a shift in the sex-typing of store work. Retail sales had been a predominantly male occupation as late as the 1880's, when only 12 percent of clerks and salespersons in New York stores were women. By 1900, the saleslady had become a fixture of the retail emporium, a much coveted position for young working women. Working as a saleswoman or store clerk was the second most common occupation of native-born single wage-earners, whether "American girls" or daughters of immigrants.[11] Other businesses catered to the work routines and pleasures of a mobile, hectic population. Restaurants and lunchrooms, laundries, hotels, beauty parlors, drugstores, and theaters offered young women desirable alternatives to domestic service.

Although small workshops and households continued to play an important role in manufacturing, the production process increasingly turned toward larger factories. In the complex world of garment-making, conditions varied in the different branches of the industry. Generally, however, production shifted from isolated homework toward small sweatshops housed in tenements by the 1880's; by 1910, as the demand for ready-made clothing grew and further mechanization of the industry occurred, it was increasingly based in large-scale factories. John Commons estimated that, while 90 percent of ready-made garments had been produced in sweatshops in 1890, 75 percent were made in factories after 1900. While the clothing trades dominated New York industry, women also found work in a variety of light assembling and operative jobs producing consumer goods. Artificial flower-making, box-making, confectionary dipping, jewelry work, and bookbinding were typical female occupations.[12]

These new patterns of labor fostered differing work expectations across generations, expectations that particularly affected the American-born daughters of immigrant parents. Although domestic service remained the foremost occupation of single women, the daughters of immigrants increasingly refused to don the maid's uniform. In her 1914 study of 370 working mothers, Katharine Anthony found that almost half had been employed in domestic service and one-third in manufacturing before marriage; as working mothers, 70 percent of them labored in domestic and personal service. In contrast, most of their daughters worked in stores, offices, and factories, with only a small fraction going into service. "The German-American child wants a position in an office," noted anthropologist

Elsa Herzfeld. "The daughter refuses to go into domestic service although her mother had formerly taken a 'position.'"[13] New immigrant groups from southern and eastern Europe repeated this pattern. As Thomas Kessner has shown for the years 1880 and 1905, Italian and Jewish wives rarely worked outside the home, but depended on homework to supplement the family income. Their daughters' work patterns changed significantly in the twenty-five year period. Italian girls' occupations shifted from unskilled labor and street trades to factory work. Jewish girls throughout the period worked in the small shops of the garment industry, but by 1905 were also finding positions in schools, offices, and department stores.[14]

Women flocked to these jobs in part because they allowed more free time and autonomy, splitting the realms of work and leisure more clearly than household-based labor. A bitter complaint about domestic service was its lack of leisure time. One woman, for example, who had turned to service after working in manufacturing, asserted, "as long as I had a trade I was certain of my evenings an' my Sundays. Now I'm never certain of anything." An investigation into the "servant question" agreed with this assessment: "Especially is objection made to the fact that her evenings are not her own, so that she may go out at will with her friends or may attend places of amusement."[15]

Among working women, leisure came to be seen as a separate sphere of life to be consciously protected. Whether their employer was exploitative or well-intentioned, women resented interference with their "own" time. Nonunionized bindery workers, for example, tried to protest overtime work that kept them on the job through Christmas Eve. Shopgirls, too, who had been urged at a public hearing to state their grievances over working conditions, complained chiefly about not getting out of work on time. "Make them close at 6 o'clock," one exclaimed, testifying that her employer rang the closing bell late, causing store workers to labor an extra fifteen to thirty minutes: "Q. And that really has the result of depriving you of your evenings—of getting to places of entertainment in time, does it not? A. Yes sir; that is right." Another store clerk observed that all the workers took turns closing up the department, so that each night one could leave early at 5:45 P.M.[16]

Those who could—predominantly the young, unmarried, and

American-born—rejected the household-based, task-oriented employments that had traditionally been women's work. They preferred to labor in stores and factories, where they sold their labor and submitted to employers' work discipline for a specified portion of time. The remainder of the day, while often limited by exhaustion and household obligations, they could call their own. This distinctive sphere of leisure, demarcated in new forms of wage-earning, grew as the hours of labor decreased from 1880 to 1920.

THE DECLINING HOURS OF LABOR

The actual time working women had for relaxation and amusement is difficult to assess, since women's occupations rarely conformed to a single standard. Variations in the size and scale of industries, the seasonal nature of many jobs, differences between piecework and hourly wages, and low levels of unionization contributed to the non-uniformity of women's workdays. The New York State Bureau of Labor Statistics in 1885, for example, in cataloguing hundreds of industrial concerns, found that women's working days ranged from eight to seventeen hours. Even within a single industry, vast differences among workers are apparent. In the cigar industry, for example, some cigar-makers, presumably unionized, worked only eight hours, while bunch-makers regularly worked fifteen to seventeen hours daily. Moreover, women doing piecework often felt compelled to labor extra hours in the factory or at home in the evening.[17]

For many, the seasonal demand for consumer goods and services created an alternating pattern of intense labor and slack work. Garment manufacturers made heavy demands on employees in the fall and spring, but laid off workers in the dull seasons after Christmas and in the summer. The work history of one milliner typifies the casual employment many women faced: from February to May she had steady work; she was then laid off and hunted for a job in June and July; from August to December, she worked a total of fourteen weeks at four different establishments. During intermittent layoffs and the month-long slack period after Christmas, she sold candy. Cigarette-makers, carpet weavers, candy-makers, and bookbinders all experienced the seasonal rush to produce goods, and department store clerks put in ten- to sixteen-hour stints during the Christmas and Easter holidays. While posted hours in New York City factories were usually less than those upstate, many women regularly worked overtime as many as three or four nights a week during the busy season.[18] These spells allowed little time for leisure, while the slack season left women with time on their hands. Many looked for employment and filled in at other jobs, but others "took it easy" during the layoffs and, like Maria Cichetti, spent their hard-earned money going to vaudeville shows and movies.[19]

The contracting of jobs in some trades created a peculiar weekly rhythm of heavy labor and slack work. In many small task shops, garment-makers worked a fourteen-hour stretch for three days and then were idle the rest of the week. Similarly, laundries often had little work on Saturdays and Mondays, but might keep their employees at labor sixteen or seventeen hours on other days. In some jobs, labor intensity varied widely during the day. Waitresses, for example, often worked "split tricks"—on duty during the busy hours of lunch and dinner, relieved in the afternoon, hardly the best time for social engagements.[20]

Despite the irregularity of women's labor, the general trend of the period from 1880 to 1920 was toward shorter working days for female wage-earners in factories and stores. In 1885, women's workday ranged from ten to seventeen hours, but by the 1910's the long stints were much less common. Millinery workers, for example, who typically worked fourteen hours in 1885, put in only nine to ten hours in 1914. Similarly, a 1911 study of workers in lower Manhattan found that almost two-thirds of the female wage-earners worked less than ten hours daily. In addition, growing numbers of businesses closed early on Saturdays, particularly in the slow summer months, to give their workers a half-holiday.[21] The movement for protective legislation, greater union activity among working women, the increased rationalization of production, and changing attitudes toward workers' leisure contributed to this overall decline.

Protective legislation to lower women's work hours was pushed by middle-class reformers seeking to safeguard women's health and reproductive capacities, and by craft unions anxious about women's growing role in the workforce. Under pressure from these groups, New York's state legislature enacted a series of laws limiting the hours of labor, beginning in 1886 with the restriction of minors and women under twenty-one from working in manufacturing more than ten hours a day or sixty hours a week. This ceiling was extended to all female factory workers in 1899. In 1912, a revised statute curtailed the working day for women in manufacturing to nine hours, and two years later, this limit covered women's work in the city's mercantile stores. The nine-hour day and fifty-four hour week continued to be the legal standard in New York well into the 1920's.[22]

Generous loopholes and ineffective enforcement limited the efficacy of these laws, however. The legislation failed to cover women who did not work in factories and stores. It also permitted mercantile and industrial employers to demand irregular hours and overtime on a daily basis, as long as they obeyed the weekly limit. Enforcement was hampered by the hostility of employers, the limited number of factory inspectors, and the perfunctory penalties for violations. Mary Van Kleeck echoed the criticism of many reformers in observing that "the limit of the law is exceeded in numerous instances and in many trades—so that it is by no means uncommon to find young girls in the factories of New York working twelve, thirteen, even fourteen hours in a day." Despite these limitations, protective legislation contributed to the gradual decline in hours by setting legal limits and popularizing the notion of the "right to leisure." Major employers of women, including large clothing manufacturers and department stores, generally adhered to the labor laws.[23]

For some women, the labor movement's demand for the eight-hour day held the most promise of greater leisure. Although the vast majority of working women were not organized in this period, the union movement made important inroads after 1905 in industries with high female employment, such as garment-making and bookbinding. Bookbinders successfully struck for the eight-hour day in 1907, while waist-makers and other clothing workers achieved shorter hours in the settlements following the famous garment strikes of the 1910's.[24] Workers in unionized shops experienced a dramatic increase in their leisure time, as this young woman attested:

The shorter work day brought me my first idea of there being such a thing as pleasure. It was quite wonderful to get home

before it was pitch dark at night, and a real joy to ride on the cars
and look out the windows and see something. Before this time it
was just sleep and eat and hurry off to work. . . . I was twenty-
one before I went to a theater and then I went with a crowd of
union girls to a Saturday matinee performance. I was twenty-
three before I saw a dance and that was a union dance too.[25]

Changes in the scale and organization of industry also hastened
the decline in hours. As they achieved greater worker productivity
through scientific management and mechanization, many major employers yielded to the shorter workday. Thus the trend in New York
City toward larger mercantile establishments and factories had a
salutary effect on lowering working hours. The reorganization of the
garment trades, for example, sharply reduced hours. When the industry was dominated by home-sewing, there were no limits placed
on the hours women might work. Workers in small task shops continued to be plagued with irregular employment and fourteen-hour
workdays, while large clothing factories offered more steady work
and a ten- to eleven-hour day. These establishments stopped work at
6:00 P.M., giving workers their evenings for rest and recreation.
Similarly, the large department stores required only nine hours of
labor except in the pre-Christmas season, in contrast to smaller
neighborhood stores, which kept late hours to serve the working-
class trade.[26]

Finally, liberalized attitudes toward workers' leisure began to
take hold by the 1910's. The philanthropic bent of some large indus-
trialists and retail merchants, joined with their desire to forestall
unionization drives, led to welfare programs and practices designed
to improve workers' health and well-being, in part by reducing
hours. Josephine Goldmark's influential study of workers and efficiency, Louis Brandeis' brief on the hazards of long hours and night
work for women, and the publicity campaigns of the Consumer's
League contributed to the growing cultural legitimacy of the short
day for women.[27]

By 1920, the hours of labor had declined sharply for many urban
working women. In 1923, three-quarters of the women surveyed by
the New York State Department of Labor worked only forty-eight
hours or less in New York City, in contrast to their upstate sisters, of

whom fewer than one-third worked such a short week. The memories of Nathan Cohen and Ruth Kaminsky, brother and sister, suggest the dimensions of change in the hours of labor. Nathan, a Russian immigrant who arrived in the United States in 1912, remembers doing little at night other than working, but his sister Ruth, who came to this country in 1921, had time to go to night school: "When I came over, they didn't work ten, twelve hours a day anymore. Tops was eight, nine, unless it was a small business, or some factories." Although she worked nine hours daily with a Saturday half-holiday in the 1910's, observed another immigrant woman, "at that time, we didn't consider it long."[28]

WORK CULTURES AND WOMEN'S LEISURE

While the shortened workday allowed more leisure time, women's experiences in the workplace reinforced the appeal of pleasure-oriented recreation in the public sphere. On one level, the desire for frivolous amusement was a reaction against the discipline, drudgery, and exploitative conditions of labor. A woman could forget rattling machinery or irritating customers in the nervous energy and freedom of the grizzly bear and turkey trot, or escape the rigors of the workplace altogether by finding a husband in the city's night spots. "You never rest until you die," observed one young box-maker, "but I will get out by marrying somebody." Indeed, factory investigators recorded the "wide-spread belief of the girls that marriage is relief from the trouble and toil of wage labor."[29]

At the same time, women's notions of leisure were reaffirmed through their positive social interactions within the workplace. In factories, stores, and offices, women socialized with other women and informally cooperated to affect working conditions. Their experience of work in a group context differed sharply from the homebound, task-oriented, and isolated situation of domestic servants, outworkers, and housewives. There developed in this setting a shared and public culture, which legitimized the desires and behaviors expressed in young women's leisure.

Like other work groups, women workers developed degrees of autonomy and control in their relationship to managers and the work process by enforcing informal work rules and production quotas, socializing new employees into these patterns of behavior, and protecting their job skills from the bosses' encroachment. Given their status as low-skilled and easily replaced workers, wage–earning women rarely commanded the control over the work process that men in the skilled trades could exert, but neither were they merely victims of capitalist discipline.[30] Department store saleswomen, for example, used their selling skills to manipulate managers, supervisors, and customers, enforcing work rules among the women to sell only so many goods each day and employing code words to warn co-workers of recalcitrant customers. Bookbinders too employed the notion of a "fair day's work," controlling the output during each stint, while other factory hands orchestrated work stoppages and job actions over such issues as sexual harassment and pay cuts. Even waitresses worked out their resentment toward employers by pilfering pins and small objects, supplying themselves liberally with ice water and towels, and eating desserts ordered for imaginary customers.[31]

In mediating the relationship between the wage-earner and the labor process, work cultures involved not only informal efforts to control work but also the daily interactions that helped pass the long hours. While women characterized the workplace as tedious and demanding, a necessity to be endured, most tried to create places of sociability and support on the shop floor. Women sang songs, recited the plots of novels, argued politics, and gossiped about social life to counteract the monotony and routine of the workday. One feather-maker, for example, described her co-workers' conversations: "We have such a good time. We talk about books that we read, . . . the theatres, and newspapers, and the things that go on about town." Pieceworkers, who had more control over their time than hourly hands, could follow their own rhythms of intense work mixed with periods of sociability. "When I was a pieceworker," recalled one garment worker, "I would sing, I would fool around, say jokes, talk with the girls."[32] Singing helped pace the work, as in one box-makers' shop where songs would rise and fall while the workers sped through their tasks:

Three o'clock, a quarter after, half-past! The terrific tension had all but reached the breaking point. Then there rose a trembling, palpitating sigh that seemed to come from a hundred throats, and blended in a universal expression of relief. In her clear, high treble Angelina began the everlasting "Fatal Wedding." That piece of false sentiment had now a new significance. It became a song of deliverance, and as the workers swelled the chorus, one by one, it meant that the end of the day's toil was in sight.[33]

Even in factories with loud machinery, women would try to converse above the noise, while lunch hours and the after-work walk home also afforded time to socialize with workmates. At Macy's, employees were "fond of sitting down in a corner and eating a pickle and pastry and a cup of tea; they can do that very quickly and can then visit for quite a long time during the rest of the noon hour."[34] Women's work cultures varied according to type of employment, ethnic and religious affiliation, and larger cultural traditions. American-born union women, believing in self-education and uplift, often mirrored their male counterparts' behavior in the shop. In one New York cigar factory, for example, female trade unionists would pay one of their members to read aloud while they worked: "First the newspaper is read, then some literary work, such as for instance Morley's 'Life of Gladstone.' "[35] Even among nonunionized workers, the rituals, rules, and interactions governing work in stores and restaurants, where interpersonal skills were utilized, differed from semiskilled production, where machinery dominated the shop floor. The women themselves had a firm understanding of the occupational hierarchy indicated by language, mores, and "tone." The saleslady's patina of style and refinement differentiated her from the rougher manner of many tobacco or garment workers. Within a single industry, ethnic patterns also shaped different work cultures; cultural and political traditions, for example, contributed to the Jewish waist-makers' readiness to organize and strike, unlike their more hesitant Italian workmates.[36] Despite these distinctive differences, we can discern important commonalities in the work cultures of women that shaped and defined their attitudes toward leisure.

In the workplace, young women marked out a cultural terrain distinct from familial traditions and the customary practices of their ethnic groups, signifying a new identity as wage-earners through language, clothing, and social rituals. "Learners" might adopt new

names from storybook romances when they entered a workplace for
the first time, and greenhorns shed their Old World names for An-
glicized ones. Fads, modish attire, and a distinctive personal style
were also encouraged, as wage-earners discussed the latest fashions,
learned new hairstyles, and tried out cosmetics and cigarettes. Indeed, employers often found it necessary to proscribe the unseemly
behavior of working women: "At Koch's there is a splendid system of
rules prohibiting the chewing of gum, rougeing and excessively
using face powder."[37]

For factory hands, talking and socializing forged links between
the world of labor and the pleasures of leisure. Some working girls,
noted Lillian Betts, "dance[d] on the street at lunch-time, in front of
their factory, singing their own dance music."[38] Part of the enjoyment inherent in the evening's entertainment lay in recounting the
triumphs of the ball or party to one's workmates. Moreover, co-
workers became a circle of friends apart from neighborhood or ethnic group ties. One Jewish garment worker observed, for example,
that "while working, [I] used to have friends—Gentile girls. Sometimes we used to go out, we used to attend weddings, [I] was in their
homes a few times."[39] Others formed social clubs comprised of co-
workers and school friends.

Department store workers too were irrepressible in integrating
work and social life through their use of language, special events,
and organizations. When extra employees were laid off at the end of
the holiday season, for example, they referred to the mass exodus as
the "cake walk," after the popular Afro-American dance and strut.
Holidays and engagements were constant excuses for parties, sup-
pers, and celebrations. A popular ritual involved cutting a Hal-
loween cake, wherein one lucky saleswoman found a ring, forecast-
ing marriage, while an unfortunate co-worker discovered a button
or thimble, threatening spinsterhood. Numerous social clubs formalized the relationship between work and leisure. At the Siegel-
Cooper department store, the workers banded together by department, forming, for example, the Foot Mould Social Club, comprised
of women in the shoe department, and the Bachelor Girls Social
Club, organized by the mail order clerks. These associations of
women workers typically sponsored dances, entertainments, and
excursions to Coney Island.[40]

In the workplace, women's conversations, stories, and songs often gravitated to the subject of dating and romantic entanglements with men, a discourse that accentuated the mixed-sex character of their leisure. During free moments, waitresses relished gossip about "the ubiquitous 'gentleman friend,' the only topic of conversation outside of the dining room interests." Women's socialization into a new workplace might involve a ritualistic exchange over "gentlemen friends." In one steam laundry, for example, an investigator repeatedly heard this conversation:

> 'Say, you got a feller?'
> 'Sure. Ain't you got one?'
> 'Sure.'[41]

One Jewish garment worker recalled daydreaming about love and marriage in the shops: "We used to even sing the songs . . . Yiddish naturally, singing the dream songs, the love songs, and this is how we dreamed away our youth and go out gay and happy."[42]

In department stores, the mixed-sex workplace became a setting for romance, trysts, and discussion of male-female relations. *Thought and Work*, the in-house magazine of the Seigel-Cooper department store, which was written by workers, evinced little interest in selling skills and business news, but resonated with gossip about eligible bachelors, intra-store courtships, wedding notices, and entertainments about town. Personal popularity, beauty, hair styles, clothing, and dancing ability were newsworthy items. Cultural practices among department store workers emerge from the breathless commentary of the newsletter: the saleslady who changes her hair color because, the gossip speculates, she "wants a man"; the competition between departments for the most engagements and marriages; the delivery of roses and mash notes to young women; the debates among idle saleswomen on such topics as kissing mustachioed men. Some department managers were portrayed more as popular matchmakers than enforcers of work discipline. "Mr. Eckle is a past master at securing husbands for the young ladies in his department," noted *Thought and Work*. "He'd rather do that than sign time cards."[43] While doubtlessly the magazine embellished the business of romance at the store, management eventually reined in its editors, ordering less copy on personal life and more articles on the business of selling.[44]

Bound to the language of romance was the frank discussion of sexuality among laboring women, a practice in the workplace that mirrored that of popular amusements. Risque jokes, swearing, and sexual advice were a common part of the work environment in restaurants, laundries, factories, and department stores. Waitresses bandied obscenities and engaged in explicit discussion of lovers and husbands before work and during breaks. As one surprised middle-class observer described the scene in a restaurant: "They were putting on their aprons, combing their hair, powdering their noses, . . . all the while tossing back and forth to each other, apparently in a spirit of good-natured comradeship, the most vile epithets that I had ever heard emerge from the lips of a human being."[45] Despite their image of gentility and upward mobility, department store workers relished a similar freedom in language and behavior. At Macy's, a store that sought to maintain strict standards of employee respectability, investigators found "salacious cards, poems, etc., copied with avidity and passed from one to another, not only between girls and girls, but from girls to men." While many workers remained aloof from such vulgarities, there was "more smutty talk in one particular department than in a dance hall."[46]

Sexual knowledge was communicated between married and single women, between the experienced and the naive. A YWCA study of the woman worker observed that "the 'older hands' initiate her early through the unwholesome story or innuendo. She is forced to think of sex matters in relation to herself by the suggestions made to her of what she may expect from suitors or find in marriage." Examples of such initiation abound in the reports of middle-class investigators and reformers. In one department at Macy's dominated by married women, for example, "there was enough indecent talk to ruin any girl in her teens who might be put at work on that floor."[47] Stripped of their moralistic overtones, such observations reveal the workplace as an arena in which women wage-earners articulated their sexual feelings and shared their acquired wisdom about negotiating the attentions of men, both on the job and in their leisure time.

It was also an arena in which they experienced sexual vulnerability, a world of harassment as well as the give-and-take of
humor and conversation. Then as now, sexual harassment limited
women's position in the workforce and maintained male privilege
and control. Wage-earning women were perceived by bosses and
male workers alike to be outside the realm of parental or community
protection. As one cigar-maker observed, behavior that in another
context would not be tolerated was given free rein on the shop floor:

> Many men who are respected—when I say respected and re-
> spectable, I mean who walk the streets and are respected as
> working men, and who would not, under any circumstances, of-
> fer the slightest insult or disrespectful remark or glance to a
> female in the streets, . . . in the shops, will whoop and give ex-
> pressions to "cat calls" and a peculiar noise made with their lips,
> which is supposed to be an endearing salutation.[48]

Women learned to tread a fine line between participating in acceptable workplace practices and guarding their integrity and respectability. Macy's clerks, who could trade obscenities and *double en-
tendres* with the salesmen, knew "just how to be very friendly,
without permitting the least familiarity," when conversing with male
customers. As one factory investigator observed, "such women
learn to defend themselves and to take care of themselves."[49] As we
shall see in later chapters, this sexual knowledge gained in the workplace informed women's relations with men in the world of leisure.

WOMEN'S WAGES AND TREATING

The work culture of women encouraged an ideology of romance that
resonated with explicit heterosexual pleasures and perils at the
same time that it affirmed the value of leisure. Still, working wom-
en's lack of financial resources posed a problem to their participation
in an active social life, particularly in the world of commercial
amusements. On the surface, low wages and little spending money
would seem to have limited women's access to leisure, thus under-
cutting the heterosocial, pleasure-oriented culture of the work-

place. Paradoxically, the material conditions of their lives at work
and at home served instead to strengthen that culture.

Working women in New York typically earned below the "living
wage," estimated by economists to be nine or ten dollars a week in
1910. Employers and workingmen alike justified women's low
wages and their exclusion from higher-paying skilled trades by
claiming that women were temporary wage-earners who worked
only until marriage. Occupational segregation of the labor market
was deeply entrenched, and women were concentrated in semiskilled, seasonal employment. As cashgirls and salesclerks, as-
semblers and machine-tenders, waitresses and servants, their average earnings were one-half of those received by men in their
employments. In New York factories in the early 1910's, 56 percent
of the female labor force earned under $8.00 a week. Despite their
higher social status, the majority of women in retail stores earned
under $7.50, although the large emporia offered higher wages than
neighborhood stores and five-and-tens. Deductions for tardiness,
poor workmanship, and other violations further depleted wage-
earners' already meager earnings.[50]

Relatively few women were able to live alone in comfort. Among
the large industrial cities of the United States, New York had one of
the highest percentages of wage-earning women residing with parents or relatives, from 80 to 90 percent. Self-supporting workers
lodging in boardinghouses or renting rooms tended to be older,
native-born women who earned higher wages than those living at
home.[51] Most found, nevertheless, that their earnings were consumed by the cost of room, board, and clothing, leaving little for
recreation.

To make ends meet, self-supporting women would scrimp on essential items in their weekly budgets. Going without meals was one
common strategy, as was sleeping three to a bed to reduce the rent.
"Some never boarded a street car for an evening's ride without planning days ahead how they could spare the nickel from their lunch or
clothes money," noted reformer Esther Packard, describing women
who lived on six dollars a week.[52] After work, the self-supporting
woman sewed and washed her own clothing, cooked meals, and pre-
pared for the next workday. Such scheduling and scrimping often

left little time or money for evening amusements: "When the women or girls were visited at night, they were more likely to be found at home busy at the wash tub or ironing board than out at a dance or the theater." A movie and occasional ball were their only forms of leisure.[53]

By scrimping and making do, young women could provide some recreation for themselves. Yeddie Bruker, a factory worker earning seven dollars a week, spent almost two dollars of that on clothing and four dollars on room and board. A union member, she spent sixteen cents weekly for union dues and a benefit association, while for recreation she allocated ten cents a week for theatre tickets. Katia Markelov, a corset maker earning ten dollars, saved thirty dollars yearly for outings, while Rita Karpovna's low wages, six to seven dollars weekly, forced her to sacrifice essential items for union dues and the "Woman's Self-Education Society": "The Union and this club meant more to Rita than the breakfasts and luncheons she dispensed with, and more, apparently, than dress, for which she spent only $20 in a year and a half."[54]

For women living at home, recreation was limited not so much by the size of their income as by access to it. In exchange for their wages, most parents gave their daughters small sums of spending money, averaging twenty-five to fifty cents each week, in addition to lunch money and carfare. Like self-supporting women, those who lived at home necessarily scrimped and depended on others for recreation. They commonly saved their allowances for lunch by eating the free food served in saloons or skipping the meal altogether. Many, like Maria Cichetti, saved carfare by walking to or from work. Maria received ten cents for the roundtrip trolley ride to her shop; by walking home with friends at night, she could save a nickel for the movies. As one investigator of West Side girls observed, "A carfare saved by walking to work is a carfare earned for a trip to a dance hall 'away out in the Bronx.'"[55]

Women also relied on co-workers and female friends to help them out with food, clothing, and recreation. The low-wage cashgirl or salesclerk was "helped by those about her in the store with gifts of clothing or even with money," observed one salesgirl. In factories, older wage-earners would aid the youngest by paying her a dime to fetch tea or lunch. A tradition of mutual aid and support can be seen in the frequency of raffles and events to raise money for less fortunate workmates.[56]

Typically, however, young women looked to men for financial assistance and gifts. "If they didn't take me, how could I ever go out?" observed a young department store worker. Treating was a widely accepted practice, especially if the woman had a fiance, or "steady," from whom she could accept food, clothing, and recreation without compromising her reputation. One woman, for example, counted on her steady for Sunday meals, exclaiming, "Why! if I had to buy all of my meals I'd never get along." Unable to save a penny of her seven-dollar weekly wage, Clara X. depended on her beau, who earned more than twice her income, to occasionally purchase her clothes and take her on vacation.[57] Rose Pasternak paid for an overcoat on installments until she was "keeping company": "I paid and paid and paid, till I got with the company with my fella. He paid eight dollars. After I was a long time married, he used to throw it in my face, 'you made so much money that I had to pay for the plush coat.'"[58] Other self-supporting women had no qualms about accepting treats from unknown men or chance acquaintances. As one observer concluded, "the acceptance on the part of the girl of almost any invitation needs little explanation when one realizes that she often goes pleasureless unless she does accept 'free treats.'"[59]

The culture of treating was reinforced in the workplace through women's interactions with employers, male workmates, and customers, particularly in service and sales jobs. In department stores, managers were said to advise shopgirls to find gentleman friends who could buy them the clothing and trinkets that their salaries could not cover. At a government hearing, one saleswoman testified: "One of the employers has told me, on a $6.50 wage, he don't care where I get my clothes from as long as I have them, to be dressed to suit him."[60] Some investigators denied the accuracy of these reports, but their widespread currency among saleswomen suggest the tacit legitimacy of treating as a means of gaining access to the world of amusements. Waitresses knew that suggestive familiarity with male customers often brought good tips, and some used their skills and opportunities to engage in an active social life with chance acquaintances. "Most of the girls quite frankly admit making 'dates' with strange men," observed a Consumer's League study. "These 'dates' are made with no thought on the part of the girl beyond getting the good time which she cannot afford herself."[61] These working women sought a way to negotiate dependency and claim some choice, autonomy, and pleasure in otherwise dreary lives. They understood, albeit hazily, that leisure was the realm in which that quest could most easily be achieved.

CHAPTER THREE

PUTTING ON STYLE

In the twentieth century, youth is regarded as a distinctive stage of life, a time of self-expression and experimentation before the experience of marriage, children, and work. Clearly applicable to middle-class teen-agers, who can nurture a separate culture in high schools and colleges,[1] this notion of youth may not seem relevant to the working-class adolescents of 1900, who felt the pinch of financial responsibility at an early age and subordinated individual desires to the family's survival. Nevertheless, working-class youth spent much of their leisure apart from their families and enjoyed greater social freedom than their parents or married siblings, especially married women. Despite maternal efforts to make the home a place of recreation, they fled the tenements for the streets, dance halls, and theaters, generally bypassing their fathers' saloons and lodges. Adolescents formed social clubs, organized entertainments, and patronized new commercial amusements, shaping, in effect, a working-class youth culture expressed through leisure activity.

Young working-class men had a long history of creating organizations for their own sociability. Militias and volunteer fire companies, for example, provided a structure for the bachelor subcultures of the mid-nineteenth century. By the 1890's, gangs and social clubs had taken over this function. Certain forms of commercial recreation in the nineteenth century, such as pool halls, billiard parlors, and dime museums, were also identified with unmarried men, particularly the lodging-house population. The pattern of age segregation among men continued after 1900; George Bevans found that young work-ingmen went chiefly to theaters, dances, poolrooms, and clubs while their fathers sought the camaraderie of saloons and lodges.[2]

Single women in New York also pursued a social life distinct from their working-class parents', but their search for pleasure in public forms of recreation was shaped not only by long-standing patterns of culture and social organization but by new conditions of family life, work, and commercialized leisure in the city. The alluring world of urban amusements drew young women away from the ugliness of tenement life and the treadmill of work. Not content with quiet recreation in the home, they sought adventure in dance halls, cheap theaters, amusement parks, excursion boats, and picnic grounds. Putting on finery, promenading the streets, and staying late at amusement resorts became an important cultural style for many working women. Entrepreneurs sought ways to increase female par-ticipation in commercialized recreation, encouraging women's fancy dress, slangy speech, and provocative public behavior, as we shall see in later chapters. These cultural forms were not simply imposed on working-class female consumers by the emergent entertainment industry, however, but were developed and articulated as well by the young women themselves. Without doubt, amusement en-trepreneurs capitalized on female fads and fancies, constructing de-sires as well as responding to them. Nevertheless, working women and men created their own forms of activity that broadly structured their social relationships and expressed a distinctive constellation of values and concerns. This process is most apparent in two noncom-mercial forms of recreation, the streets and social clubs, which working-class youth colonized as their own social spaces.

SOCIAL LIFE IN THE STREETS

The city streets were public conduits of sociability and free ex-pression for all working-class people, avenues for protest, celebra-tion, and amusement. Still, children and young people claimed ownership of the streets, despite intensified efforts by police and reformers to eradicate unruly revelry and unsanctioned behavior from the mid-century onward. Young working-class women throughout the nineteenth century were among those who flocked to the streets in pursuit of pleasure and amusement, using public spaces for flamboyant assertion. Although such "rowdy girls" had long been targets of public commentary for their supposed immorality and wanton behavior, young women continued to seek the streets to search for men, have a good time, and display their clothes and style in a public arena.[3]

Working-class girls were more supervised than boys, whose choice of activities was seemingly endless: exploring the neighborhoods, scavenging in alleys, shooting craps, playing baseball, masterminding petty robberies, lighting election night bonfires, chasing ambulances, harassing peddlars. Gang organizations were rampant throughout the working-class districts of the city, where groups of boys held sway over specific blocks, fighting interlopers and rival gangs.[4] Although girls did not enjoy this level of activity and organization, the streets offered countless diversions. As Sophie Ruskay recalled, "We shared the life of the street unhampered by our parents who were too busy to try to mold us into a more respectable pattern."[5] Even when saddled with minding a younger sibling, girls could still play sidewalk games, chat with friends, revel in the city's sights and sounds, or gather around itinerant musicians to try out their dancing skill. Girls did not form their own gangs, but some of the more adventurous joined in the boys' fun, roaming the streets and playing tricks on passers-by. As one study noted, "individual girls are frequently attached to boys' gangs and are sometimes real factors in the gang-government."[6] More important, the streets were alternative environments that taught children a repertoire of manners and mores they did not learn in school. Attitudes toward sexuality, marriage, and women's work were conveyed in street games and rhymes.[7]

In their teens, young women and men used the streets as a place to meet the other sex, to explore nascent sexual feelings, and carry on flirtations, all outside the watchful eyes and admonitions of parents. "Doing nothing"—small talk, scuffling, joking, and carrying on—was infused with meaning for working-class youth. With no supervision but the cop on the beat, young women could be unladylike and unrestrained on street corners and in doorways. To Maureen Connelly, an Irish immigrant to the Yorkville section of Manhattan, "fun was standing at the door with boys and girls and kidding around—this was a big thing in our life—until the policeman came and chased us."[8] Some adolescent girls, whom parents and reformers labelled "tough," spent their evenings on street corners and in alleys and gang hangouts until late at night. More respectable young women might promenade the local commercial streets or parks in a group or with a gentleman friend, enjoying the walk, window-shopping, and chatting. Each working-class neighborhood had its place to be seen: Eighth Avenue, with its gaudy movie houses and flashing lights drew crowds of West Side Irish, German, and native-born youth; the Bowery, Grand Street, and 14th Street attracted the inhabitants of the lower East Side; and First Avenue near 72nd Street was known as the Czech Broadway to its promenaders.[9]

SOCIAL CLUBS

The streets offered uninhibited space for youth activity; social clubs and amusement societies offered an organizational structure. Social clubs evolved from several traditions of associational life, including the lodge, political club, and gang. By the late nineteenth century, street gangs were increasingly being transformed into social or pleasure clubs throughout the working-class neighborhoods of Manhattan, as police and reformers cracked down on gang activity. Social clubs often had the patronage of political associations like Tammany and were places where budding politicos learned to become part of the party machinery. As the *Civic Journal* observed, "To move into public life under local conditions a man must 'play monkey' to the political hand-organ of his party, and it is a *club* that turns the crank."[10]

With names like the Go-Aheads, the East Side Crashers, the Round-Back Rangers, and the Limburger Roarers, the clubs ranged from the respectable to the marginally criminal. University Settlement observed that the social instinct in the lower East Side "[found] its gratification in countless "Pleasure Clubs," the height of whose ambitions is a chowder party in summer and a ball in winter."[11] Clubs contained approximately twenty-five to fifty members, youths fifteen to eighteen years of age who attended school or worked in factories and offices. These clubs usually met once a week in a rented hall, saloon, or tenement basement to discuss business and organize dances and entertainments. Other nights club members might gather in a cigar store or cafe to drink, smoke, play cards, and gamble.

Young women's involvement in social and pleasure clubs varied. Some joined clubs that functioned like the lodges and associations of older working-class men. The Roumanian Young Folks' Social Club and the Independent Bukowmaer Young Men's and Young Ladies' Benefit Society were typical *landsmanschaft* organizations of the lower East Side. These proffered mutual assistance, sick benefits, and burial plots while encouraging immigrant youth to remain close to their traditional cultures through sociable gatherings. "We had a social club from our city," recalled Ruth Kaminsky. "We used to go to meetings every second week or meet in our house."[12] However, most young women did not join mutual benefit societies to the same degree as their fathers and brothers. Only saleswomen joined in large numbers, but these associations were usually sponsored by the department stores. The five to ten cents a week other wage-earners customarily spent on insurance and death benefits was often paid into a private insurance company whose function was entirely commercial rather than recreational and communal.[13]

More often, youth organizations tended to be oriented toward amusement and mixed-sex sociability rather than mutual aid, education, or political action. Significantly, social clubs were often called "pleasure clubs" by their patrons, to differentiate them from the more serious-minded lodges and benefit societies. As one investigator testified, women's organizations "seem to be largely social; they belong to little societies; they tell me they belong to a 'Heart and Hand Club,' a social club; nothing for the study of their own wage conditions at all."[14] Women were admitted to auxiliaries of young men's pleasure clubs or formed their own, adopting such outrageous names as the Lady Flashers, the Lady Millionaires, and the Lady Liberties of the Fourth Ward. Organizing social clubs was a simple task. "You get together a number of people, you know, youngsters, . . . in the neighborhood and you just open up a social club," recalled Rachel Levin, who lived in the lower East Side. "We set . . . up our own programs," observed Ida Schwartz, a Russian-born milliner who joined a club when she was seventeen. "We made an organization, and we had a little dues, and then we used to make affairs and you made dances and met people, like young people do."[15] Her club was typical of these organizations; its primary aim was to sponsor elaborate social gatherings for itself and rival clubs, hold dances in rented halls, and congregate at the city's picnic parks and beaches.

These single-sex and mixed-sex clubs structured social interaction by engineering the introduction and rendezvous of working-class youth. Schwartz noted that her club was comprised of men and women from school and work, whose friendship often led to marriage: "We were about twenty couples, and then of course when we got older, we were married . . . among the girls."[16] To parents, allowing a daughter to step out with the crowd was more acceptable than permitting her to go out alone on a date. Young women too sought safety in numbers. Around the time that she graduated eighth grade and entered the workforce, Maureen Connelly joined the Friends of Irish Freedom, an ostensibly political organization, but one which, she noted, "was more social than anything else." The group had meetings every Friday night, followed by a dance, which was "the highlight of our lives." She had little interest in what they did for Ireland, but "most of the girls joined—and of course you didn't go with a boy when you were seventeen. They were there and we danced with them and laughed about them, but you didn't take them serious."[17]

The importance of social clubs as mediators of urban courtship may also be seen in a short story, "Schadchen's Luck," written by a member of the Henry Street Settlement, Samuel Lewenkrohn. In this story, a matchmaker tries unsuccessfully to bring together two young East Siders, who resist his efforts and demand the freedom to seek a mate of their own choosing. The young man's social club runs a ball, and the woman attends with her girl friends to represent their club. The two meet, he asks her to dance, true love triumphs—and the relieved matchmaker claims to have fulfilled his end of the bargain.[18]

The activities that young working-class women pursued in their leisure were largely heterosocial in orientation, directed toward meeting men, dating, romance, and fun. Reformer Belle Israels summed up the attitude of many working girls when she noted, "No amusement is complete in which *he* is not a factor."[19] At the same time, it would be misleading to view the consciousness of most young women solely in terms of a desire for marriage and to argue that their leisure activities simply affirmed the world of their fathers, a traditional patriarchal order.

Ambiguously, young women marked out their leisure time not only as an opportunity for romantic entanglement but also as a sphere of autonomy and assertion. The Bachelor Girls Social Club, composed of female mail order clerks at Siegel-Cooper, addressed this paradox when they were accused by several male co-workers of being "manhaters" and of "celebrat[ing] Washington's Birthday without even thinking of a man." The club heatedly responded: "No, we are not married, neither are we men haters, but we believe in woman's rights, and we enjoy our independence and freedom, notwithstanding the fact that if a fair offer came our way we might not [sic] consider it."[20] Young women's desire for social freedom and its identification with leisure activities spilled over into behavior unsanctioned by parents and neighbors, as well as middle-class reformers. Clubs, for example, could be gathering places for sexual experimentation. A club member familiar with the organizational life of young East Siders reported to the University Settlement that "in all [clubs] 'they have kissing all through pleasure time, and use slang language,' while in some they 'don't behave nice between young ladies.'" Similarly the street corners and doorways were spaces for kissing, hugging, and fondling, free and easy sexual behavior "which seem[s] quite improper to the 'up-towner,'" but was casually accepted by working-class youth.[21]

CLOTHING, STYLE, AND LEISURE

Streets and social clubs, as well as such commercial forms of amusement as dance halls and theaters, became the spaces in which young women could carve out a cultural style expressing these complex and often contradictory values. It was in leisure that women played with identity, trying on new images and roles, appropriating the cultural forms around them—clothing, music, language—to push at the boundaries of immigrant, working-class life. This public presentation of self was one way to comment upon and mediate the dynamics of urban life and labor—poverty and the magnet of upward mobility, sexual assertion and the maintenance of respectability, daughterly submission and the attractions of autonomy and romance, the grinding workday and the glittering appeal of urban nightlife.

Promenading the streets and going places with the crowd, young working-class women "put on style." Dress was a particularly potent way to display and play with notions of respectability, allure, independence, and status and to assert a distinctive identity and presence. Genteel reformers noted with concern the tendency of young working women to present an appearance fraught with questionable moral and social connotations. Mary Augusta LaSelle lamented the use of low decolletage, gauze stockings, high-heeled shoes, freakish hats, and hair dressed with "rats" and "puffs," or artificial hair pieces—"in too many cases a fantastic imitation of the costly costumes of women of large incomes."[22] To such middle-class observers, working women were seeking upward mobility, dressing like their betters in order to marry into a higher class. This interpretation, while not without foundation, obscures the more complex role of fashion and style in the social life of working women.

Proper clothing in working-class culture traditionally helped to define respectability. As Lillian Betts observed of the workingman, "He, with the mother, has one standard—clothes."[23] Among laboring families hard pressed for income, dress divided itself into two types, work clothes and Sunday clothes. Work clothing necessarily varied with the requirements of job and employer, from the crisp white aprons and caps of waitresses to the hand-me-down garments worn by factory hands. Sunday clothes, however, were visible displays of social standing and self-respect in the rituals of churchgoing, promenading, and visiting. Appropriate attire was a requirement of social participation. Elena and Gerda Nakov, two impoverished needlewomen, considered "their clothing [to be] so poor that they were ashamed to go out on Sunday—when everybody else put on 'best dresses'—and would sit in their room all day."[24] For newly arrived immigrants, changing one's clothes was the first step in securing a new status as an American. When Rose Pasternak landed at Castle Garden, her brother took her directly to a hat store: "They said in this country you don't go to work without a hat."[25]

Clothing was only the palpable aspect of competing cultural

styles among young working–class women. Patterns of speech, manners, levels of schooling, attitudes toward self-improvement, and class consciousness differentiated groups of women beyond the obvious divisions of ethnicity and religion. In workshops, stores, clubs, and dance halls, observers noted the cliquishness of adolescent girls around these considerations. In the moralistic language of one reform committee, "The several floors of a large factory often mean as many degrees of respectability or demoralization" among working women.[26] Journalist Mary Gay Humphreys described the New York girls of the 1890's who took themselves seriously as independent and thoughtful workers, and reflected this view in their public style. Women strikers in a thread-mill, for example, linked fashion—wearing bonnets—to their sense of American identity and class consciousness, contrasting their militancy to Scottish scabs who wore shawls on their heads. Believing in the labor movement's ideology of self-improvement, organization, and workers' dignity, these women devoted their leisure to lectures, evening school, political meetings, and union dances. While they sewed their own ball gowns and loved display, they also agreed that ribbons were a "foolish extravagance."[27]

For other young women, dress became a cultural terrain of pleasure, expressiveness, romance, and autonomy. "A girl must have clothes if she is to go into high society at Ulmer Park or Coney Island or the theatre," explained Sadie Frowne, a sixteen-year-old garment worker. "A girl who does not dress well is stuck in a corner, even if she is pretty." Similarly, Minnie saved her earnings in order to "'blow herself' to an enormous bunch of new hair, which had transformed her from what she called 'a back number' to 'something dead swell.'" As another working woman succinctly put it, "If you want to get any notion took of you, you gotta have some style about you."[28]

Stylish clothing—a chinchilla coat, a beaded wedding dress, a straw hat with a willow plume—was an aspect of popular culture that particularly tugged at women's desires. Maria Cichetti lovingly remembers hats and the sense of being "dressed": "They were so beautiful, those hats. . . . They were so rich. A woman looked so dressed, you know, in the back, with the bustle. . . . I wanted to grow up to wear earrings and hats and high heels."[29] The demands of fashion caused Rose Pasternak to be docked for lateness:

That time they wear the big puffs on the hair, you know, like
wigs. Until I put on the girdle—my brother and my cousin used
to pull the laces for me, you know—until I fix the hair, till I
walked to the place to work. . . . I was ten minutes late, five
minutes late. . . . On four dollars a week, I never had a full pay.[30]

Many department store clerks, observed a saleswoman, were restrained and sensible in their clothing, but "there are others of us
who powder and paint, who bleach our hair, whose bodies suffer for
food because every penny goes for clothes."[31] Even newsgirls who
could ill afford a presentable shirtwaist might splurge on an outrageous hat. To be stunningly attired at the movies, balls, or entertainments often counted more in the working woman's calculations
than having comfortable clothes and shoes for the daily round of toil.

The fashions such young women wore often displayed aristocratic
pretensions. Grand Street clothing stores cheaply produced the
styles found in exclusive establishments. Working women read the
fashion columns, and many could observe wealthy women in department stores and the streets for inspiration in their dressmaking.
This seems to have been one manifestation of a broader pattern
whereby working-class youth played with the culture of the elite.
Etiquette demanded, for example, that they refer to their closest
comrades as "lady friends" and "gentleman friends." Jacob Riis even
reported the organization of a boys' club which called itself the Gentlemen's Sons' Association. Similarly, romance novels such as *Woven
on Fate's Loom,* in which wealthy heroes and long-suffering young
heroines underwent the turns of fortune, were popular reading. The
female box-makers whom Dorothy Richardson observed even
adopted storybook names that connoted wealth and romance, such
as Henrietta Manners and Rose Fortune.[32]

Working women's identification with the rich seems to have been
more playful and mediated than direct and calculated, as much a
commentary on the rigors of working-class life as a plan for the future. Significantly, women did not imitate *haute couture* directly,
but adapted and transformed such fashion in creating their own
style. While they could ill afford the fine cloth or exquisite decorations of the wealthy woman's dress, there was no purely economic
reason why they chose to wear flashy colors, gaudy hats, and cosmetics. Indeed, imitation of "ladies of leisure" might involve admir-

ing the style of prostitutes as well as socialites. As Ruth Rosen has argued, much of the appearance of twentieth-century women, including their use of make-up and wigs, was common among prostitutes before becoming accepted by "respectable" females.[33] In the promiscuous spaces of the streets, theaters, and dance halls, prostitutes provided a cultural model both fascinating and forbidden to other young working-class women. Tantalized by the fine dress, easy life, sexual expressiveness, and apparent independence, while carefully marking the boundary between the fallen and respectable, a working woman might appropriate parts of the prostitute's style as her own. So-called "tough girls," as Lillian Wald described the assertive and rowdy working girls of her community, played with the subculture of prostitution: "Pronounced lack of modesty in dress was one of several signs; . . . their dancing, their talk, their freedom of manner, all combined to render them conspicuous."[34]

The complex dynamics of working women's self-definition is suggested in Rose Schneiderman's recollections of her adolescence. The future labor leader and activist voraciously read the romance literature so popular among young working women, and, internalizing its messages, worried that her hair and figure did not fit the fashion of the day: "All the romantic novels I consumed made me a most romantic young woman, and when I looked at myself in a full-length mirror I was very unhappy." Popular culture also helped define ideals of masculinity, although this was mediated by the realities of working-class experiences and expectations: "From the books I read I had also developed a special taste in men. Among other traits, I wanted them well-read and cultured. I never dreamed of marrying a rich man. That was entirely out of my ken." Personal pleasure in dancing outweighed her interest in romance and courtship: "My idea of what a man should be didn't quite match up with the boys Ann Cypress and I were meeting at the Saturday night dances in the neighborhood. . . . I didn't enjoy their company, but I did love to dance and was pretty good at it, so I put up with them."[35]

Putting on style seemed to fly in the face of the daily round of toil and family obligation—an assertive flash of color and form that belied some of the realities of everyday life. Yet this mode of cultural expression, linked to the pleasures of the streets, clubs, and dance halls, was closely shaped by the economic and social relations of working-class life. Maintaining style on the streets, at dance halls, or at club functions was an achievement won at other costs—going without food, sewing into the night to embellish a hat or dress, buying on installment, leaving school early to enter the workforce, and forcing confrontations within the working-class family.

THE FAMILY ECONOMY AND CONFLICT OVER LEISURE

No investigation on the order of George Bevans' *How Workingmen Spend Their Spare Time* provides the detailed information necessary to correlate working women's leisure activities with their family situation, ethnic background, residence, or occupation. Government surveys and reformers' reports provide ample statistical data on women's work, but comparable sources on leisure do not exist. However, the evidence of reformers, observers, journalists, and working women themselves does allow us to explore the parameters within which different young women made choices about their amusements and social life. Cultural practices rooted in religious, ethnic, and class traditions suggest the varying definitions of appropriate behavior for unmarried women in Manhattan's working-class communities. Whether one lived in a family or alone in a boardinghouse were important determinants of social freedom. Relations within the family, too, shaped the choices women could make, as did their access to money and other resources.

Most young women negotiated leisure within the dynamics of the family economy, which was both a strategy for survival and a working-class cultural ideal. In an industrial system dominated by low-paying unskilled and semiskilled jobs, the inadequacy of men's wages necessitated the economic contribution of daughters, sons, and wives, thus reinforcing the interdependency of family members. In a 1914 study, for example, the typical working-class family of five contained three wage-earners.[36] Such economic strategies were supported by cultural traditions within working-class communities that legitimated and reinforced notions of mutual obligation, filial responsibility, self-sacrifice, and family unity. The impact of these expectations could be profound, as Lucy, a twenty-three-year-old Italian box-maker supporting her mother and brother, discovered: "The other week my mother turned away a good offer of marriage because she said I must work until my brother is old enough to work."[37] Custom demanded that daughters contribute all or a substantial part of their earnings to the family. In 1888, 72 percent of female factory workers interviewed gave all their earnings, and this figure remained relatively unchanged into the 1910's, when three-quarters to four-fifths handed their pay envelopes over to their parents unopened.[38]

Parents made a distinction between the contributions—and independence—of sons and daughters. Boys were less pressured to contribute all their earnings, often paying half for board and keeping the rest for themselves. Before the 1920's, girls under twenty-one could not make the same arrangement without risking family conflict. Flower-maker Theresa Albino, the daughter of Italian parents, gave all her earnings to her mother, while her eighteen-year–old brother contributed three or four dollars a week. "But you know how it is with a boy," she explained. "He wants things for himself." Similarly Maureen Connelly, an Irish-born saleswoman, observed that her brother paid only board, but "I gave all, I'd be afraid to say I'd give board. The idea never even entered my mind."[39]

Mothers also expected their daughters to help them with housework or tend their younger siblings, an expectation not placed on sons, who had more freedom to roam the streets, play sports, and seek adventures with their gangs or clubs. In an 1888 survey of three thousand female factory workers in Manhattan, for example, three-quarters assisted with the housework after their day of wage labor.[40]

The degree to which parents permitted daughters an independent social life in the public sphere varied among different immigrant groups. Chaperonage remained an important institution among East Side Jews, but parents considered it appropriate for their daughter to go for walks and to dances with men, as long as the parents knew about the excursion beforehand and had met the young man. Young Jewish women often attended theaters, clubs, and dances weekly and, according to one investigator, had greater freedom in spending their income than German or Italian girls.[41] A survey of the favorite amusements of fifteen hundred wage-earning women conducted by sociologist Annie MacLean also suggests ethnic differences. She found that over 50 percent of Jewish girls preferred theaters, concerts, or dances to other forms of entertainment, while a somewhat lesser number of Americans and Germans, approximately 40 percent, did so. Irish women, according to this study, did not attend musical entertainments, but 35 percent preferred theater trips or dancing. In contrast, Italian girls were most likely to engage in home-centered amusements or to state no preference at all; fewer than 30 percent listed a commercial form of leisure as their preference.[42]

More than other working-class youth, unmarried Italian women found their social participation curtailed by conservative cultural traditions regulating women's familial roles and affirming patriarchal authority. Parents ordered daughters to come home directly from their places of employment, turn in their pay envelopes unopened, and help with the housework. Chaperones usually accompanied young women who went out in the evening, and the modern concept of dating was alien to most Italian parents. The requirements of courtship assumed that a woman went out only with the man she would ultimately marry. Rather than attending dances and theaters, the couple would visit at her home several times a week until the courting year had ended. Even when a young woman was permitted to go out, and exceptions were allowed especially for movies, an early curfew was set. These practices reflected the common belief tersely expressed by two Italian parents: "The daughter has [a] better chance at marriage by staying away from public amusements."[43] In the case of Italian girls at least, parental control and daughterly submission extended far beyond the need to ensure the family's economic survival.

Yet this notion of the family economy as the determining structure of young women's experience simplifies the dramas of control, resistance, acquiescence, and subterfuge that occurred within many working-class families. While daughters may have accepted the family claim to their wages and work, struggles often ensued over their access to and use of leisure time. Participation in social life, parental supervision, spending money, and clothing were common issues of conflict. As wage-earners and contributors to the family, they sought to parlay their new-found status toward greater autonomy in their personal lives.

In an example of this familial drama, Louisa, a young woman

living in a West Side Irish neighborhood around 1910, discovered
that working in a candy factory for five dollars a week gave her power
within the family. Her economic contribution enabled her to claim
the privilege of going to dance halls, staying out late with men, and
purchasing extravagant suits and hats. Social investigator Ruth True
observed of Louisa that "the costume in which she steps out so tri-
umphantly has cost many bitter moments at home. She has gotten it
by force, with the threat of throwing up her job." Her distraught
mother decried such undutiful behavior: "She stands up and an-
swers me back. An' she's comin' in at 2 o'clock, me not knowin'
where she has been. Folks will talk, you know, an' it ain't right fer a
girl."[44] Indeed, a bargain was struck in many families, with daughters bartering their obedience in turning over wages for the freedom
to come and go as they pleased. Reformer Lillian Betts found that
the American-born girls she studied viewed independence not as a
privilege but a right: "Beyond the fact that some of them must be at
home at ten or half-past, there was no law but their own will."[45]
Indeed, Maureen Connelly threw caution to the wind when she
violated her parents' curfew: "If I went out and I knew I'd get hit if I
came in at twelve, so I'd stay out till one."[46]

Even in Italian families, young women carved out spaces in their
lives for privacy, independence, and unsupervised social interaction. When parents forbade a young man's visit, a daughter might
slip out into the streets to meet him. Antoinette Paluzzi, who came
to New York from Sicily in 1920 when she was thirteen, was not
allowed by her father to date. Her mother, however, permitted her
to walk with a girl friend to the local park, where she would meet
her beau, being careful to obey the stipulation that she return home
before her father's workday ended. Similarly, Angela Defina and her
fiance were chaperoned whenever they went out, but occasionally
they took an afternoon off from work to visit the Hippodrome, despite Angela's fears that her father would find out. Some adolescent
Italian women even defied cultural tradition by frequenting commercial dance halls. Observing women on the balcony of the Excelsior, a cafe and dance house, a Committee of Fourteen investigator
noted that "2 appeared to be respectable Italian girls."[47]

Attitudes toward autonomy differed even between sisters. In the
early 1920's, Sophia Margolis dutifully stayed close to home, turning

over her pay envelope and sharing her leisure with her mother. In contrast, her sister would take a few dollars of her own wages to spend on clothing and entertainment, and eventually demanded and received the right to pay only board. More independent than Sophia, she stayed out late at Roseland Ballroom's costume parties, risking the neighbors' gossip about her notorious behavior. "My sister would have a good time," recalled Sophia, "going out dancing, going bathing, going to Coney Island by herself."[48]

At its extreme, young women's rebelliousness was expressed in the subculture of "tough girls." At the Lexington Cafe, a saloon on the corner of East 116th Street and Lexington Avenue, a vice investigator observed an eighteen-year-old "Italian street corner tough" conversing with an intoxicated man:

> The girl had no hat on and had probably just left her house to go on an errand when she met this man[.] I heard her say, my mother will think I got lost I was supposed to go to the drug store she wouldn't know what became of me. The man was under the influence of liquor and was trying to put his hands under her skirts, she resisted at first but afterwards let him go as far as he liked.[49]

Although the investigator does not describe this incident and its participants in great detail, the vignette suggests the powerful allure of leisure as a realm of assertion, sexual experimentation, and escape from parental demands.

Family controversy over young women's leisure was compounded by the problem of space and privacy in tenement apartments, where the "parlor" served as kitchen, dining room, and bedroom. New York housing ranged from abysmal rear tenements to "new law" apartments with indoor plumbing and adequate ventilation, but overcrowding remained a dominant characteristic of working-class neighborhoods. Dumb-bell tenements, the prevailing housing type between 1879 and 1901, usually contained several apartments per floor, in a five- to seven-story walk-up. In 1900, an average of eight families lived in each tenement house, and the mean size of households was 4.3 individuals, usually crowded into two or three rooms. Although housing conditions improved after 1900 with the construction of new law tenements, families still had to contend with small rooms and, often, the presence of boarders. Consequently, "privacy could be had only in public," and young people sought the streets, clubs, and halls in order to nurture intimate relationships.[50]

Contention over leisure, social freedom, and dating was also heightened by the inevitable cultural conflicts between the American-born or educated youth and their immigrant parents, who clung to Old World traditions. Lillian Wald noted that the Americanized wage-earning daughter "willingly gave her earnings and paid tribute to her mother's devotion and housekeeping skill, [but] said she felt irritated and mortified every time she returned to her home." Sadie Frowne, a young garment worker, observed that immigrant women criticized her for spending her income on fashionable clothes: "Those who blame me are the old country people who have old-fashioned notions, but the people who have been here a long time know better."[51]

The emergent consumer culture, with its beguiling modernity, challenged parental authority over manners and mores. Women attentively read the advertisements and commentary about personal appearance printed in the working-class dailies, even in the socialist press: the *Jewish Daily Forward* noted in 1915, for example, that facial hair "makes a bad impression"; to eliminate it, women should "go immediately to your druggist and for one dollar buy Wonderstone." Some women apparently pondered such counsel carefully; one young East Sider asked the *Forward*'s "Bintel Brief," an advice column: "Is it a sin to use face powder? Shouldn't a girl look beautiful? My father does not want me to use face powder. Is it a sin?"[52] Increasingly, as young people chose forms of entertainment identified with American culture, parents who had previously decried cheap dance halls and theaters slowly acquiesced to them.[53]

RECREATION AND THE "WOMAN ADRIFT"

Although most adolescent working-class women lived at home, a sizable number—as many as sixty-eight thousand in 1910—lived alone, lodging in boardinghouses or renting rooms.[54] Style and amusement were important aspects of their lives as well, but the "woman adrift," as she was called, experienced the culture of the streets, clubs, and dance halls in a different context from those who resided at home. Women who lived outside families trod a fine line between asserting independence and guarding respectability in their everyday lives. Many chose to live with relatives or board in the houses of strangers rather than risk their reputations living alone. Foreign-born women especially tended to seek a room with a "Missus," occupying a passageway or sharing a folding bed in the parlor at night. Among the Italian women whom Louise Odencrantz studied, only one-eighth were not living at home, and of these, the majority resided with kinfolk. This arrangement often created a surrogate family for young women, a necessity for those in low-paying or seasonal jobs. As "daughters," they might help out with cooking or child care and in turn would receive the family's assistance when in need. Since living alone spelled immorality among many immigrants, this strategy also ensured that a woman's respectability would be maintained.[55]

For these women, familial and cultural norms often affected leisure as much as they did women living with their parents. Old World tradition kept most Italian women off the streets and out of public amusements at night, whether they lived at home or not; visiting friends, attending church, going to movies and occasional balls or theatrical events comprised the bulk of their amusements. For one Italian living on her own, decorating a small tenement apartment was her major form of entertainment:

> The room was decorated with several shelves of gay dishes. The images of 18 different saints adorned the head of the bed, bright pictures of the rulers of Italy, advertising calendars and panels, an alarm clock, and a guitar hung on the wall. The care of her room was a daily joy and her only recreation.[56]

Other "women adrift" found housing in noncommercial boarding homes organized by churches and philanthropic agencies, which usually established house rules for recreation and sociability and occasionally organized their own leisure activities. Their residents came mainly from American and "old immigrant" stock, especially English, German, and Irish backgrounds, who were more often employed as office workers, servants, teachers, and nurses than as factory workers or salesclerks.[57] The gentility and bourgeois standards of such homes may well have attracted migrants from small American towns or girls who were otherwise exposed to dominant middle-class notions of domesticity and womanhood.

Still, by 1915, many boarders complained heartily about the regulations on social life enforced in the homes. Women's sense of self-respect was eroded not only by taking charity but by the restrictions imposed on their time and leisure—the enforced quiet, prohibitions on dancing and popular music, limited space to entertain friends, and evening curfews. Locking the doors at ten or eleven o'clock, for example, hampered young women's leisure in a city "where the theatre rarely is over until eleven, and where parties seldom begin until nine."[58]

Many refused to live in the homes, citing their opposition to charity, forced sociability, and a stultifying female culture. "A place like that should have a strictly hotel basis; no Christian stuff; and a decent name," observed one Irish girl. Freedom, to such women, meant such simple acts as choosing one's dinner at a restaurant rather than eating the planned meals of the home, and seeing male faces instead of a roomful of women: "Now I live in a furnished room house and I go into Childs' and I'm as good as the next fellow," said one former resident. Heterosocial relationships were of utmost concern to them. "I don't want to live in a place with a lot of hens," said several women, explaining:

> Everybody calls those Homes the "Old Maids' Retreat" and they're just about right. It's not that I'm crazy about men, that I don't want to live there, but just because I'm normal. If you live in a furnished room house you meet men sometimes and if you don't meet them, at least you see them going in and out, which is something. It must be awful depressing to live with a bunch of gossipy women all the time.[59]

Many young women sought lodging in commercial rooming houses and apartments for greater social freedom, in order to come and go as they pleased. In the 1890's, many New York dwellings were converted into boardinghouses; Mary Gay Humphreys estimated that there were fifteen thousand furnished rooms for rent from Washington Square to Central Park in the blocks between Fifth and Sixth Avenues. "For a young man or young woman whose expenses must be kept within $10 a week, there seemed to be no other mode of existence." Young women pooled their resources to live together in apartments, in "a new order of feminine friendship" that combined autonomy, sociability, and mutual aid.[60] It was often difficult for women to find such rooms, since landladies preferred renting to men, who had larger incomes and smaller reputations to preserve. Still, lodging houses offered a woman the advantages of having her own place and, as a Czechoslovakian domestic servant observed, the opportunity to go out dancing evenings and Saturdays without parental restraint.[61]

Living conditions in these furnished room apartments often drove women into the commercial amusements of the city. Rooms were small, bleak, and cold, and houses usually lacked public parlors or reception rooms where women could socialize with their friends. Moreover, women entertaining men ran the gauntlet between landladies' disapproving stares and the knowing glances of male boarders. For boardinghouse keepers concerned with decency, "the most commonly used device is the rule that one may entertain only 'steadies' in one's room. . . . The working girl who numbers among her acquaintances more than one man is looked upon askance." Thus women combatted the loneliness of the furnished room by seeking out the movie houses, dance halls, cafes, and even saloons as places of rendezvous, diversion, conviviality, and courtship.[62]

Whether they lived at home or alone, young women's notion of a "good time" was intimately linked to the public spaces of the streets, clubs, and commercial amusement resorts. Clearly not all women could pursue these forms of leisure activities. With tiring labor and few resources, many had little opportunity to enter the social whirl. "When the girls get home they're too tired to do anything," observed one bookbinder, a statement confirmed by female workers in restaurants, garment shops, and other businesses.[63] Family responsibilities kept others at home. Investigator Mary Van Kleeck, for example, interviewed Katie, a twenty-two-year-old machine operator in a bindery, who was washing the dishes as her younger sister dressed for a wedding: "Katie said that she used to go to dances and weddings when she was young, but she is too tired to go now."[64]

Other women held strict notions of respectability that limited their participation. Two poor but genteel working sisters defended their reputations when it came to social activities: "Evening amusements we cannot go to for want of clothes and beaux, and in fact we do not care for the company of that class of young men who we *can* know." The demands of the family economy often left women dependent on unsavory men for amusements, an arrangement many rejected. Commented a working girl who gave her weekly wages to her mother, "We have not the money for pretty clothes to attract the boys who would really care for us and of course we have no money to pay for our own amusement, and as a result we stay at home." Some obviously craved the world of popular amusements to which they could not belong. "Never have I been to a moving picture show or taken out," lamented Celia, a young immigrant. "The excursions that leave the pier make me jealous sometimes. . . . Only to be out like everybody else!"[65] Within the varieties of working -class cultural experience, Celia's words suggest that those who could indulge in the city's cheap amusements stood out as a model for other young working women.

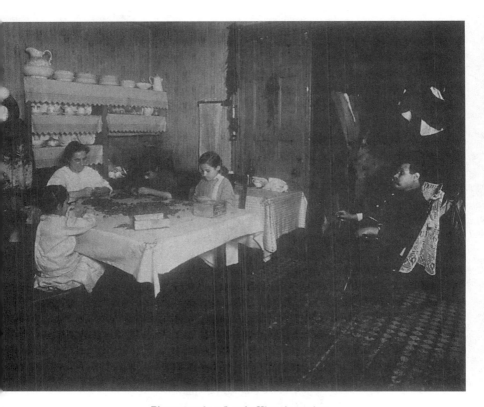

Photographer Lewis Hines' caption,
"everybody works but . . . ,"
comments on the sexual division of labor
in this immigrant household.
The room's decor shows that poverty
did not stop women's efforts
to beautify their homes.

The Edward L. Bafford Photography
Collection, Albin O. Kuhn Library and
Gallery, University of Maryland
Baltimore County

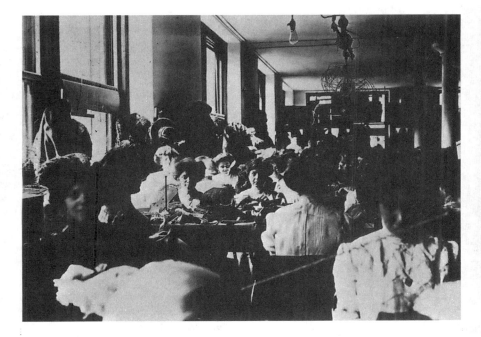

In this millinery factory,
long hours of toil were mitigated
by a lively peer-group culture
that fostered a new sense of
identity among young working women.

U.S. History, Local
History & Genealogy Division,
The New York Public Library,
Astor, Lenox and Tilden
Foundations

The workplace presented new opportunities for sociability;
female factory workers converse with shopmates off the job.

A young wage-earner and her gentleman
friend meet during a lunch break.

Stylish working women share confidences
in a city park.

Putting on style: Four sisters
from the lower East Side make elegance
and respectability part of the
"public presentation of self" in
this studio portrait.

Courtesy of Joan Korenman

Dreams for sale: Division Street clothing shops offered
working women inexpensive versions of high-fashion designs.

Museum of the City of New York

Steeplechase Park enticed
crowds of working women and men
with the promise of
"ten hours fun for ten cents."

Museum of the City of New York

On hot summer days, family
groups and young people flocked
to Coney Island beaches; in
the evenings, the dancing pavilions
(shown in the background)
attracted young working-class
"spielers."

Museum of the City of New York

To get a needed respite from the sweltering city, tenement
dwellers went on free seashore excursions sponsored by civic
groups and reformers, in addition to commercially run outings.

Didactic amusement in the form of
"practical talks" at the 38th Street
Working Girls' Club was geared to
promoting middle-class standards
of respectability and cross-class sisterhood.

General Research Division,
The New York Public Library,
Astor, Lenox and Tilden
Foundations

CHAPTER FOUR

DANCE MADNESS

Of all the amusements that bedazzled the single working woman, dancing proved to be her greatest passion. After the long day laboring in a factory or shop, young women dressed themselves in their fanciest finery, put on their dancing shoes, and hurried out to a neighborhood hall, ballroom, or saloon equipped with a dance floor. The gaily decorated hall, riveting beat of the orchestra, and whirl of dance partners created a magical world of pleasure and romance. Thousands of young women and men flocked to such halls each week in Manhattan. By the 1910's, over five hundred public dance halls opened their doors each evening throughout greater New York, and more than one hundred dancing academies instructed 100,000 neophytes yearly in the latest steps. As one reformer exclaimed, "the town is dance mad."[1]

The dance hall was the favorite arena in which young working women played out their cultural style. Their passion for the dance started early, often in childhood, as girls danced on the streets to the tunes of itinerant musicians. In a 1910 survey of one thousand public school children aged eleven to fourteen, nearly nine out of ten girls reported that they knew how to dance, in contrast to only one-third of the boys. By the time they were teen-agers, dancing had become a pervasive part of women's social life. The vast majority of women attending dance halls were under twenty years of age, and some were only twelve or thirteen. Their male dance partners tended to be slightly older; dancing was even more popular with them than

were saloons and pool halls.[2] For both sexes, going to the city's
dance halls marked a particular stage in the life cycle. Participation
rose during adolescence, when dance halls offered "the only opportunity in the winter for unrestrained, uncramped social intercourse
between the young people of the two sexes."[3] Attendance at the
halls lessened considerably when girls started "keeping company"
with a beau and ceased upon marriage. Josie, a sixteen-year-old hab-
itue of the dance halls, told Ruth True, "When I'm eighteen or nineteen I won't care about it anymore. I'll have a 'friend' then and won't
want to go anywheres."[4]

Young women's attendance at dance halls followed the general
patterns of their participation in street life and social clubs. The
evidence is too limited to show the specific social composition of the
dancers—their ethnicity, family life, or work experience. No ethnic
enclave seems to have had a monopoly on dancing. The lower East
Side was riddled with dance halls, and Russian and Polish Jews delighted in balls and affairs. In the heart of this district—between
Houston and Grand Streets and east of the Bowery—a settlement
worker counted thirty-one dance halls, one for every two-and-a-half
blocks, more than any other area in the city.[5] Other surveys indicate
that dancing was popular throughout Manhattan's working-class
neighborhoods, whether the locale was an upper East Side block of
Italians and Jews or a West Side tenement district inhabited by
American, German, and Irish working people. Although we cannot
enumerate the occupations of the dancers, women who worked in
typical female jobs, including garment workers, domestic servants,
and saleswomen, were commonly seen in the city's halls.[6]

What was the role of the dance hall in the lives of young working-
class women? From an anthropological perspective, dance is a form
of structured, expressive movement that articulates and conveys
cultural information to its participants, helping them to make sense
of their world. While dance hall culture is only a piece of working-
class experience, and a relatively small one, it is a window on cultural issues and social dynamics that are usually obscured.[7] Ethnographic description of dance halls—dance steps, ballroom etiquette, drinking customs, clothing styles—illuminate aspects of the
cultural construction of gender among working-class Americans.
These forms of expression dramatize the ways in which working-

class youth culturally managed sexuality, intimacy, and respectability.

This dance hall culture, and its embodiment of sexual ideology and gender relations, must also be situated in a broader social context. The organization of dancing underwent important changes in the late nineteenth century, as the commercialization of leisure challenged older patterns of working-class recreation. Once a family amusement and neighborhood event, dancing was transformed as its setting changed. New ballrooms and dance palaces offered a novel kind of social space for their female patrons, enhancing and legitimating their participation in a public social life. The commercial culture of the dance halls meshed with that of working-class youth in a symbiotic relationship, reinforcing emergent values and "modern" attitudes toward leisure, sexuality, and personal fulfillment.

THE SOCIAL ORGANIZATION OF WORKING-CLASS DANCE

Dance madness thrived in the back rooms of dingy saloons, in large neighborhood halls, and in the brightly lit pavilions of amusement parks. The character of working-class dances from 1880 to 1920 varied considerably with the type of hall, the organization of the dance, and the social composition of the participants.[8] The traditional working-class dance of the late nineteenth and early twentieth centuries, however, was the "affair" held in a rented neighborhood hall. At public dance halls, "receptions, 'affairs,' weddings, and balls are given or take place three or four nights a week in a majority of them and on Saturday and Sunday afternoons," observed the University Settlement. "These are given by reputable organizations and the weddings are usually family parties."[9] Local fraternal lodges, mutual aid societies, political associations, and unions "ran off" dances on an annual or occasional basis. The affair not only raised money for charitable purposes, but strengthened group spirit for members and their families.

Many of these dances originated in kinship ties and Old World customs. Weddings held in neighborhood halls provided frequent opportunities to dance and visit among family and friends. At the East Side's Liberty Hall, which held three weddings each week, young and old danced at the receptions to Russian melodies until the early hours of the morning.[10] Traditional folk dances, such as the annual Bohemian Peasant Ball, were transplanted to New York, reinforcing immigrant bonds. Those in attendance wore national costumes, with some participants representing folk characters. A receiving line of Bohemian societies was formed, and a mock marriage ceremony performed, followed by a dance that lasted until dawn.[11] In addition, the immigrant residents of lower Manhattan often gathered in the back room of corner saloons for dancing, drinking, and socializing. The saloon dance hall, observed one settlement worker, was a "veritable neighborhood rallying-place, where young and middle-aged of both sexes crowd in the stuffy room together; where English is little spoken; and mental and physical atmosphere suggest a medieval inn."[12]

Organization affairs and traditional balls took place in an environment controlled at least partially by familial supervision and community ties, although without the strict proprieties and chaperonage of a middle-class dance. This was particularly the case at smaller dances, observed one settlement worker, where "greater respectability is maintained, because there is a closer acquaintance among those who attend."[13] Usually the sponsoring organization issued formal invitations and sometimes appointed floor managers to oversee the dancing and drinking. For example, when the Hudson River Railroad Association held a ball at the Manhattan Casino, they hired a special officer to prevent shimmying and improper dancing.[14]

Young women attended affairs or weddings with their families or an approved escort, expecting to see friends and neighbors. With the exception of Italian immigrants, who sharply restricted the public activities of women, most parents considered these dances relatively safe for their daughters. West Side girls whose Irish and native-born parents strictly guarded them were permitted nevertheless to go to an occasional lodge sociable, church dance, or wedding. Similarly, in the lower East Side, "an invitation to a public ball or wedding once in two weeks may reasonably be expected by the unmarried girls of the district." Sarah Wiseman recalls travelling to lower Manhattan to attend the balls of different societies and clubs: "I was going downtown, those years it was customary [to have] balls on Saturday night, each *landsmanschaft*."[15]

The traditional affair, linked to the extensive network of working-class voluntary organizations, remained a common form of amusement well into the twentieth century. In the 1890's, however, new ways of organizing dancing, spurred by the growth of a working-class youth culture, developed alongside the traditional ball and affair. The "racket," a dance organized by social clubs and amusement societies, increasingly enticed young pleasure-seekers. In the tenement districts, the Barn Stormers, Fly-by-Nights, Lady Sheriffs, and other clubs vied with each other to hold the best ball of the social season.[16]

Rackets differed greatly from the lodge affair or benefit society ball, in which dancing was associated with neighborhood supervision, philanthropy, and intergenerational sociability. Clubs evinced little interest in controlling admissions and chaperoning the dance floor. Promotional posters like the following, advertising a dance of the Schiller Young Men's Benevolent Association, plastered tenement walls and saloon windows:

Full dress and Civic Ball
given by
Schiller
Y — M — B — A
Grand Living Palace
214–20 Broome Street,
March 25,
Music by Prof. L. Uberstein,
Brass Band
Dancing commencing at 7:30 o'clock sharp.[17]

Observed a social investigator, "One day in walking not more than three blocks on Grand and Clinton Streets, I counted nineteen different posters advertising nineteen different balls and entertainments which were to be given in the near future."[18] Extensive advertising and the indiscriminate sale of tickets often brought crowds of seven hundred to eight hundred dancers to a single event. "Almost any one may buy a ticket," young women from the West Side informed Elsa Herzfeld. "If the racket is to be a large one you must expect 'a mixed crowd.'"[19] At such dances, proper working-girls in

their neat shirtwaists might find themselves mingling with the flashily dressed and "tough."

Participating in this social round became a familiar practice for
the young women and men who belonged to clubs and amusement
societies. One reformer observed that "the same people are frequently found at the different dance halls. . . . It appears that the
boxes are all reserved by different 'clubs.'"[20] Rackets offered not
only pleasure but profit: the sale of tickets produced enough money
to finance excursions and vacations for club members. The Rounder
Social Club, for example, ran an affair every year in order to rent a
bungalow at Rockaway Beach each summer.[21] With these incen-
tives, the club dance became increasingly widespread throughout
the working-class sections of the city.

THE COMMERCIALIZATION OF DANCING

An interlocking network of commercial institutions and voluntary
societies structured working-class dancing. Whether the dances
were lodge affairs or club "blow-outs," the dance craze was intensified by the expansion and commercialization of Manhattan's public
halls. For the working-class population packed into small tenement
apartments, large halls that could be rented for dances, weddings,
mass meetings, and other gatherings were a requirement of social
life. The number of public halls in Manhattan rose substantially in a
short period; business directories listed 130 halls in 1895 and 195 in
1910, an increase of 50 percent. While some of these, like Carnegie
Hall, were cultural spaces of the privileged, most were located in
working-class districts. The largest East Side halls, such as the New
Irving, Progress Assembly Rooms, and Liberty Hall could hold five
hundred to twelve hundred people and were always in great demand.[22] Moreover, the directories do not include countless saloons
that expeditiously added a back room or upstairs hall for dancing
and meetings. In the Trinity Church area of downtown Manhattan,
for example, investigators found many private dance halls situated
over saloons, even though public dance hall licenses from the city
had been denied.[23]

The "liquor interests" spurred the growth of large public halls

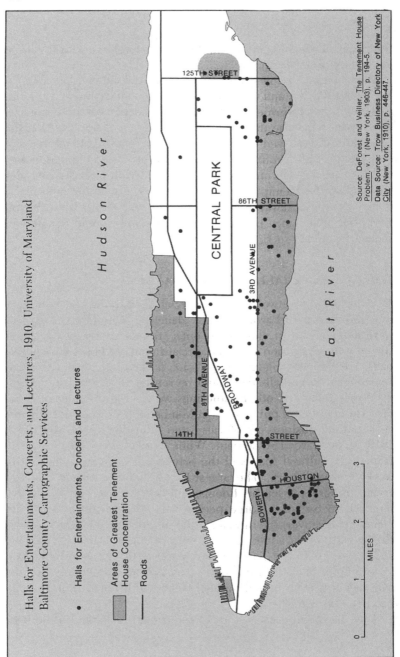

Halls for Entertainments, Concerts, and Lectures, 1910. University of Maryland Baltimore County Cartographic Services

• Halls for Entertainments, Concerts and Lectures

▨ Areas of Greatest Tenement House Concentration

— Roads

Source: DeForest and Veiller, The Tenement House Problem. v. 1 (New York, 1903). p. 194-5.
Data Source: Trow Business Directory of New York City (New York, 1910). p. 446-447.

that could accommodate dances for hundreds of people. In the lower East Side, 80 percent of the dance halls surveyed in 1901 were adjacent to saloons, and the sale of alcohol formed the foundation of their business. A social club could hire New Irving Hall, for example, for thirty dollars a night, and if its dances were known to be money-making ventures, the owner might offer it free for the next engagement. The club would sell tickets and hat checks to swell its coffers, while the hall owner dispensed liquor to enlarge his. Other halls based their rentals on a sliding scale, determined by the amount of alcohol consumed.[24] With the hall owner's profits pegged to alcohol consumption, dancing and drinking went hand in hand, as typical dance programs suggest. In the small saloon dance hall with no admission fee, a dance might last three or four minutes, followed by a fifteen- to twenty-minute intermission period devoted to drinking. In a respectable dancing academy or lodge affair, ten minutes were permitted for dancing, with a shorter intermission for rest and refreshment.[25] Quenching the thirst of dancers became a profitable business, and amusement resorts rushed to rent spaces to clubs, lodges, and benefit societies. As a waiter at the Central Casino observed, "They have about four balls a week and that[']s what makes this place pay."[26]

By the 1910's, the old multiple-purpose neighborhood hall and saloon no longer could meet the demand for dance space, and huge metropolitan halls and ballrooms designed specifically for dancing sprang up. The first dance palace, the Grand Central, was built in 1911, and five others, including Roseland Ballroom, followed in the next ten years. Ranging in capacity from five hundred to three thousand patrons, the large halls were usually located in the commercial amusement zones of the city, in such areas as 42nd Street and Broadway, 14th Street, and 125th Street, serving a city-wide clientele. Dance palaces attracted people of all nationalities, but they appealed more to factory and office workers than to middle-class and elite amusement-seekers, who flocked to Gotham's cabarets and restaurants. Large working-class organizations often rented these halls for their yearly gatherings. In the 1910's, at least twenty unions held annual balls with over three thousand people in attendance. Huge affairs by such groups as the Metropolitan Street Railway Employees or the Stationary Firemen packed the Palm Garden, Terrace Garden, Manhattan Casino, and other dance resorts.[27]

In the large commercial halls, the continuing presence of a sponsoring club or organization conferred legitimacy on the dance, even as the activity moved away from its traditional working-class form. Hall managers even created their own clubs to encourage a steady clientele and add a veneer of respectability to the dance. The Manhattan Casino, for example, formed the Tiger Social Club, which held basketball games and rackets every Sunday afternoon.[28] The illusion of sponsorship remained important to hall owners, who hoped to bury the unsavory reputation of the commercial dance house, which dated back to the Victorian era. These had been part of an extensive male subculture with links to prostitution, gambling, and the "sporting" life. In the mid-nineteenth century, for example, numerous dance halls run by Germans and frequented primarily by sailors could be found in the 1st Ward; these employed "decoy dancers" or "taxi-dancers" as female companions for the patrons. Dressed in scanty costumes, some of the women also earned money as prostitutes, soliciting the men's business as they waltzed. Prominent commercial dance houses of the 1860's and 1870's, such as John Allen's and Harry Hill's, also were primarily the cultural territory of men. These drew female curiosity-seekers and the demimonde, but respectable women anxious to preserve their reputations would not attend.[29]

The gulf between commercial and sponsored dances lessened by 1900, and hall owners increasingly ran dances without the mediation of an organization or club, throwing open their doors to anyone paying the price of admission. A popular strategy was to advertise the hall as a dancing academy, teach the latest steps during the day, and offer open public "receptions" in the evenings and on Sunday afternoons. Such East Side halls as the Apollo and the Golden Rule, for example, operated primarily as dancing schools.[30]

Commercial dance halls remained morally suspect to some parents and their daughters. Irma Knecht, for example, differentiated between the respectable social evenings of the *landsmanschaft* societies and the promiscuous public halls: "We didn't go to these dance halls, [we] used to go to organization affairs."[31] Others, however, had no qualms about attending the public halls. Ruth Ka-

minsky, for example, exclaimed, "As single girls we went dancing . . . in dancing halls, we went dancing, we used to have a nice
time, to meet fellows."[32] Girls who were not closely supervised by
their parents went to public dances and social club parties at least
one evening a week, and some attended as many as three or four.
Hutchins Hapgood noticed that some East Side shopgirls "dance
every night, and are so confirmed in it that they are technically
known as 'spielers.'"[33] For these women, the emergence of the
large commercial dance hall, whether run through general admission fees, through social club rentals, or as a dancing academy, created an alternative to the traditional affair of the fraternal lodge and
benefit society. The intergenerational integration that was possible
in the locally based dance rarely occurred in the new ballrooms and
dance palaces. Rather, this expanding network of commercial dance
halls became the territory of working-class youth.

DANCE HALL CULTURE

With the commercialization of dancing, hall owners and entrepreneurs especially promoted the participation of young women. Halls
lowered their admission prices for unescorted women, charging ten
to fifteen cents, as opposed to the usual fee of twenty-five or fifty
cents per couple; some even admitted women free. Charges for
checking hats and coats show a similar differential: "Ladies ten
cents, gentlemen a quarter."[34] This policy implicitly recognized the
subordinate economic status of women, at the same time that it
urged them to attend ballrooms with or without an escort.

The hall owners' pitch was not primarily an appeal to thrift, however, but rather a promise of excitement, glamour, and romance. In
the late nineteenth century, working-class dances had often taken
place in small, dingy saloons, crowded with dancers who simply
ignored the unpleasant surroundings. The new commercial dance
halls, however, were large structures that enticed their patrons with
bright lights, blaring music, and a festive atmosphere. "The sounds
of a waltz or two step pounded on the piano and emphasized by an
automatic drum flow out to a passer-by," while hall managers stood
in the streets and declaimed, like circus barkers, upon the splendors
inside.[35] In the hall, a large, polished dance floor, bounded by a

stage at one end and a bar at the other, drew crowds of youth. Often a balcony ringed the dance floor, containing chairs and tables for patrons to relax and watch the dancers. Banners and mirrors gave a festive air to the halls, and the "Professor" and his band warmed up the crowd with the latest ragtime tunes. As one investigator observed at a lively ball, "Everybody was full of joy asking them to repeat the same dance."[36] Weekday dances ended no earlier than one or two o'clock, and on a Saturday night they continued well into the early morning.

Where young women saw an aura of sensual pleasure, middle-class observers of the commercial halls found immorality, drawing a lurid connection between working girls' recreation and vice. The press was filled with dramatic accounts of innocent daughters tempted by glittering dance halls, seduced and drugged by ruthless "cadets" or pimps, and held against their will in brothels. Beyond the sensationalism, their views had some basis in fact. As historian Ruth Rosen has shown, incidents of white slavery did occur in the nation's large cities. The Committee of Fourteen, a reform agency formed to battle urban prostitution and vice, sent undercover investigators to the city's saloons and dance houses in the 1910's. While their primary concern lay in the clean-up of notorious resorts, their reports reveal in rare detail the culture of many commercial dance halls frequented by working-class youth.[37]

The large public halls they described were territories where the promiscuous interaction of strangers was normative behavior. Classes and cultures mingled in New York's commercial halls. At a Turnverein ball in 1917, for example, a vice investigator reported the entrance of two gentlemen in evening dress and top hats seeking prostitutes at what was primarily a working-class dance.[38] Indeed, by the 1910's, it was often difficult to distinguish the dress and style of respectable women from prostitutes at dances. As one waiter explained to a vice investigator who wished to be "introduced" to any available women, "The way women dress today they all look like prostitutes and the waiter can some times get in bad by going over and trying to put some one next to them, they may be respectable women and would jump on the waiter."[39]

Clearly the middle-class distinction between respectable working-class women and prostitutes polarized a more complex social

reality. At the Turnverein ball, for example, the investigator acknowledged that the crowd was a more reputable one than the usual
patrons of Remey's, but his description belied the usual bourgeois
standards of conduct. He described the scene in the hall's barroom,
as patrons sought refreshment between dances:

> I saw one of the women smoking cigarettes, most of the younger
> couples were hugging and kissing, there was a general mingling
> of men and women at the different tables, almost every one
> seemed to know one another and spoke to each other across the
> room, also saw both men and women leave their tables and join
> couples at different tables, they were all singing and carrying on,
> they kept running around the room and acted like a mob of luna-
> tics let lo[o]se.[40]

At a dance hall frequented by Irish domestic servants and motor-
men, the investigator noted that the easy familiarity of asking
strange women to dance or drink did not indicate vice or prostitution: "This changing of tables was not a case of open soliciting but
just a general mixing." To prove his point, he exclaimed with some
frustration that he had tried for forty-five minutes to pick up some of
the women, "but there was nothing doing."[41] At another dance,
held under the auspices of the National Brotherhood of Bookbinders, kissing, hugging, singing, shouting, and other familiarities were
simply accepted as routine conduct. The presence of several young
girls, twelve to fourteen years of age, who "appeared to be respectable and came here with their parents or guardians," attests to the
normality of these scenes.[42]

Ribald language and bawdy behavior were encouraged by many
commercial halls and social clubs. These dances could be distinguished by their advertising, which took the form of "throw-
aways" or "pluggers." The sponsoring club or hall would flood the
neighborhood with small printed cards announcing the particulars
of the dance, accompanied by snatches of popular songs or rhymes.
As vice reformer George Kneeland described the throwaway:

> These latter intimate the character of the proposed frolic. They
> all appeal to the sex interest, some being so suggestive that they

are absolutely indecent. During the progress of a dance in St. Mark's Place, a young girl, hardly above seventeen years of age, presented a boy with a printed card advertising a ball soon to be held. When the card is folded, it forms an obscene picture and title.[43]

Although his sensibilities were sorely offended, these suggestive advertisements were carefully preserved and valued as mementos of dances by their young patrons.

DANCING STYLES

The sexual expressiveness of working-class youth at the commercial halls was particularly apparent in the styles of dancing. Anxious to maintain their good reputations with working-class parents and placate civil authorities, many hall owners sought to contain promiscuous sexuality by patrolling the dance floor. The Women's Municipal League praised a respectable dance hall in the Murray Hill district, patronized by people of different nationalities: "Signs are displayed calling attention to the fact that orderly demeanor must be observed in the dancing and the patrons appear to be well-disposed and well behaved. The dances taught are the waltz, two-step, etc."[44] These dances, which required specific body positions and had established standards to recommend them, symbolized respectability to parents and reformers.

In the unrestrained commercial halls, however, dancing styles took less traditional forms. In the 1890's and early 1900's, "pivoting" or "spieling" captivated working women. "'Spieling' is the order of the evening," observed a West Side study in 1906.[45] In this dance, the couple, held tightly together, would twist and spin in small circles on the dance floor. One observer at a Coney Island dance house described two stereotypical pivoters:

Julia stands erect, with her body as rigid as a poker and with her left arm straight out from her shoulder like an upraised pump-handle. Barney slouches up to her, and bends his back so that he can put his chin on one of Julia's shoulders and she can do the same by him. Then, instead of dancing with a free, lissome, graceful, gliding step, they pivot or spin, around and around with the smallest circle that can be drawn around them. [46]

Pivoting, which was a loose parody of the fast waltz, was diametrically opposed to the waltz in intention. In nineteenth-century high society, the waltz was initially scandalous because it brought the sexes into closer contact than in dances of previous eras, but the dance form itself countered that intimacy with injunctions toward stiff control and agile skill. The speed of the dance demanded self-control and training to achieve the proper form. The major innovation of the dance was that a woman and man placed their hands on each other, but instructors insisted that partners' shoulders be three to four inches apart and that the distance between their bodies should increase downward. The proper position for the waltz meant that "each dancer will be looking over the other's right shoulder," not directly into each other's eyes. [47]

The spieling dance, in parodying this form, was performed not with self-control, but as a dance out of control, its centrifugal tendencies unchecked by proper dance training or internalized restraint. Instead, the wild spinning of couples promoted a charged atmosphere of physical excitement, often accompanied by shouting and singing. Reformer Julia Schoenfeld, reporting on working girls' amusements, observed that in New York halls "vulgar dancing exists everywhere, and the 'spiel,' a form of dancing requiring much twirling and twisting, . . . is popular in all." In her view, spieling "particularly cause[d] sexual excitement" through "the easy familiarity in the dance practiced by nearly all the men in the way they handle the girls."[48]

The sexual emphasis of the dance was even more pronounced in a style known as "tough dancing," which became popular after 1905. Tough dancing had its origins in the houses of prostitution on San Francisco's Barbary Coast and gradually spread, in the form of the slow rag, lovers' two-step, turkey trot, and bunny hug, to the "low resorts" and dance halls of major metropolitan areas. Ultimately much transformed and tamed, it became by the 1910's the mainstay of the middle-class dance craze, the one-step. In the commercial dance halls, however, unrestrained versions of the grizzly bear, Charlie Chaplin wiggle, "shaking the shimmy," and dip would be joyously danced to the popular ragtime tunes of the day.[49]

Tough dances differed significantly from earlier dances like the waltz or two-step, in which partners held each other by the hands or around the waist. "Bodily contact has been conventionalized to an unprecedented degree," observed one reformer, while another elaborated, "Couples stand very close together, the girl with her hands around the man's neck, the man with both his arms around the girl or on her hips; their cheeks are pressed close together, their bodies touch each other."[50] The dancers' movements ranged from a slow shimmy, or shaking of the shoulders and hips, to boisterous animal imitations that ridiculed middle-class ideals of grace and refinement. Performed in either a stationary or a walking position, such dances were appropriate for a small, crowded dance floor. Moreover, they were simple to learn, requiring little training or skill, while permitting endless variations on the basic easy steps. Indeed, one of the common complaints of reformers was that these dances had no standard positions, and dancers could simply walk and glide over the dance floor.[51]

Tough dancing not only permitted physical contact, it celebrated it. Indeed, the essence of the tough dance was its suggestion of sexual intercourse. As one dance investigator noted obliquely, "What particularly distinguishes this dance is the motion of the pelvic portions of the body, bearing in mind its origins [i.e., in houses of prostitution]." What troubled such reformers was that the dance, whether wild or tame, became an overt symbol of sexual activity, which the dancers, operating outside the usual conventions of dance, were free to control: "Once learned, the participants can, at will, instantly decrease or increase the obscenity of the movements, lowering the hands from shoulders to the hips and dancing closer and closer until the bodies touch."[52] More than other dances, the tough dance allowed young women to use their bodies to express sexual desire and individual pleasure in movement that would have been unacceptable in any other public arena.

Working girls were not the only New Yorkers who revelled in the modern dances, for the new dance steps also charmed members of the elite and middle classes. "Everybody's Overdoing It," complained one writer, punning on a popular song title of the day.[53] The dancing mania that swept segments of the middle class points to a new level of sensuality and expressiveness within the dominant culture. As Lewis Erenberg observes, however, these cultural forms did not give vent to unrestrained expression, but rather were carefully controlled and refined to meet middle-class standards of respectability.[54]

The contrast in class attitudes toward the new dances is suggested by the frontal attack on tough dancing made by leading dance masters. Irene and Vernon Castle, who most popularized expressive dance forms of the teens, insisted that their Castle Walk, or one-step, bore "no relation or resemblance to the once popular Turkey Trot, Bunny Hug, or Grizzly Bear." Restraining the creative and individualistic qualities of these dances, the Castle Walk eliminated "all hoppings, all contortions of the body, all flouncing of the elbows, all twisting of the arms, and above everything else, all fantastic dips."[55] Bodily contact between dancers was unnecessary, observed one instructor, proclaiming that the "new dances do not require 'hugging' and crossed arms to make them enjoyable. Insist that the couples stand from 1 to 4 inches apart." Another commanded imperiously, "Do not rag these dances."[56]

The intention of these instructions was to reduce the sexual symbolism and individual expression inherent in the dance, setting clear boundaries for behavior in the promiscuous environment of the dance floor. Dancing masters hoped to fend off criticism from religious and civic leaders, at the same time fearing the infectious popularity of the new dances among liberal members of the middle class. "Our girls will spend hundreds of dollars taking grace lessons, and as soon as a ragtime piece of music starts up, they will grasp a "strange' man in any outlandish position that often will put the lowest creature to shame," one complained.[57] Maintaining class distinctions as well as respectable relations between the sexes could be achieved through proper dance form. "Our aim is to uplift dancing, purify it and place it before the public in its proper light," asserted the Castles.[58]

Given their criticism of middle-class daughters' unbecoming dance steps, it is clear that dance masters' prescriptions should not be equated with behavior. However, tough dancing remained a controversial form within the middle class, the boundary at which most people drew the line. While more sensual than earlier dances, the middle-class dances of the 1910's did not exhibit the blatant sexuality expressed in tough dancing. The subtle distinctions in dance styles may be seen, for example, in a description of a businessman and his respectable date at the Ritz Cabaret: "They dance, the girl with her arm about the fellow's neck—the way many society girls do it now a days. It is not exactly tough but it brings the cou[pl]e rather close together."[59] Similarly, the Committee on Amusements and Vacation Resources of Working Girls, concerned that working women were finding legitimation for tough dancing in the society pages of the newspapers, went to a debutante's ball to see for themselves. They saw no tough dancing at the ball they attended, although they did report hearsay "evidence of *modified* 'turkey trot' and 'grizzly bear' being danced by members of the younger set" at other affairs.[60] While such modifications were also practiced at smaller, chaperoned dances in the tenement districts, in the anonymous spaces of the commercial dance halls neither floor managers nor social conventions restrained the sexual implications of the dance movement.

CONSTRUCTING HETEROSEXUALITY IN THE PUBLIC HALLS

Control over dancing styles was only one aspect of the larger problem of regulating heterosexual relations at dances. The popular middle-class resorts, cabarets, and cafes tended to mediate promiscuous contact by imposing elaborate rules on their clientele. Many cabarets not only outlawed suggestive dancing, but often barred unescorted women and men from the premises. The intermingling of strangers was taboo at the Parisien, a fashionable resort that did not allow "men from different tables to take women for a dance and won't allow any one to change tables."[61] After a vice raid, another cabaret did not permit women into the hall alone, prevented sensual dancing, and stopped the music precisely at 12:55 A.M. Nor were performers permitted to mix with the crowd: "The lady entertainers were sitting on the platform with the musicians and didn't drink or dance with any of the men here."[62] The careful scrutiny of vice squads led to increasingly subtle markers of respectability. The owner of the Park View Hotel, for example, did not "allow the men to put their arms around a girl[']s chair and don[']t allow the women to put their hands on men['s] chair."[63] Moreover, as Lewis Erenberg cogently argues, the placement of tables and the stage in middle-class cabarets created a structure that limited contacts between unacquainted women and men. These measures placed barriers between friends and strangers, as well as audience and performers, and censured the presence of the lone individual, who still connoted the prostitute or her customer.[64] The "couple on a date" became an increasingly important cultural construct for the middle class, since it provided a way to structure potentially promiscuous heterosocial relations at the new resorts.

The commercial dance halls frequented by working-class youth varied in the types of behavior their managers would tolerate, particularly those concerned with vice raids. Unlike the middle-class resorts, however, many hall owners simply ignored the unruly revelry of the crowds and the close physical contact of women and men. At one wild New Year's Eve party at the Princess Cafe, a dance hall and saloon, an undercover investigator observed that "the manager was on the floor all the time but did not interfere or prevent them from doing what ever they pleased."[65] Investigations by the Committee on Amusements and Vacation Resources of Working Girls cited numerous instances of dance halls with little supervision by the management, concluding that "the proprietors of these places not only permit the young men and women who visit the places to do about as they please, but often encourage their lascivious and immoral tendencies."[66] Balconies, for example, were accepted zones of free behavior, and women could be observed on men's laps, hugging and kissing in the dark corners of the hall.

In contrast to the pleasure-seekers at middle-class cabarets, working-class youth often did not attend dances as heterosexual couples, heightening the problem of control. When a working-class woman or man found a "steady," attendance at balls tended to drop. Instead, young people arrived at the halls alone or with members of their own sex, expecting to "couple off" during the dance. At a huge ball held by the Mohawk Club, for example, the vice investigator thought that "the majority of the women came here unescorted and got doubled up in here."[67] The halls themselves devised schemes to facilitate heterosocial interaction. A number of downtown dance academies and halls employed men called "spielers" who danced with unattached women. "It is the business of the spieler to attract and interest young girls," observed Belle Israels. Waiters were also encouraged to play a role in matching up and introducing young women and men.[68]

More commonly, finding a partner occurred through the custom of "breaking" women on the dance floor. At the beginning of a dance, women would dance together, with men watching them from the sidelines; then "the boys step out, two at a time, separate the girls, and dance off in couples—the popular form of introduction in the popular dance hall." The Committee of Fourteen investigators confirmed this practice, often reporting that they "saw women dance alone on the floor and saw men break these girls while on floor."[69] The etiquette of the hall required that a woman remain with this partner at least until the end of the dance.

The scorn for proper introductions reflects the widespread practice of "picking up" unknown women or men in amusement resorts or the streets, an accepted means of gaining companionship for an evening's entertainment. Indeed, some working-class social clubs apparently existed for this very purpose. In his endless search for prostitutes and loose women, an undercover vice investigator was advised by a waiter to "go first on a Sunday night to 'Hans'l & Gret'l Amusement Society' at the Lyceum 86th Str & III Ave, there the girls come and men pick them up." The waiter carefully stressed, however, that these were respectable working women, not prostitutes.[70] Nor was the "pick-up" purely a male prerogative. Journalist Hutchins Hapgood found that "tough" girls "will go to some dance-hall, which may or may not be entirely respectable, and deliberately look for men to dance with."[71]

Such social customs as "picking up" and "breaking" suggest the paradoxical nature of dance hall culture for women. Women enjoyed dancing for the physical pleasure of movement, its romantic and sensual connotations, and the freedom it allowed them. The commercial dance halls were public spaces they could attend without escorts, choose companions for the evening, and express a range of personal desires. Nevertheless, the greater freedom of expression women found in the dance halls occurred in a heterosocial context of imbalanced power and privileges. Picking up women and breaking dancers were more often male prerogatives in a scenario where women displayed themselves for the pleasure of male eyes. "Two men are sure to 'break' provided the girls are good looking and dance well," observed Ruth True.[72] Moreover, the custom of treating, which enabled many women to participate in the life of the dance hall, undercut their social freedom. Women might pay trolley fare out to a dance palace, or purchase a dance ticket and hat check, but they often relied on men's treats to see them through the evening's entertainment. Making a virtue out of economic necessity, young women learned to prize male gifts and attentions. As Belle Israels remarked, the announcement to one's friends that "he treated" was "the acme of achievement in retailing experiences with the other sex."[73] Under these conditions, the need to strive for popularity with men came to be a socially defined—and ultimately restricting—aspect of female expressiveness and desire.

To win male attention in the dance halls, working women fully elaborated their eye-catching style. Chicago women, for example, placed powder puffs in their stocking tops and ostentatiously flourished them to attract male attention on the dance floor.[74] Their New York sisters could hardly be outdone, wearing high-heeled shoes, fancy ball gowns, elaborate pompadours, hair ornaments, and cosmetics. Louisa, who so distressed her Irish working-class mother, proudly wore her "flossy attire" to the West Side dance halls. "She cannot boast a ball dress to be sure. But her scant suit of brown serge with its sateen collar is trim and new," Ruth True observed. "A great encircling hat of cheap black straw reaches to the middle of her back and bends under the weight of an enormous willow."[75] Fancy dress and masquerade balls were held frequently in the middle West Side during the winter months, with prizes given for the best costume or prettiest woman, subsidized by the hall management or social club. This practice reinforced women's objectification, but it also allowed them an outrageous expressiveness prohibited in other areas of their lives. Significantly, Louise de Koven Bowen found that many Chicago girls attended masquerade balls in male attire, cross-dressing being perhaps the most assertive fashion statement they could make.[76]

Women's popularity was also predicated on willingness to drink. In many dance halls and saloons, economic considerations militated against abstinence, and any woman not drinking or encouraging others to imbibe was made unwelcome by the manager or waiters. In some places, prizes were offered the woman who had the most drinks to her credit.[77] Inventive cocktails helped to make drinking a more acceptable female activity. "Beer and other five-cent drinks are not fashionable at these places," observed Belle Israels. "The young man wants to make an impression and therefore induces the girl to drink Mamie Taylors, cocktails and other insidious mixtures." Women who refused to drink might also be obstracized by men. The connection between popularity and drinking in the company of a male companion put an observable social pressure on women; Israels noted that between dances "girls not being entertained at the tables rush over to the dressing-rooms to avoid being seen on the floor."[78]

The approved cultural style of dance hall women involved other forms of uninhibited behavior as well. Loud talk, boisterous laughter, and cigarette smoking all helped women gain attention and status in the halls. Smoking was still a controversial form of female behavior in the 1910's, symbolic of the modern and somewhat risque woman. While some lit their cigarettes in the open, others, like the young women at the Grand Union Hotel's dance hall, smoked covertly: "The men held the cigarettes and the women snatched a puff now and then."[79] Participation in kissing rituals was also emblematic of the "game girl." "Now the kissing parties are starting in," observed a waiter at Remey's New Year's Eve dance, "it appeared to be contagious, when one started kissing they all started." The search for popular attention even led to aggressive and frank sexual advances to men. At another end-of-the-year ball, for example, "one of the girls while in the middle of a dance stopped on [the] floor and went to different tables and kept saying 'You didn't kiss me for New Year's.' "[80]

TREATING AND SEXUALITY

For these women, treating was not always a one-way proposition, but entailed an exchange relationship. In the male subculture of the

saloon, treating rounds of beer asserted workingmen's independent
status while affirming common ties among a group of equals. Wom-
en, however, were financially unable to reciprocate in kind and instead offered sexual favors of varying degrees. Most commonly, cap-
italizing on their attractiveness and personality, women volunteered
only flirtatious companionship. "Pleasures don't cost girls so much
as they do young men," asserted one saleswoman. "If they are ag-
greeable they are invited out a good deal, and they are not allowed
to pay anything." Reformer Lillian Betts observed that working girls
held themselves responsible for failing to finagle men's invitations,
believing that "it is not only her misfortune, but her fault; she
should be more attractive."[81] Not all working-class women simply
played the coquette, however. Engaging in treating ultimately involved a negotiation between the desire for social participation and
adherence to cultural sanctions that strongly discouraged premarital
sexual intimacy. One investigator captured the dilemma women
faced in their dependency on men in their leisure time: "Those who
are unattractive, and those who have puritanic notions, fare but ill in
the matter of enjoyments. On the other hand, those who do become
popular have to compromise with the best conventional usage."[82]

The extent of sexual intimacy involved in treating and the nature
of the social relations surrounding it are difficult to establish. Du-
alistic middle-class categories of "respectability" and "promiscuity"
do not adequately describe the complexity and ambiguity of working-class sexual norms, norms that were complicated further by ethnic, religious, and generational differences. The Italian daughter
who stayed out late at ballrooms or an unmarried Irish girl who
became pregnant might equally be stigmatized by their respective
communities. Reformer Lillian Betts, for example, cites several
cases of women turning their backs on co-workers or neighbors
whom they suspected of immorality. Settlement workers observed,
however, that for many young women, censure was more instru-
mental than moralistic. "The hardness with which even the suggestion of looseness is treated in any group of working girls is simply
an expression of self-preservation," Betts observed.[83] Another investigation found a profound ambivalence in young women's attitudes toward premarital pregnancies, their criticism of the wrong-
doer being more "conventional than sincere and deep-seated;

and . . . not always unmixed with a certain degree of admiration for the success with the other sex which the difficulty implies."[84]

Working-class women received conflicting messages about the virtues of virginity in their daily lives. Injunctions about chastity from parents, church, and school might conflict with the lived experience of urban labor and leisure. Working in factories and stores often entailed forms of sexual harassment that instructed women to exchange sexual favors for economic gain, while talk about dates and sexual exploits helped to pass the working day. Crowded tenement homes caused working-class daughters to pursue their social life in the unprotected spaces of the streets, while those living in boarding homes contended with the attentions of male lodgers. The pleasure and freedom young women craved could be found in the social world of dance halls, but these also carried a mixed message, permitting expressive female sexuality within a context of dependency and vulnerability.

Negotiating this world produced a range of responses. While many women carefully guarded their reputations, attended chaperoned dances, and deflected the attentions of men, others engaged in looser forms of behavior. Women who had steady male friends they intended to marry might justify premarital sexual intimacy: "A girl can have many friends," explained one woman, "but when she gets a 'steady,' there's only one way to have him and to keep him; I mean to keep him long."[85]

Other women fully bought into the culture of treating, trading sexual favors of varying degrees for male attention, gifts, and a good time. These women were known in underworld slang as "charity girls," a term that differentiated them from prostitutes because they would not accept money in their sexual encounters with men. As vice reformer George Kneeland found, they "offer themselves to strangers, not for money, but for presents, attention and pleasure, and, most important, a yielding to sex desire." A thin line divided these women from "occasional prostitutes," women who slipped in and out of prostitution when unemployed or in need of extra income. Many respectable working women apparently acted like Dottie: "When she needed a pair of shoes she had found it easy to 'earn' them in the way that other girls did."[86]

Charity girls were frequent patrons of the city's large public dance halls, finding in them the pleasure and freedom they craved, and perhaps the anonymity they needed. Undercover vice investigators were informed by a waiter at one racket that the women present were "game" and "lively," but not prostitutes, and that the "majority . . . are here every week, they take in every affair that takes place at this hall." Often they comprised more than half of the dancers: "Some of the women . . . are out for the coin but there is a lot that come in here that are charity." At La Kuenstler Klause, a restaurant with music and dancing, a waiter confided to the investigator, "girls could be gotten here, but they don't go with men for money, only for [a] good time." The latter sketched the cultural style of such women, reporting that "most of the girls are working girls, not prostitutes, they smoke cigarrettes, drink liquers and dance dis[orderly] dances, stay out late and stay with any man, that pick them up first." Meeting two women at a bar, another investigator remarked, "They are both supposed to be working girls but go out for a good time and go the 'Limit.' "[87] These women flocked to the dance halls not necessarily as an environment for courtship, but for the pleasures of dancing, flirtation, and sexual encounters.

This evidence points to the presence of charity girls at dance halls, but it tells us little about their numbers, social background, working lives, and relationship to family and community. The vice reports suggest that the women were young, some not over fifteen or sixteen; as one investigator indicated, "Some of these girls had their hair down in a braid." The jobs they held were typical of other working women—waitresses, domestic servants, garment-makers. While some lived alone, others resided with their families, which made sexual encounters difficult. One man, who picked up charity girls at a dance hall, remarked, for example, that "he sometimes takes them to the hotels, but sometimes the girls won[']t go to [a] hotel to stay for the night, they are afraid of their mothers, so he gets away with it in the hallway."[88]

It is important to note that the vice investigators generally attended the larger halls, such as the Manhattan Casino and the Harlem River Casino, oriented to a metropolitan rather than a neighborhood clientele. Not knowing the extent to which charity girls chould be found at the smaller rented halls in the tenement districts makes it impossible to assess how visible or tolerated this behavior was within Manhattan's working-class communities. Nor is there evidence about pregnancy and birth control, and what occurred to these women as they aged. Whether they took the "downward path" toward prostitution, as reformers warned, or married into respectability can only be a matter for speculation.

Whatever the specific numbers of charity girls, many more women must have been conscious of the need to negotiate sexual encounters if they wished to participate in commercial amusements. Clara Laughlin, for example, reported the story of an attractive but decorous working girl who could not understand why men dropped her after a few dates. Finally a co-worker gave her the worldly advice that social participation involved an exchange relationship: "Don't yeh know there ain't no feller goin' t'spend coin on yeh fer nothin'? Yeh gotta be a good Indian, Kid—we all gotta!" While some women self-consciously defined their own respectability against the culture of treating, others clearly relished the game of extracting gifts and favors. A vice investigator offered to take one woman, a department store clerk and occasional prostitute, to the Central Opera House at 3:00 A.M.; he noted that "she was willing to go if I'd take a taxi; I finally coaxed her to come with me in a street car." Sociologist Frances Donovan found similar concerns in the conversations of waitresses, "talking about their engagements which they had for the evening or for the night and quite frankly saying what they expected to get from this or that fellow in the line of money, amusement or clothes."[89]

The intricacies of this negotiation—the balancing act between social respectability, female desire, and male pressures—created subtle and flexible standards for personal conduct. The hat check girl at Semprinis dance hall carefully walked this line in a conversation with a vice investigator, who noted that "she appears to be game and . . . is not a church member." Answering his proposal for a date, she "said she'd be glad to go out with me but told me there was nothing doing [sexually]. Said she didn't like to see a man spend money on her and then get disappointed." Commenting on the charity girls who frequented the hall, she remarked:

These women get her sick, she can't see why a woman should lay down for a man the first time they take her out. She said it wouldn't be so bad if they went out with the men 3 or 4 times and then went to bed with them but not the first time.[90]

The culture of the commercial dance hall—the anonymity of its spaces, tolerance of uninhibited behavior, aura of romance, and peer pressure to conform—supported the social relationship of treating. It induced young women to engage in freer forms of sexuality and perhaps glamorized the notion of a sexual exchange. While treating gave some women opportunities for social participation they otherwise would have lacked, it remained a situation of vulnerability and potential exploitation.

One way women exerted some control over their interactions with men was by attending dances and other leisure activities in the company of a "lady friend." Young working-class women's friendships were structured relationships between girls who usually met at school, at work, or on the streets. Unlike their brothers, who often joined gangs or clubs, young women would cultivate a single friend, or at most a small clique. The formality of these relationships was observed by Ruth True: "It is very constant and means that the two share most of their pleasures together. There are distinct requirements; one must 'call up' and 'wait in' and not 'go round' too much with anyone else."[91] The lady friend enhanced social occasions, as a companion to share the fun of a dance and a confidante for whispered gossip. At the same time, she performed another function, serving as an implicit protector whose presence helped to deflect unwanted sexual attentions. At a racket for the Drivers' Sick and Benevolent Fund, the Committee of Fourteen investigator "tried to get next to some of the women but couldn['t, they travel in pairs and it[']s hard for one man to pick any of them up." Even when a woman had a steady, outings might include a lady friend for pleasure and protection; Lillian Betts reported that "one would rarely hear of plans that did not include two beside the couple engaged or willing to be. Sometimes two girls were to complete the party."[92] However, True notes that the special obligations of lady friends to be with each other fell by the wayside when one woman began keeping company with her gentleman friend.[93]

The lady friend symbolically drew the line of respectability at a time in women's lives when heterosexual contact was at its most promiscuous and dangerous, when meeting men in dance halls, amusement resorts, and the streets. The single woman alone might be taken for a prostitute, but hunting in pairs permitted women to maintain their respectability in the aggressive pursuit of pleasure. The function of working-class lady friends clearly differs from the nineteenth-century pattern of middle-class female friendships, which emerged in the shared experience of a woman-centered realm, fed by the rituals of the home and the female life cycle.[94] The working women's friendships as described by reformers and settlement workers occurred in a context that strengthened women's ability to negotiate the public, heterosocial world of commercial amusements rather than maintain a privatized female one.

In the commercial dance halls, single working-class women found a social space that reinforced their emergent cultural style and offered an opportunity to experiment with unconventional sexual and social roles. In a few hours of dancing and camaraderie, they could seemingly escape the social relationships and expectations tying them to their household responsibilities, jobs, and ethnic communities. What mattered in the dance hall—popularity, dancing ability, fashionable clothes, and male attention—was a modern style that promised independence, romance, and pleasure. Nevertheless, the realities of working-class life persistently intruded; women's situation in the labor force and family undercut their social freedom, and treating underscored their material dependency. And within the halls, an ideology took shape that fused notions of female autonomy and pleasure with heterosexual relationships and consumerism. This formulation, which ultimately limited female possibilities and power, increasingly defined the cultural construction of gender in the twentieth century.

CHAPTER FIVE

THE CONEY ISLAND
EXCURSION

If dancing was working women's winter passion, then excursions were the height of the summer season. A network of picnic grounds, beach resorts, and amusement parks ringed Manhattan, attracting thousands of young women like Agnes M., a twenty-year-old German immigrant who had worked as a milliner, dressmaker, and domestic servant. "I have a great many friends in New York and I enjoy my outings with them," she observed in 1903. "We go to South Beach or North Beach or Glen Island or Rockaway or Coney Island. If we go on a boat we dance all the way there and all the way back, and we dance nearly all the time we are there." Her favorite resort, though, was Coney Island, "a wonderful and beautiful place." The special appeal of Coney's amusement resorts to working women is suggested in Agnes' description of an outing with a German friend, newly arrived in New York. "When we had been on the razzle-dazzle, the chute and the loop-the-loop, and down in the coal mine and all over the Bowery, and up in the tower and everywhere else, I asked her how she liked it. She said: 'Ach, it is just like what I see when I dream of heaven.'"[1] Coney took young women out of the daily round of tenement life and work, but at the same time, it allowed them to extend their culture to the resort, whose beaches, boardwalk, and dancing pavilions were arenas for diversion, flirtations, and displays of style.

Agnes did note that her passion for Coney Island was not shared by those of higher social standing, who questioned the resort's respectability and gentility. "I have heard some of the high people with whom I have been living say that Coney Island is not tony." Symbolically understanding this cultural issue in terms of dance, she implied that her betters repressed desire and were unable to express or enjoy themselves. "The trouble is that these high people don't know how to dance," she exclaimed. "I have to laugh when I see them at their balls and parties. If only I could get out on the floor and show them how—they would be astonished."[2]

In the early twentieth century, many middle-class people, if not Agnes' employers, began to go to Coney Island and enjoy it. In his study of Coney Island, John Kasson brilliantly traces its evolution from a Victorian resort to the home of the modern amusement park. This transformation, Kasson argues, both exemplified and fostered the decline of genteel cultural hegemony and the rise of a new, expressive urban culture. Coney's thrilling mechanical devices and spectacular exhibits constituted a liberating experience for the middle class, a contrast to the normative demands of conventional bourgeois society. In this way, amusement parks "emerged as laboratories of the new mass culture," where middle-class attitudes toward leisure, sexuality, and the social relations of women and men were forged.[3]

As Agnes' narrative suggests, however, Coney Island's amusement parks also resonated with pleasure for working-class people, particularly its youth subculture. Working-class participation at Coney followed a different trajectory from that of the middle-class patrons who rejected Victorian gentility and adopted a new expressive culture. Rather, Coney Island was initially incorporated into a tradition of working-class excursions and outings, which like other forms of leisure were closely integrated into the life of the community. However, the way laboring people experienced the beach resort changed with the intensified commercialization of leisure. Less obvious, perhaps, is the impact of working-class culture on the design of the new "mass culture" realized in the amusement parks. Not only did Coney symbolize the conflict between Victorian and "modern" culture, it embodied a subtle debate over what forms that new culture should take. Amusement entrepreneurs and showmen developed different strategies for attracting the crowds, drawing upon alternative traditions of popular amusements that were linked to class-based cultures. In this debate, the desires of such working women as Agnes M., who loved to dance, see the men, and have a good time, shaped the emergent mass culture.

THE WORKING-CLASS EXCURSION

Saloons, clubs, dance halls, and the streets figured prominently in the everyday recreation of working-class New Yorkers; the excursion was a special occasion. The outing to a picnic park or beach resort was a brief outdoor respite from tenement apartments, crowded neighborhoods, and busy workshops. On their days of rest—Sundays and summer holidays and, for increasing numbers, the Saturday half-holiday—working people relished a day of fresh air, eating, games, and socializing. Unlike a visit to a local park or square, the excursion usually involved some expense, at least the cost of carfare. Robert Coit Chapin found that three-quarters of the working-class families he questioned went on excursions. While many reported excursions simply to parks or friends' homes, typically families took a major outing—to Coney Island or Fort George—once or twice during the summer months. Such trips were even more common among the more prosperous households, as well as the American, German, and Italian populations of Manhattan. Nevertheless, poorer households could manage to afford excursions by some cost-saving strategies. As one West Side boy observed, "When our whole family goes to Jersey, . . . all of us kids sneak in that way. My father buys tickets and then we walk through the gates and he refuses to pay for us because he don't know us."[4]

Family outings often took the form of day excursions, particularly to the public parks. The huge expanse of Central Park was a pre-eminent location for picnics and outdoor fun, accessible to working-class visitors by foot or streetcar. "The working classes fill the street-cars, and throng the Central Park," observed one writer in the 1870's. "In the summer whole families of laboring people go to the park early in the morning, taking a lunch with them, and there spend the entire day."[5] Several decades later, Rachel Levin, a Russian immigrant, recalled the special quality of such outings: "Sunday usually you know we'd get the family together and go to Central Park—that was a holiday."[6]

Besides the family get-together, there were massive outdoor gatherings sponsored by fraternal and social organizations for their members' families and friends. Like the lodge affair and benefit society ball, these excursions and picnics were incorporated into the working-class social system that provided insurance and mutual aid, integrating recreation with social services and community welfare. In the summertime, banners and posters advertising picnics were hung in the tenement districts, parades would form, and thousands boarded boats to enjoy inexpensive recreation, sociability, and a brief escape from the hot city. These excursions cost their participants relatively little. "The voluntary societies," Robert Coit Chapin observed, "often furnish means of recreation, such as social gatherings, picnics and excursions, and expenditure for recreation is sometimes not differentiated from dues and payments to the society."[7]

Political organizations, unions, and social clubs also organized outings. To encourage tenement dwellers to support their ticket, Tammany Hall ran free excursions every two weeks in the summer. "So many people, especially children and their mothers, desired to go on an excursion," recalled Samuel Chotzinoff, "that by five in the morning a queue many blocks long had already formed at the wharf."[8] Unions sponsored annual picnics for their members, and these events often attracted masses of people. "The picnic on Sunday was the most successful affair our local ever held," Timothy Healy, the president of the Brotherhood of Stationary Firemen, reported. "We sold nearly six thousand tickets at the gate, and had in the neighborhood of ten thousand out before the affair came off."[9]

Working-class pleasure-seekers travelled to beaches on Staten Island and Long Island and sailed up the Hudson. "In the mild season," said one observer, "the adjacent rivers and the harbor are thronged with pleasure boats filled with excursionists."[10] Closer to home, lodges and societies took their members to the city's commercial picnic parks. Privately owned picnic groves dotted the landscape in and around Manhattan in the nineteenth century. The earliest of these was Jones' Woods, located along the East River between 70th and 75th Streets, which offered families and organizations a place for parties, socializing, and fresh air. Other picnic groves later sprang up in the more rural terrain of upper Manhattan, New Jersey, and the Bronx. A group of fraternal and social organizations developed Scheutzen Park in New Jersey in 1875. Its Grand Volkfests drew as many as 150,000 Germans, who marched from "Little Germany" on Manhattan's East Side to the trans-Hudson ferries, where they boarded boats for an outing to the park.[11]

More commonly, picnic groves were outdoor versions of Manhattan's public halls, commercial enterprises linked to saloons, roadhouses, or hotels in outlying areas. In 1895, there were seventeen picnic grounds in upper Manhattan and the Bronx alone, many of them run along the lines of German beer gardens, with bands, singers and fireworks. Unlike municipal parks, which banned alcohol and offered limited recreational facilities, the commercial picnic grove encouraged beer drinking and dancing, two favorite working-class activities. Typically an organization hired a boat and picnic grove, charged a fee for the excursion, and served up chowder and sandwiches to its hungry patrons. The park's owner sold drinks to the excursionists or charged a single admission fee, which included all the beer they could drink. Picnic parks always had a platform, where, Lillian Betts observed, "all day dancing goes on."[12] The entertainment at the old-fashioned picnic ground often included athletic competitions, games of chance, shooting matches, and fireworks. At the Stationary Firemen's picnic, for example, the union's president claimed that "some of the best athletes in the world performed at the games."[13]

Picnic groves were popular with working women as early as the mid-nineteenth century. Settlement workers and journalists noted that even women who had little opportunity for amusement nevertheless enjoyed excursions. West Side girls, for example, in the 1890's went on "occasional picnics in warm weather at Lion or Sulzer's Park, up in Harlem." Belle Israels, whose Committee on Amusements and Vacation Resources of Working Girls did the most extensive study in 1909, found that "the picnic park utilized for the outing, the chowder and the summernight's festival" was among the most popular spots for summer entertainment, after the amusement park and beach resort.[14]

Summer picnics and chowder parties sponsored by working-class voluntary organizations often supervised behavior and reinforced community bonds for the people in attendance. Even when tickets were sold indiscriminately, they usually carried a higher price during the daylight hours—from one to five dollars in 1909—which prevented many young people from attending alone. Belle Israels observed, "Many families go to these picnics, and, during the day, the crowd is quite respectable."[15] Some picnic parks affirmed specific ethnic ties. Schuetzen Park, for example, catered to German immigrants, while Celtic Park appealed to an Irish clientele. Maureen Connelly went there on Sundays, and saw only those from the Old Country: "I guess I thought there was nobody but Irish."[16] Some outings were elaborately staged and chaperoned events, as was the case at a union picnic. "It is as formal in its routine as an uptown cotillion," observed journalist Mary Gay Humphreys. "The lady floor managers are intent on their duties; the grand promenade that opens the festivities is a gravely decorous and imposing rite." For young women, these were occasions to dance, socialize, and show off their fashions, not simply for pleasure's sake but to strengthen consciousness of class interests. "No girl is expected to dance with a man who does not belong to a union unless he promises to join," Humphreys reported, "for a picnic is also a proselyting occasion."[17]

Other outings, particularly those held by social clubs, tended to reinforce the youth culture of the streets and dance halls. Commercial parks drew a youthful clientele especially at night, when many reduced their admission prices to twenty-five cents. Israels' committee sent one investigator to a number of these privately operated picnic groves. "At one Long Island park different men told me that decent girls get out of the park at eight o'clock," reported Julia Schoenfeld. "In this same park, I saw many girls under sixteen, boisterous, 'fresh,' and some already showing the signs of dissipation."[18]

Indeed, the life of the commercial dance hall often spilled out into the grassy picnic groves. The Manhattan Casino, for example, was a large entertainment complex comprised of a saloon, dance hall, and picnic grounds, which was rented by fraternal orders and other voluntary societies. The Drivers' Sick and Benevolent Fund hired it for an afternoon picnic and dance, attracting over four hundred people, who, the waiter observed, "were all out in the park lapping up the beer." At a Bookbinders' affair one Sunday afternoon, the crowd caroused indoors, while in the picnic grounds, "there was quite a little crowd here. . . . Some of them were sitting in cliques around barrells of beer and drinking." Respectable women mingled with charity girls and some prostitutes, and the free-and-easy sociability, drinking, and flirtations of the hall seem simply to have flowed out of doors. [19]

THE COMMERCIALIZATION OF EXCURSIONS

By the 1890's, the development of commercial excursions and the extension of transportation lines had begun to alter the working-class outing. New transportation networks made day trips cheaper and easier for families and individuals. Steamship companies continued to rent their facilities to organizations, but they also started to run regular excursion boats for anyone paying the price of admission. These charged fifteen to twenty-five cents for a round trip to Coney Island in 1901, and other commercial boats took passengers up the Hudson or to New Haven for outings. Streetcar lines were extended to the outer regions of the city, and by 1895, one could reach Coney Island for only five or ten cents by trolley. [20]

Young women's opportunities for the pursuit of pleasure were heightened as excursions became commercialized. Irma Stein, who took outings with her family, recalled that "at that time everything was so cheap. . . . We took subway rides, double-decker trolley, boat riding." [21] Some trolley lines connected directly with picnic groves and amusement parks like Fort George, where a woman could enjoy an unsupervised afternoon or evening. Women could afford to use trolleys much as they had the streets, as spaces to court and socialize with men. Like Zetta, a woman with little spending money was "obliged to turn to trolley rides and walks and various kinds of excursions,—literally to the streets,—for hospitality, when she received a man's visit." [22]

With the development of inexpensive and regular commercial excursions, young women travelled on their own to beach resorts. At North Beach, one of the more notorious amusement resorts, Israels interviewed a young girl who observed, "My mother doesn't know I go out here; but I want some fun, and it only costs ten cents." [23] The excursion boats themselves also provided an opportunity for flirtations and amusement, without the chaperonage of parents. Israels' committee condemned the moral atmosphere of the all-day excursion boats as far worse than that of the late weekend boats from Coney Island or Rockaway Beach, charging that some boats rented staterooms to couples for short periods and "their purpose is not one of rest or comfort."[24] Like other forms of working women's amusements that took place outside of a familial or community context, the excursion boats combined sexual perils with the pleasures women craved.

Commercialization not only altered the mode of transportation; it also affected the social spaces in which young women and men enjoyed their outings. The number of old-fashioned picnic grounds began to decline in the early twentieth century; in 1910, there were only ten remaining in Manhattan and the Bronx, as residential and commercial development transformed the metropolis. Trying to meet a growing demand for new sensations and entertainment, many picnic parks began to offer a wide range of popular amusements, including concert halls, penny arcades, and mechanical rides. By the 1890's, the organized working-class excursion to a picnic grove increasingly gave way to a new cultural and commercial phenomenon, a trip to a modern amusement park.[25]

THE WORKING-CLASS PRESENCE
AT CONEY ISLAND

The changes wrought by the commercialized outing are most evident at Coney Island, whose checkered history involved an important working-class presence even before the advent of its famous amusement parks. In the mid-nineteenth century, Coney Island was a desolate beach, attracting only a few wealthy patrons who sought quietude and the sea air. By 1870, small inns and bathhouses dotted the shore, but tales of swindlers and roughnecks roaming the island deterred many travellers. Not until the late 1870's did Coney emerge as New York's leading amusement resort. Railroads linked the beaches with Manhattan, while regular steamship service began by 1880. On the east end of the island, exclusive hotels and restaurants sprang up along Manhattan Beach, where society's upper crust, "chiefly New York and Boston nabobs," frequented the elegant Oriental Hotel. Just to the west, Brighton Beach beckoned middle-class vacationers to its family hotels, shore dinners, and open-air bands.[26]

Discernible patterns of participation by class and sex marked Coney Island's early days. Middle- and upper-class women and children summered at the exclusive hotels and beaches, while businessmen remained in the city, paying occasional weekend visits to their families. While the east end of Coney Island catered solely to the respectable, its far west end was notorious as a hangout for underworld figures and gangs. Norton's Point became a center for horse racing, prize-fighting, and prostitution, offering leisure activities oriented to a "sporting" male subculture that crossed class lines. In the late nineteenth century, Coney Island's geography not only offered a "linear, visual study in American class structure," as Robert Snow and David Wright have written,[27] it also reflected the Victorian organization of social life by gender.

Between these two poles, West Brighton, at the midpoint of the island, emerged as the playground of the masses. More than 80 percent of Coney's sixty thousand visitors clustered there on hot Sunday afternoons. Ignored by big real estate developers in the 1870's and 1880's, West Brighton was an amalgam of different amusements, including restaurants, saloons, bathhouses, and circus sideshows, dominated by Lucy the Elephant, at once a hotel and a major landmark of the area. Some of these resorts, like Feltman's Pavilion, catered primarily to middle-class lodges and voluntary organizations.[28] Other attractions, however, appealed to the sensibilities and pocketbooks of the laboring classes. "Seeing the elephant" involved incorporating Coney's resorts into working-class culture.

Even in the days before the modern amusement parks dominated Coney Island, working women and men sought out its rollicking resorts and cool beaches. Their presence is impossible to document statistically, but a number of witnesses confirm the popularity of working-class outings to Coney Island. As early as the 1870's and 1880's, three hundred different societies were said to "indulge in at least one pic-nic during the summer" there.[29] The cool sea air attracted crowds of women and children, who would wait until the last train or steamship to take them back to Manhattan. On one particularly steamy day, one thousand "apparently respectable" workingmen were permitted to sleep overnight on the beach. "The crowd was so great," observed the New York *Tribune*, "that extra cars were put on to accommodate those who wanted to start for the city to their work." By 1900, Coney Island was thronged with as many as 300,000 to 500,000 on Saturday afternoons, Sundays, and holidays.[30]

Not only did working-class people flock to West Brighton, but by the 1890's, many of the resorts had taken their character from working-class cultural activities and commercial amusements popular in the tenement districts. Variety shows, inexpensive beer saloons, and penny arcades beckoned to the working-class crowds, while boardwalk pushcarts hawked such popular Coney Island cuisine as clams, hot corn, and chowder to the passing throngs. Like men of other classes, workingmen went to the prize fights, concert saloons, and other arenas of male culture, causing one union leader to complain, "If the working man would only show half the interest in the bread and butter question that he showed in the recent slugging battle at Coney Island, he would be doing something to benefit himself and those dependent upon him."[31] People from the tenement districts, a journalist observed, particularly liked the free dancing pavilions and bathing beaches, where they revelled in such indecorous behavior as screaming and chasing through crowds.[32] The free-and-easy culture of working-class Manhattan's streets, clubs, saloons, and public halls found expression at this summer resort.

The nature of West Brighton before the rise of the great amusement parks is best characterized by the Bowery, a lane of amusement concessions laid out by the area's leading entrepreneur, George Tilyou. Like its Manhattan namesake, it teemed with arcades, penny slot machines, shooting galleries, kinetoscope shows, freak shows, and dime museums, as well as numerous dance halls and variety houses. And while its visitors were of many classes, its hurly-burly ambience was much like the Bowery in the city, a street mingling working-class saloons, commercial amusements, and a rowdy and gregarious atmosphere. "Life is strenuous on the Bowery," one guidebook warned. "It is no place for the weak-hearted or the languid."[33] The cultural style of West Brighton mimicked that of its working-class visitors rather than the more high-flown tastes of the middle-class end of the island. A journalist observed that West Brighton's patrons "have set aside money sufficient for a day within sound of Seidl's orchestra, yet they prefer the oom-pah bands of rusted brass. They would rather have a luncheon of Frankfurters and lager and a dinner of roasted clams and melted butter."[34] This area was the center of attraction to Coney's visitors before the creation of the large amusement parks and, even after, drew crowds loving uninhibited excitement.

At the same time that a working-class presence developed at West Brighton, its patronage subtly changed in terms of gender. Many resorts at Coney Island had been havens for a male subculture of gambling houses, saloons, brothels, and taxi-dance houses. By the 1890's, the concert halls, dance pavilions, and variety shows sought members of both sexes. Open-air stages and beach pavilions were particularly popular, offering melodrama, sentimental plays, and slapstick comedy. Originally entertainment for men only, concert halls like Koster's emphasized risque titillation, having its soubrettes wear short skirts and sing suggestive lyrics. By the 1890's, such shows were drawing a mixed-sex audience. Men continued to attend, but were joined by "mothers with babies and whole hordes of youngsters [who] would suddenly pounce upon and occupy a table in these halls." The entertainment had become tamer, but still challenged proper middle-class sensibilities. "The singers in the concert halls and the variety shows have lengthened their dresses and abbreviated their misbehavior," noted one journalist, "but it is still the seat of a delirium of raw pleasure."[35]

WORKING WOMEN'S CULTURE
AT CONEY ISLAND

For young working women, an excursion to Coney Island was the apotheosis of summer entertainment. The diversions ranged from sideshow attractions and vaudeville shows to restaurants and the boardwalk. Not unexpectedly, the most popular gathering places were dancing pavilions, open-air structures built on piers or on the beach, which rollicked with music and spieling from 7:00 P.M. until the last boat back to the city each night. The pavilions attracted "pivoters," those "thousands of girls who are seized with such madness for dancing that they spend every night in the dance halls and the picnic parks."[36] Working women could find eight large dance

halls at Coney Island, ranging from regulated places to more disreputable saloons with a dance floor, each having a discernible cultural style. Beatrice Stevenson, examining the working girls' amusements at Coney Island, catalogued these halls:

> At the largest and most exclusive, Saturday night sees an enor-
> mous crowd of elaborately dressed girls and men of good ap-
> pearance and grooming. At other places girls are more plainly
> dressed, wear shirt waists and street hats, and at still others the
> girls are of coarse appearance and are flashily dressed. The forms
> of dancing and behavior vary at the three grades of halls; in the
> most fashionable there is a good deal of promiscuous intercourse,
> flirting and picking up of acquaintances, but the dancing itself is
> usually proper and conventional; in the most Bohemian, behavior
> is free and pronouncedly bad forms of dancing are seen. [37]

Even after the new amusement parks were built, numerous dance
houses and concert halls could be found in the seedy places of the
Bowery that continued to attract young working women on Saturday
and Sunday nights. "They know the bad reputation of some of
them," Belle Israels observed in 1909, "but the dancing floor is
good, there are always plenty of men and there are laughter and
liberty galore."[38]

Many of the social forms so familiar to young women in the city's
dance halls and streets simply carried over to Coney Island. By rely-
ing on the system of treating, women could enjoy a day at Coney's
resorts with their only expense being transportation: "It only costs
fare down and back, and for the rest of it the boys you 'pick up,'
'treat.'"[39] Some working women's manipulation of this relationship
was suggested by a journalist, who overheard two young women at
an unguarded moment discussing their male escorts:

> "What sort of a time did you have?"
> "Great. He blew in $5.00 on the blow-out."
> "You beat me again. My chump only spent $2.55."[40]

Such customary practices as picking up a date and breaking dancers
could be seen in the dancing pavilions of West Brighton. "Any well-

seeming youngster may invite any girl to dance" at Coney Island, observed one journalist, "an arrangement long since sanctioned by that maelstrom of proletarian jollity, the 'social,' where tickets . . . connote partners and more partners, till everybody knows everybody else." Lillian Betts concurred, noting that at dancing pavilions "the buying of a drink gives the right of the floor to any man."[41]

West Brighton's Bowery, the dancing pavilions, and the boardwalk were social spaces women used for flirtations and adventure, but like their urban counterparts, they held sexual risks. The typical shopgirl at Coney, one journalist asserted, was "keen and knowing, ever on the defensive, she discourages such advances as perplex her. . . . Especially she distrusts cavaliers not of her own station." At other amusement parks, too, unescorted women could expect verbal harassment and advances. At Fort George, claimed Israels, "no girl or group of girls can walk along the street there or through the park without being repeatedly accosted by men."[42] Young women sought Coney's diversions with a friend of the same sex, the protective arrangement that better allowed them to strike up innocuous acquaintances with young men.

THE MODERN AMUSEMENT PARK

By 1900, commercialization had altered the customary patterns of working-class leisure at the beach resort with the development of the amusement park. In 1896, Captain Paul Boyton's Sea Lion Park became the first amusement park at Coney Island, drawing in the crowds with marine animals and shoot-the-chutes. For the first time, a developer had enclosed a large area of land at West Brighton and established a variety of mechanical and other amusements based on a specific theme. Witnessing the commercial potential of this venture, George Tilyou purchased Coney Island property and created Steeplechase Park in 1897, cramming it with mechanical rides and fun-house laughs. Steeplechase was followed by two spectacular parks, Luna Park and Dreamland.[43]

The amusement parks brought a new measure of permanence to Coney's amusements. Owners invested heavily in land, buildings, and machinery. They consolidated control over entertainment in the parks by leasing the amusement concessions within their boundaries, which allowed them to determine the content and style of the exhibitions. Charging only ten to fifteen cents for admission, they sought the common denominator of the crowds, knowing that large profits would come from people who would return again and again to the parks. These entrepreneurs consciously created entertainment to fit their conception of a mass audience and what it wanted to experience.

In the eyes of the middle-class commentators who travelled yearly to West Brighton, the creation of the amusement park produced unexpected—and welcome—results. Not only did the parks offer mechanical thrills, hilarity, and new sensations, but they apparently engineered the social and moral transformation of Coney Island. Journalists tested the moral tenor of the amusement park and judged it wholesome. To court a new public, showmen now eschewed the old con games, the fake sideshows, and the criminal element. "Its laundered diversions attract a laundered constituency," one writer observed. "A permanent amusement park can't afford out-and-out swindles." The new moral atmosphere even extended to West Brighton's rollicking saloons and concessions, where another journalist found that "a careful scrutiny of the Bowery and adjacent lanes fails to discover evidences of the vicious resorts found there in recent years."[44]

The result of the improvements, observed these commentators, was a new clientele for Coney Island, a shift in its composition by class and gender. "Time was when the place was shunned by ultra-respectable New Yorkers, who went instead to Manhattan Beach," one wrote, "but nowadays Coney is visited by all classes."[45] Journalists were impressed with the refinement and courtesy of this new crowd, "as handsome and charming to gaze upon as any to be found at Newport or Long Branch or along the board walk of Atlantic City" and a far cry from the rowdy pleasure-seekers of previous decades.[46] The new amusement parks were seen as family entertainment, and the male culture that permeated the resorts and sideshows abated. One writer observed, "The man who formerly came with a gang of fellows from his office or shop to enjoy a relapse into rowdyism now brought his womenfolk and was decent."[47]

There is no doubt that the owners of Steeplechase, Luna, and Dreamland energetically sought to attract a respectable audience, wooing the middle-class patrons who had formerly attended Manhattan and Brighton Beaches. In a departure from the old Coney Island, several parks sold only soft drinks within their boundaries and entertainment was toned down for a family audience. Determined to offend no one, George Tilyou posted the following warning to vaudeville performers appearing at Steeplechase Park:

> Performers playing in this house are requested not to use any *Vulgarity* or *Slang* in their act and to kindly omit the words *Damn* or *Liar* or any saying not fit for *Ladies* and children to hear. . . Our audiences are mostly ladies and children, and what we want is only *Polite Vaudeville.*[48]

Within the category of "respectability," however, the showmen and park owners sought the widest possible range, including working-class women and men in their idea of a mass audience. One guidebook stressed that "it is now possible for every sort and condition of people to find opportunities for rest and healthful recreation and all without the expenditure of too much money."[49]

Amusement park owners used different strategies to attract the new mass audience, with differing degrees of success. The three large amusement parks, Steeplechase, Luna Park, and Dreamland, did not wage a unified assault on vulgarity and immorality, but rather fought a subtle battle over the nature of popular amusements and early mass entertainment. These parks drew upon different cultures in designing and presenting their amusements, with Luna and especially Dreamland oriented toward a middle-class model and Steeplechase using and transforming cultural forms prevalent in working-class life, especially in its youth subculture. These choices particularly affected the ways in which park owners handled sexual expression and social relationships in their mixed-sex amusements.

ATTRACTING A MIDDLE-CLASS AUDIENCE AT LUNA AND DREAMLAND

The amusement parks that garnered the most public attention and admiration were Luna and Dreamland, described by one journalist as an "enchanted, story book land of trellisses, columns, domes,

minarets, lagoons, and lofty aerial flights. . . . It was a world removed—shut away from the sordid clatter and turmoil of the
streets."[50] Luna Park opened its colorful, oriental buildings in 1901,
while Dreamland, all in white, followed a few years later. As John
Kasson explains, these parks owed much to the example of the Chicago World's Fair of 1893. Two ideas melded together from this exposition, the spectacular, unified vision of the White City and the
eye-catching, raucous Midway, with its Ferris Wheel, sideshows,
and exotica. Believing that the public would rather be amused than
edified, the showmen who built Luna and Dreamland stressed mid-
way-style fun and sensation within their grounds.[51]

Luna Park was the more successful of the two. When Luna
opened, it was applauded by journalists and the middle-class visitors who flocked to its gates, attracted by its thrilling mechanical
rides, scenic displays, and midway, the first built in a permanent
amusement park. Visitors marvelled at Fire and Flames, a staged
enactment of a tenement house fire that would have been familiar to
some but not all of Luna's patrons. Eskimo and German villages
gave New Yorkers a taste of foreign cultures, while the Delhi marketplace, to which "three hundred natives . . . have been brought
over to lend local color," satisfied their cravings for the exotic. The
stress on spectacle and sensation at Luna was epitomized by one
amusement, the Dragon's Gorge, in which the "passenger starts
from the North Pole and visits in rapid succession Havana Harbor,
Port Arthur in winter, the Rocky Mountains, the bottom of the sea
and the caverns of the lower regions besides experiencing a dash
under a great cataract and numerous other sensational adventures."[52] The formula in these attractions, derived in part from the
World's Fair, was to offer imaginary journeys, re-enactments of current events, and exotic views of foreign lands.

Luna Park displayed the hallmarks of the modern amusement
park, thrilling patrons with chutes, sending them screaming on roll-
er coasters, and encouraging romance on the Old Mill and Canals of
Venice. It avoided the moralizing and edification generally associated with Victorian middle-class leisure, just as it rejected the immoral and vulgar amusements of late nineteenth-century Coney Island. In many ways, however, Luna seems the culmination of
nineteenth-century forms of entertainment, not the breakthrough

into twentieth-century culture that commentators and journalists acclaimed. The middle-class interest in exotic foreign travel, science, and realism in the Victorian era found expression at the amusement park. Like stereopticon shows and lyceum speakers, Luna Park brought the experience of foreign lands home to millions who could not travel beyond Coney Island. Such exhibits as baby incubators and re-enactments of naval battles and tenement fires served the middle-class public's interest in scientific advances and newspaper events.[53] In its conception of recreation for the masses, Luna alternated between forms of amusement derived from nineteenth-century middle-class forms and a twentieth-century sensibility based on humor and excitement.

Dreamland sought to challenge Luna's success, creating an architectural grandeur out of plaster that was unrivalled at Coney Island. Its founders, who were not showmen but politicians, did acknowledge the popular desire for pure amusement and met it with such fun-house attractions as the Haunted Swing, the Funny Room, and a human obstacle course, as well as technological sensations, including the Leap Frog Railroad, in which "passengers in breathless excitement momentarily anticipat[e] disaster." Far outnumbering these concessions, however, were the scenarios of exotic life and re-enactments of current events. To compete with Luna, Dreamland offered the Fall of Pompeii, a Japanese building "showing real life in Japan," scenic trips through Switzerland and the Venetian canals, a dramatization of warfare, as well as the omnipresent baby incubators and Fighting the Flames, a "most realistic production of a city fire."[54] Even more than Luna, Dreamland defined the mass appeal of its entertainments in terms of spectacular exhibits, realistic drama, and sensation.

Dreamland went much further than Luna, however, in its moralizing efforts to win a respectable audience. Two of its most elaborate attractions, for example, were The Creation and The End of the Earth, designed to inspire visitors with the imagined grandeur and terror of those events. Dreamland's middle-class morality suffuses these exhibits. As described by Maxim Gorky, the scenes of Hell became a lesson in contemporary morals: a pretty young woman buys a new hat and tries it on before a mirror, when two demons seize her and throw her into a fiery pit. The announcer pointedly observes that, "if people do not want to be the victims of Satan . . ., they should not kiss girls to whom they are not married, because then the girls might become bad women." He continued by condemning women pickpockets and liquor drinking, while recommending churches over saloons: "Not only [are they] more beneficial to the soul but they are cheaper."[55] Dreamland's advocacy of virtue and abstinence directly opposed the emergent popular culture of the early twentieth century, which affirmed more expressive sexual and social relations between women and men. Unlike the earlier, notorious Coney Island, the amusement park in Dreamland's formulation was to be mass entertainment that upheld middle-class standards of propriety, catering to both sexes without making sexuality an integral part of the amusement.

The paradox of such a position was noted by Gorky, who observed of the announcer that "he himself does not seem to believe in what he is told to preach."[56] Dreamland was never as popular as Luna or Steeplechase Park, and when it burned to the ground in 1911, its owners decided it was not worth rebuilding. One of its directors, George Dobson, voiced the essential problem of Dreamland: its attempt to be the beautiful, edifying White City could not lure the masses. "We sought to appeal to a highly developed sense of the artistic, but it did not take us long to discover that Coney Island was scarcely the place for that sort of thing," he observed. "Architectural and decorative beauty were virtually lost upon the great majority of visitors, with the result that from year to year Dreamland was popularized, that is to say, the original design abandoned."[57]

SEXUAL CULTURE AT CONEY

Luna and Dreamland based much of their appeal on spectacle and sensation, inspiring surprise, awe, laughter, and delight in the experiences they orchestrated for the public. They intentionally rejected the "old" Coney Island's sexual culture. Still, many of Coney's visitors, including working women, continued to gravitate to the rowdy streets, alluring concession stands, and bawdy sideshows that flourished under the shadow of the big amusement parks. Hundreds of questionable dance resorts and music halls remained in the Bowery,

Belle Israels charged in 1909: "Not even belittling the fact that 'nice' people dance in the Dreamland ball room, the fact remains that the average girl has small powers of discrimination."[58]

While journalists touted the wholesome respectability of the "new" Coney Island, middle-class reform groups found much to criticize. In 1901, the Women's Branch of the Brooklyn City Mission crusaded against immorality and prostitution at Coney. When police denied that such activities occurred, a New York *Tribune* reporter investigated the moral condition of the resort. He condemned the "disgusting photographs" displayed in kinetoscope shows, noting that "the most pathetic sight was the number of women with daughters and sons that patronized the places where these machines were."[59] Another study of vice at the island's resorts was conducted in 1910, while in 1912, a reform group called the West End Improvement League of Coney Island crusaded for more beach front, a boardwalk, and an improved moral tone. One Reverend Mortenson, of the Society of Inner Mission and Rescue Work, was outraged by the rowdyism at night, the sideshows and bawdy concert halls, the suggestive moving picture machines, and, not least, the immorality of the beach on Sunday afternoons: "The nudity and unproper behavior of many of the people there are, mildly speaking, shocking."[60] Indeed, some New York City guidebooks continued to advise middle-class tourists to stick to the safe and refined Manhattan and Brighton Beaches, warning that the individual who went to West Brighton "should look out for his pocket-book and not be too curious to visit all the 'midway attractions,' some of which are to be avoided."[61]

The freer sexual expression of the dance halls, beaches, and boardwalk, which had long appealed to working women, increasingly became commodified in the amusement concessions of West Brighton. Many sideshows promoted familiarity between the sexes, romance, and titillation to attract crowds of young women and men. Penny arcades, for example, had machines to measure the ardor of a couple's kiss. The Cannon Coaster, which shot people out of a cannon onto a slide, advertised itself with the come-on, "Will she throw her arms around your neck and yell? Well, I guess, yes." Rides that sent their patrons into dark, winding passages—the Canals of Venice and the Tunnel of Love, for example—proliferated.

Said the manager of one of these mazes, "The men like it because it gives them a chance to hug the girls, the girls like it because it gives them a chance to get hugged." One Coney Island dance master summed up the prevailing commercial attitude: "If you haven't got the girls, you can't do business! Keep attracting 'em. The fellows will come if the girls are there."[62]

STEEPLECHASE

George Tilyou's Steeplechase Park, the third of the large amusement parks of Coney Island, exemplifies the commercial potential of making sexuality and romance the focal point of amusement. Tilyou's inspiration came as much from the world of cheap amusements as it did from the middle-class exposition. He built Steeplechase in 1897 on different principles from those underlying Luna and Dreamland, being much less concerned with grandeur, artistic design, and awe-inspiring sensation. Advertised as "The Funny Place," Steeplechase featured hilarity, symbolized by a vulgar, grinning, slightly sinister clown face above its entrance gates, which by 1905 "was causing sensitive folk to wince as they passed by."[63] With none of the attractions of Luna Park or Dreamland—no exotic villages, scenes of natural disasters, or re-enactments of current events, Steeplechase relied on fun houses, mechanical sensations, and circus-type sideshow attractions. Tilyou rarely allowed his patrons to be passive viewers. Instead, the patrons were whirled through space and knocked off balance, their hats blown off, skirts lifted, sense of humor tried. The patrons themselves became the show, providing interest and hilarity to each other.

At Steeplechase, visitors often experienced the unexpected in a sexual context. Some attractions simply encouraged closeness and romance. Men and women customarily sat together on the mechanical horses for the Steeplechase Ride. More inventive were such novelties as the Razzle-Dazzle, also known as the Wedding Ring. This attraction was simply a large circle of laminated wood suspended from a pole, which would be rocked back and forth, causing the patrons to lose their balance. The Wedding Ring made instant acquaintances of strangers and gave women and men a perfect excuse to clutch each other. Similarly, the Barrel of Love was a slowly revolving drum that forced those in it to tumble into each other. Tilyou's intentions were made clear in the advertisement, "Talk about love in a cottage! This has it beat a mile." Meanwhile, the Dew Drop, a parachute ride, never failed to lift women's skirts to the delight of onlookers.[64] Audience participation, the interaction of strangers, and voyeurism were incorporated into Tilyou's conception of mass entertainment.

Significantly, Tilyou never changed this formula, even with the moral cleansing of Coney Island and competition from the other amusement parks after 1900. Fire destroyed much of Steeplechase in 1907, and Tilyou energetically rebuilt it, playfully constructing a temple to exhibitionism, humor, and heterosocial relations called the Pavilion of Fun. The Pavilion featured novel and ingenious methods of placing people in compromising positions, never giving its victims any relief. The human pool table, for example, was placed at the foot of the Dew Drop. Instead of landing safely on solid ground after the parachute ride, the patrons found themselves on a spinning disk that threw them wildly into one another, with the expected results of flying clothes and revealed limbs.[65]

Tilyou's most inspired and popular work, built after the 1907 fire, was known as the Blow-Hole Theater. The stage was placed at the end of the Steeplechase Ride, and the only exit from the ride was through a tunnel leading into the theater. The suspicious patrons would move onto a stage, dimly perceiving an expectant audience in the darkness. They were soon confronted by a dwarf and clown, who urged them forward toward the exit sign. As they walked across, the embarrassed victims encountered innumerable obstacles and tricks, the most popular being a system of compressed air jets that raised women's skirts and blew off men's hats. Eventually the confused participants were allowed to stumble their way off stage, where they found that they could enter the theater as members of the audience and watch the next group of unsuspecting victims.[66]

While social classes mingled at the different amusement parks, Steeplechase attracted a less well-to-do crowd than Luna or Dreamland. Indeed, Tilyou actively promoted it among laboring women and men, advertising in working-class newspapers, including the New York *Call*, a socialist paper, as well as the regular dailies. Affordable entrance fees offered "10 hours of fun for 10 cents," and

Tilyou alone offered a combination ticket that for twenty-five cents admitted visitors to the park and sixteen attractions as well.[67] Moreover, Steeplechase incorporated into its notion of mass entertainment cultural patterns derived from working-class amusements, street life, and popular entertainment. Like them, the park encouraged familiarity between strangers, permitted a free-and-easy sexuality, and structured heterosocial interaction. This culture was not adopted wholesale, but was transformed and controlled, reducing the threatening nature of sexual contact by removing it from the street, workplace, and saloon. Within the amusement park, familiarity between women and men could be acceptable if tightly structured and made harmless through laughter. At Steeplechase, sexuality was constructed in terms of titillation, voyeurism, exhibitionism, and a stress on couples and romance.

Steeplechase was the most enduring of the three parks. The more pretentious Dreamland was never as popular as Luna Park and Steeplechase, and Luna's fortunes declined after 1920. In part, this was due to the financial and personal problems of its founders, but in many ways, Luna emerged at the end, not the beginning, of an era. Its scenic railways and re-enactments of current events were the culmination of Victorian ways of seeing and experiencing. With the rise of the movies and the automobile, Luna's spectacles seemed increasingly old-fashioned, until the amusement park finally closed in the 1940's. Steeplechase, however, remained popular through much of the twentieth century.[68]

CONEY AND CULTURAL CHANGE

At Coney Island, the commercialization of leisure entailed a complex cultural process. Steeplechase, the Bowery, and, to a lesser extent, the other amusement parks articulated new attitudes toward sexuality, gender, personal expressiveness, and pleasure. Entrepreneurs like Tilyou encouraged working-class women's participation by appealing to this cultural constellation, at the same time that they sought to tame and contain it for a middle-class clientele. The sexual culture of these commercial amusements affirmed many aspects of working-class youth culture in its encouragement of flirtation, permissiveness, and sexual humor. But in managing female-male relations, Steeplechase's formula allowed for a non-threatening sexuality that excited but never crossed "forbidden" limits, a sexual ideology that would be increasingly accepted by the middle class. Tied to this was the notion of packaging sexuality and romance for the paying public, a concept that would become a primary tool of consumer industries. The commercialization of leisure, at least in the amusement parks, made playing with heterosexual expressiveness not only respectable but a privilege for which women and men gladly paid.[69]

Thus Coney Island exemplifies not only the decline of a genteel middle-class cultural hegemony, as John Kasson has persuasively argued, but the rise of a heterosocial culture that owed its form in part to the structure of working-class social life. The cultural transformation of these decades must be seen not only in terms of changes within middle-class culture but in terms of changing relationships among class- and gender-based cultures. The Coney Island of the nineteenth century offered amusements that were geographically delineated by social group. For middle-class families, especially women and children, its east end provided a comfortable retreat from the city. For excursionists, West Brighton was an extension—albeit a spectacular one—of the social organizations, picnics, and outings that formed an integral part of working-class life. For men across class lines, the west end preserved the male subculture of gambling, athletics, and prostitution.

With the creation and expansion of the amusement park, a new phase began. Class distinctions did not entirely disappear, for the three amusement parks, as well as the Bowery sideshows, catered to somewhat different social groups. But the incorporation of the amusements into specific class and gender cultures lessened. The fashionable resorts on Manhattan and Brighton Beaches began to decline, with the two landmark hotel-palaces, the Manhattan Beach and the Oriental, closing in the 1910's. The male subculture also diminished as a separate entity on Coney Island and seems rather to have been toned down and mingled with the other amusements. Finally, Coney's place in the organization of working-class amusements changed. Increased numbers of working-class patrons visited the resort in the early twentieth century, and with the extension of the subway from Manhattan to Coney Island in 1920, it became an easily reached haven for the masses. With this new access, however, the group experience of the excursion and outing declined, and working-class people increasingly went to Coney as individuals or as family groups.

These changes grew out of the commercial transformation of popular amusements, including those of a new middle class that gloried in the midway and rejected genteel culture. Just as significant to this development, however, were the popular amusements of working-class youth. In Coney Island's Bowery they recognized their street life, in the dance halls and variety shows familiar customs and behavior, and in the new amusement parks the celebration of sexuality and romance that was so much a part of youthful social life. Amusement park owners adopted these cultural forms and tamed them for a new mass audience that was more responsive to an expressive, heterosocial culture.

CHAPTER SIX

CHEAP THEATER
AND THE NICKEL DUMPS

In the Vitagraph film "The Veiled Beauty," a young woman covered in a veil is approached by several male "mashers," who seek to force their attentions on her. After beating up his rivals, one suitor pursues the woman, who enters Dreamland amusement park, rides the miniature railroad and airship, and explores other attractions, all the while ignoring the young man's attentions. He finally succeeds in inviting her to dinner, where she raises her veil, only to reveal an ugly and horrifying face.[1] In 1907, when this movie was made, an audience composed primarily of working-class women and men would have laughed heartily at the masher's misfortune and the young woman's deception, delighting in this comic vignette of treating, heterosocial relations, and urban leisure.

Many early silent movies projected stylized images of women and men that expressed the heterosocial world of commercial recreation and urban life. Picture shows, as well as working-class vaudeville, drew upon the fads and crazes, free-and-easy sexuality, and celebration of pleasure that "Americanized" working-class youth pursued with enthusiasm. At the same time, they reinterpreted and broadcast new cultural forms for other young women and men to imitate. The general cross-fertilization between theatrical entertainment and youthful crazes is suggested by Belle Israels' observation: "The boy who is seated at the burlesque show tonight and is seeing the latest form of the Grizzly Bear . . . is tomorrow presenting these things as the latest smartness to the girl with whom he is dancing—perhaps at the church sociable."[2]

The cultural commentary embedded in the early movies was all the more powerful because it was accessible to most working-class women, whatever their marital status, ethnic background, or cultural style. Attendance at dance halls and amusement parks often entailed financial dependency on men and rebellious assertions to parents, conditions that not every woman could accept. Even the cheap theater, as reformers called working-class variety and vaudeville entertainment, played to a restricted female audience. Everyone, however, went to the movies. If popular amusements can reinforce particular values and identity within a community, then the early movies, which encapsulated urban social forms popular with working-class youth, expressed and helped to legitimize a heterosocial culture.[3]

WORKING-CLASS THEATER
BEFORE THE MOVIES

Even before the rise of the movies, theater-going was a popular form of entertainment among many working-class women. Victorian melodrama was common at the Bowery theaters before 1900, with such plays as "The Two Orphans" and "East Lynne" stirring the audience with their stylized tales of dastardly villains, threats to womanhood, and the ultimate triumph of virtue. "I go to the theater quite often, and like those plays that make you cry a great deal," observed one sixteen-year-old garment worker. "'The Two Orphans' is good. Last time I saw it I cried all night because of the hard times that the children had in the play."[4] On Saturday nights, the Grand and Old Bowery Theaters drew crowds of working-class women and men, young and old, saleswomen and factory girls: "Many of these men sit in their shirt-sleeves, sweating in the humid atmosphere. Women are giving suck to fat infants. . . . Division street milliners, black-eyed, rosy cheeked, and flashily dressed sit close to their jealous eyed lovers."[5]

Many commentators point out the intimacy and sense of community of these theaters, suggesting the cohesive cultural role they played in working-class neighborhoods. Theater-goers prompted actors, hissed villains, and warned heroines of oncoming danger, creating a sense of identity between the performers and the members of the audience. Cheap theaters were impromptu social centers, where gossip, singing, footstomping, and vendor's cries contributed to the theatrical experience. One writer observed, for example, that during intermission at the Grand Theater, "the orchestra plays 'Harrigan' and the gallery sings the chorus. There is much neighborly stepping to and fro, a hum of conversation, and no little munching of caramels."[6]

For immigrant women and men, foreign-language theater offered an even more central focus for social life. As Irma Knecht observed, "Yiddish theater was my meat."[7] In the late nineteenth century, Jewish theaters on the East Side performed serious dramas and realistic plays, including the classics of Western theater, productions of contemporary Yiddish playwrights, and biblical plays, as well as the lighter *lebensbilder,* or portraits from life, which dealt with the immigrant's experience in the Old World and New. These theaters, which often gave performances to benefit different societies and lodges, were closely integrated into the institutional life of the East Side. "Over six hundred organizations annually make use of 'benefits,'" noted the playwright Jacob Gordin.[8]

Marionette shows played a similar role in the Italian community. In storefront theaters in Greenwich Village and the East Side, "heroic tales of chivalry, bloody melodramas of the Italian civil wars, and morality and mystery plays" evoked serious discussion, involvement, and solidarity in the audience. While some of these were patronized only by workingmen, others attracted family groups. "The Marosi theater was a neighborhood center for three blocks around," observed a People's Institute report. "It was regularly patronized by several hundred Italians."[9]

While both sexes attended the melodrama and immigrant theater, another popular form of theatrical entertainment—the music hall—was closely tied to the male subculture of public amusements. In the 1850's, some saloon owners converted their back rooms and cellars into small concert halls and hired specialty acts to amuse their patrons and encourage drinking. By the 1860's, over two hundred concert-saloons had spread along Broadway, the Bowery, and the waterfronts, catering to a heterogeneous male clientele of laborers, soldiers, sailors, and "slumming" society gentlemen. The conventions of polite society were put aside in these male sanctuaries, where crude jokes, bawdy comedy sketches, and scantily clad singers entertained the drinkers. Perhaps the chief attraction of these halls were the "waiter girls," who worked the tables, flirted with men, and often made assignations with favored customers. As one newspaper reported, music hall patrons "wear their hats and caps at pleasure, smoke cigars and pipes, and conduct themselves generally in accordance with the popular song of 'We'll be free and easy still.' "[10] By the 1890's, these music halls had grown larger, but many retained their raw atmosphere.

THE EMERGENCE OF A FEMALE AUDIENCE

In the late nineteenth century, a number of showmen and impresarios sought a more broadly based, respectable, and mixed-sex audience, calling their entertainment "variety" and "vaudeville" to eradicate the connotations of the concert-saloon. As early as the 1860's and 1870's, Tony Pastor began the movement to make theatrical performance, rather than barroom drinking, the main attraction of the variety house. He sought to entice women into the theater by running matinees, sponsoring a "Ladies' Invitation Night" when women were admitted free, and offering such household necessities as coal, flour, and dress patterns as prizes. Pastor maintained a saloon inside the theater, but permitted drinking only during intermission. His "hearty and racy" shows refrained from vulgar songs and obscene skits.[11]

By the 1890's, the active promotion of "refined vaudeville," divorced from its notorious antecedents in the concert-saloons and low variety shows, was attracting middle-class crowds. Theater owner B. F. Keith, for example, systematically cleaned up variety acts to make popular theater respectable for women and children. Keith completely removed the saloons from his theaters and constructed lavish vaudeville palaces. At the same time, he maintained greater control over his entertainment by organizing vaudeville into booking syndicates and creating a star system of performers. His theaters were known as the "Sunday-school Circuit" and censored disreputable vaudeville turns. Keith not only directed his performers to excise inappropriate language and suggestive stage business, but also instructed his audiences in proper theater behavior, admonishing them not to talk or stamp their feet during the show. [12]

Still, much of the patronage for variety and vaudeville came from tenement dwellers. Variety underwent a surge of popularity among working-class audiences, who increasingly turned away from the traditional "blood and thunder" dramas and plays of immigrant experiences in favor of comedy. By 1900, even the Bowery theaters had succumbed:

> Cheap variety is now about the only staple of the American Bowery theater. Time was, and not so very far back, when the spectacular melodrama, lurid, coarse grained and silly at times, but always essentially sound in its ethical teachings, was popular. But it appears to have had its day. Now it is the "smart" thing which goes. [13]

Similarly, vaudeville besieged the foreign-language theater. Marionette shows, the live Italian stage, and the Chinese theater fell to popular variety acts. By 1900, even the vibrant Yiddish theater was challenged by the American style of comedy and sketches. Yiddish vaudeville grew so rapidly in converted saloons and reconstructed dance halls that by 1905 "every important street on the Lower East Side has its glaring electric sign which announces 'Jewish Vaudeville House' or 'Music Hall.'" [14] According to one survey, 60 percent of the vaudeville audience in 1910 was working class, with only 36 percent coming from the "clerical" class. Many theaters were located in the commercial and amusement zones within or fringing working-class residential neighborhoods, on such streets as 14th Street, 125th Street, Eighth Avenue, Grand Street, and the Bowery. [15]

Working-class women and girls continued to avoid the concert-halls and Bowery variety shows that maintained their links to male saloon culture, but they attended vaudeville theaters in large numbers, comprising one-third of the audience in 1910. According to a survey of young New York working women, theater-going was among the most popular of all amusements, rated the favorite by nearly one-quarter of the women interviewed. This was a more heterogeneous group than the dance hall crowds. Married women, sometimes with their children, attended an occasional matinee or evening performance. Despite the expense, a Greenwich Village study reported, "some of the women go regularly every week all winter to Proctor's, Weber and Field's, or the Fourteenth Street Theatre, but rarely to an uptown theatre."[16] Still, women's participation remained more limited than men's. Unlike the audience for the legitimate stage, which tended to be mixed parties of men and women, in the vaudeville theater "men of all degrees come trooping in; some alone, some in batches, and some accompanied by women, or more often by one woman."[17]

The cost of these shows precluded many women from attending more than occasionally unless they were treated. Vaudeville theater tickets ranged in price from ten cents to a dollar, with most seats costing twenty-five to fifty cents. Only higher-income families could afford to go regularly. Robert Coit Chapin's study found that over half of the working-class families earning over nine hundred dollars yearly attended theater performances, spending twenty to thirty cents on their visits each week. In contrast, only one-quarter of those families earning six and seven hundred dollars could afford such trips. The American-born were most likely to attend vaudeville and variety shows, although poor immigrant families did find ways to circumvent the high price of admission. East Siders, for example, commonly cajoled free passes to the Grand Theater from local merchants.[18]

While cost curtailed women's attendance, the character of cheap vaudeville, which often reflected its origins in saloon culture, may have restricted the participation of some women. Working-class vaudeville was a mixture of the sentimental and the suggestive. Songs and monologues explicitly expressed the Victorian construction of gender, celebrating domesticity and women's virtue, while tests of strength affirmed men's virility and power. Particularly popular in the upper East Side variety shows, one observer noted, were "songs concerning childhood scenes, recollections of the old home, love of mother, and descriptions of heroic deeds, conveyed to the audience by means of stereopticon views, in songs, or by dramatic sketches."[19] These were juxtaposed, however, with sexual innuendo and raucous familiarity. At the Yiddish music halls, observed one settlement worker, "the songs are suggestive of everything but what is proper, the choruses are full of double meanings, and the jokes have broad and unmistakable hints of things indecent." While this observer noted "the number of young girls and children who are always to be found in the audience, thoroughly enjoying themselves,"[20] many parents carefully screened these shows from their daughters. "It is only recently that the Concert-Halls have been filled up with Jewesses," noted an East Side observer. "Even now most Jewish parents are particular to allow their daughters to go only to reputable places."[21] The images expressed in the mixed-sex variety shows were subdued versions of those presented in the male world of burlesque, concert-saloons, and dime museums. Cheap vaudeville moderated the tradition of male-oriented variety as it encouraged heterosocial participation, but it retained much of its raw character. In the early twentieth century, however, there emerged a new form of theatrical entertainment—the moving picture show—which transformed working-class women's participation in commercialized recreation.

THE ADVENT OF THE MOVIES

In the 1890's, motion pictures were shown primarily to vaudeville audiences, first as a novelty and later as "chasers," which signalled the audience to leave the theater. At this time, movie equipment was sold only to vaudeville theaters, and established booking syndicates distributed films. The impetus to develop movies as a separate form of entertainment came not from vaudeville, but from the amusement parlor and penny arcade. Around 1900, numerous arcades could be found on such commercial streets as the Bowery, 14th Street, and 125th Street, crammed with slot machines, phonographs, muscle-testing apparatus, automatic scales, and fortune-telling machines. Their most popular attraction, however, was the kinetoscope, a moving picture peep show that was often known as the "penny vaudeville." These amusement parlors drew a predominantly male clientele; as People's Institute investigator John Collier noted, "The penny arcade has resembled the saloon, from which the family has stayed away."[22]

In the early 1900's, the owners of amusement arcades began to close off a section in the back of the hall and project movies on a screen, charging five to ten cents for admission. By 1905, small storefront theaters, or "nickelodeons," spread throughout Manhattan's tenement districts, encouraged by the peculiarities of the city's licensing laws. A "common show" license, which could be purchased for twenty-five dollars, permitted seating capacities of up to three hundred people, but did not require adherence to the rigid building and fire codes required for a regular theater license. Thus movie exhibitors could cheaply rent a storefront or small dance hall, outfit it with a projection booth, screen, and wooden benches, and charge a nickel for a show of one-reelers.[23]

In only a few years, "nickel madness" had swept the city, drawing a broad working-class audience. A study of recreation found that almost three-fourths of all movie-goers in 1910 were working class, although a substantial minority of white-collar workers went as well. The nickel theaters sprang up in the tenement neighborhoods and commercial amusement streets of the metropolis. By 1907, two hundred nickelodeons could be found in Manhattan alone, with over one-third located below 14th Street, an area dominated by the immigrant working class. Similar trends could be observed in other parts of the city. "In one street in Harlem the writer counted as many as five to a block. . . . They run from early morning until midnight, and their megaphones are barking before the milkman has made his rounds."[24] In 1910, weekly attendance in greater New York was estimated at one-quarter of the city's entire population, almost 1.5 million people.

In many ways, the rise of the movies marked a decisive break in the pattern of working-class amusements, comprising, as observers were fond of reporting, the "great theatre of the masses in New York."[25] According to George Bevans, while working-class patrons of the live theater tended to have relatively high incomes and short working days, approximately 60 percent of all workingmen, whatever their earnings or hours of labor, went to the movies. Most important, the movies required little outlay of money, even when compared to the vaudeville theater, since a nickel or at most a dime purchased an evening's entertainment. In Bevans' study, workingmen typically spent fifteen cents a week on movies, but those who attended theaters often spent three times as much. While

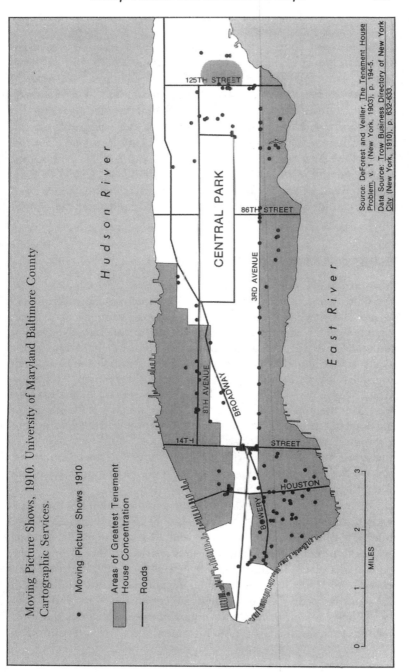

Moving Picture Shows, 1910. University of Maryland Baltimore County Cartographic Services.

- Moving Picture Shows 1910
- Areas of Greatest Tenement House Concentration
- Roads

Source: DeForest and Veiller, The Tenement House Problem, v. 1 (New York, 1903), p. 194-5. Data Source: Trow Business Directory of New York City (New York, 1910), p. 632-633.

movie fans were permitted to sit through repeated screenings of the one- and two-reel films, most picture shows lasted only an hour, making them appealing even to workers who labored long hours.[26] The movies attracted recently arrived immigrants of all nationalities, in contrast to the stage, which was most frequently visited by native-born workingmen. "The audiences are composite in the highest degree," a report by the People's Institute found. "On the Bowery we have seen Chinamen, Italians and Yiddish people, the young and old, often entire families, crowded side by side."[27] Language proved no barrier to immigrants' patronage of the silent films, and all could enjoy the mimed actions and understand the simple plots.

WOMEN'S CULTURE AND THE MOVIES

Most strikingly, movies altered women's participation in the world of public, commercial amusements. When pictures moved from the arcade's kinetoscopes to nickelodeon screens, women's attendance soared; women comprised 40 percent of the working-class movie audience in 1910. Unlike the commercial dance halls, movie attendance transcended generational lines and marital status. As one journalist noted, "Many middle-aged and old women are steady patrons, who never, when a new film is to be shown, miss the opening." Another observed that "few of these modest show places, in Harlem, for instance, can be found where the entrance is not encumbered with go-carts and perambulators."[28] Wives with their husbands and mothers with children crowded into the movie houses, breaking down the segregated and noncommercial orientation of married women's leisure.

Movie producers and exhibitors were well aware of the impact of women's attendance on their industry. "The wonderful growth in numbers of so-called 'store shows' and 'Nickelodeons' in the past twelve months has been due to a great extent to the patronage accorded this class of amusement by the women and children," observed one trade journal in 1907. Another advised exhibitors to "Play to the Ladies" by not showing objectionable films.[29] Between reels, nickelodeon owners encouraged women's participation, projecting such enthusiastic announcements as "We are aiming to please the ladies," "Bring the children," and "Ladies without escorts cordially invited."[30]

The popularity of moving pictures among married women was in large part due to the cheapness of the entertainment. A few nickels could be eked out of the family budget to enable a mother and her children to attend a weekly show. The movies' widespread availability and close proximity to working-class residential districts also proved an important attraction, much as the saloons were for their husbands. At the same time, this novel form of entertainment was not intimately linked to male culture and could be incorporated into the social world of married women. Movie exhibitors encouraged and played upon this aspect of movie-going.

Despite the standardized product, the experience of the movies took on the flavor of the surrounding neighborhood. The early nickelodeons seemed extensions of street life, their megaphones and garish placards competing with the other sights and sounds of urban streets. Inside the storefront theaters, the atmosphere seemed a heightened version of life in the tenement districts. "The majority of the fifty places examined were found to be badly overcrowded . . . with the aisles completely blocked by standing spectators," wrote an inspector, whose middle-class sensibilities were assaulted by the nickelodeons. "In many places attendants went through the room with an atomizer spraying perfumery on the crowd to allay the odor."[31]

On a scale unmatched by the vaudeville houses, nickel theaters became community gathering places. "Certain houses have become genuine social centers where neighborhood groups may be found any evening of the week," a journalist observed, "where the 'regulars' stroll up and down the aisles between acts and visit friends."[32] Inside the theater, friends gossiped and children played while awaiting the show. Unlike the middle-class theater audiences, the working-class crowd audibly interacted with the screen and each other, commenting on the action, explaining the plot, and vocally accompanying the piano player. Nickelodeon programs often featured vaudeville skits and sentimental or patriotic songs with illustrative slides thrown against the screen, during which the audience was encouraged to sing along. Exhibitors also targeted vaudeville acts to the ethnic composition of the audience. Thus in the Jewish lower

East Side, movie house owners offered vaudeville in Yiddish, while
the nickelodeons of Greenwich Village presented Italian singers and
comics.[33]

This localism helped to affirm the movie theater as a public and
commercial space that married women could incorporate into their
own culture of kinship, neighborhood, and church ties. Mary Heaton Vorse captured this experience in her description of Italian mothers, among the most home-centered of immigrants, who went to the
movies after evening church services: "Prayers finished, you may
see a mother sorting out her own babies and moving on serenely to
the picture show down the road."[34] The casual and neighborly atmosphere of the movies contrasted to more formal occasions for leisure. One observer suggested, for example, that "mothers do not
have to 'dress' to attend them," an important consideration, since
mothers often sacrificed their own wardrobes to ensure that their
husbands and children were properly clothed.[35]

Nickelodeons also offered an additional space in the public
sphere where women could safely leave their children. Many seem
to have thought of the nickel theaters as day care centers. While
some West Side mothers believed that "them places is the worst
thing that ever happened to New York, settin' b'ys to gamblin' and
stealin'," others observed that "a b'y's got t'do somethin' an' I don't
see no harm in a good show that keeps him off the streets."[36] Many
East Side parents similarly acceded to their children's presence at
the movies, at least their sons': at the Windsor Theater at 10:00
P.M., for example, investigators found numerous young boys without guardians, even though this violated the law. Another survey
estimated that forty thousand children in greater New York attended
movies daily without a parent or guardian.[37]

Many reformers praised the movies as the one form of commercial recreation that brought the entire family together, seeing it as a
substitute for the saloon. According to movie reformer Orrin G.
Cocks, there were 530 fewer saloons in New York City in 1914 than
in 1909, which he attributed to the popularity of the motion picture.[38] If the movies indeed took away saloon business, then many
working-class women too must have seen wider advantages in the
movies than simply their own enjoyment.

Single working women also attended picture shows, integrating them into their culture of treating and style. Like dance halls and social clubs, movie houses offered convenient places for meeting men, courting, and enjoying an inexpensive evening's entertainment. The accepted place of the movies in young women's pursuit of pleasure is suggested in a boardinghouse matron's description of Mary, a respectable working girl. "The other night she flirted with a man across the street," she worried. "It is true she dropped him when he offered to take her into a saloon. But she does go to picture shows and dance halls with 'pick up' men and boys."[39] Crowds of young people milled around the theaters, and young women commonly "linger[ed] with a boy companion 'making dates' for a movie or affair." The theater's darkness and the vocal familiarity of the audience encouraged opportunities for intimacy and "spooning." As one observer wrote, "Note how the semi-darkness permits a 'steady's' arm to encircle a 'lady friend's' waist."[40]

Indeed, many middle-class reformers and writers expressed a concern that the nickelodeons, like the dance halls, would quickly become public spaces for undue familiarity between the sexes. This perception caused an apocryphal story to circulate in the press about "attacks on women through the use of a supposed poisoned needle with which the victim was pricked in the semi-light of a moving picture hall." While this story of "white slavery" apparently had no basis in reality, according to an investigation of the Committee of Fourteen, the idea that movie houses were arenas of promiscuity and danger for women was a strangely potent one. Helen Weinstein, a middle-class Polish immigrant, remembered this incident vividly fifty years later, associating it with a more famous sexual crime: "There was plenty killing at that time, too—plenty—Jack the Ripper—somebody who sat in a movie would give you a needle and you'd be different."[41] Concerned civic leaders also pointed to such moral hazards as the lack of chaperonage, suggestive posters advertising the shows, and bawdy vaudeville interspersed between the films. Others feared "the likelihood that the much more easy conversational relations among spectators will lead to improvised and clandestine acquaintance with men."[42]

However, these middle-class fears obscure some important differences between the movies and other amusements frequented by young working women. The cheap price of the nickelodeon, its ap-

peal across generations, and its firm basis in working-class neighborhoods mitigated the potential for uninhibited familiarity between women and men. While young women often made the
nickelodeons an arena of sexual expression and romance, this was
developed as much in the imagery of the movies as in the social
space of the theater.

The movies attracted single women of various backgrounds and
cultural styles, a more diverse group than the habitues of the dance
halls. The young girl who put on style in flamboyant clothes mingled
with the genteel working woman concerned with respectability. The
"settlement girl" or working girls' club member, who would have
little to do with amusement parks and dance halls, nevertheless
went frequently to the movies. The Girls' Friendly Society, a
church-related organization for uplift of working women, found that
"our girls go to the 'movies' by thousands."[43]

Similarly, young women of every ethnic background were movie-
goers. Immigrant parents who traditionally restricted female activity agreed more readily to their daughters' attendance at the
movies than at other forms of amusement. There was a widespread
perception that the movies were a safe environment for daughters,
in part because entire families attended in a neighborhood setting.
Historian Elizabeth Ewen, for example, cites an Italian garment
worker who observed that "the one place I was allowed to go by
myself was the movies. . . . My parents wouldn't let me go out any-
where else, even when I was twenty-four." The movies were also the
primary form of recreation for Italian women who lived alone, with
some visiting once a week, and others attending only three or four
times a year.[44]

Other young women who could not participate in the "treating
culture" of the dance halls and amusement parks found refuge in
movie theaters. Ruth True observed that there were "tough girls" in
the West Side neighborhood who did not go to dance halls because
"they have not even the small amount of money that would take
them there, nor the one suit of good clothes that would make them
presentable among the others." These young women "have the two
universal amusement places—the street and the nickel 'dump.'"
Because of this, perhaps, movies may have had less status among
young women than dance halls or theaters; True notes that the more
expensive vaudeville was even more popular than the picture

shows.[45] At the same time, young women could experience the movie theater as a safe neighborhood institution, without the direct sexual risks and flirtatious interaction of the dance halls or amusement resorts. Those with little spending money could usually find the price of a movie ticket, and they did not need to depend on men friends to treat.

For these women, movie manufacturers and exhibitors played up the glamour, sensations, and romance of motion pictures. The movies quickly generated a young women's culture oriented around the adulation of movie stars and being a fan. In the movie's infancy, film makers insisted on the performers' anonymity, but movie audiences soon picked out favorite players and demanded their names and personal information about them. As Orrin Cocks observed, "The children of New York are sophisticated and among other things they know quite as much about motion picture stars and latest productions."[46] Film companies responded to this interest with fan magazines as early as 1908. Exhibitors posted advertisements that played up the sexual attractions one could vicariously experience in the theater, a tendency that occasionally took absurd dimensions, as reformer John Collier discovered: "Why, I saw the Passion Play in moving pictures recently advertised by a poster showing the elopement of a modern couple in evening dress over a garden wall."[47] Yet the movie stars, posters, and plots could become an important part of young women's social life, experienced without the direct intervention of men. On Eighth Avenue, observed Ruth True, the "flashing, gaudy, poster-lined entrances of Hickman's and of the Galaxy . . . supply the girls with a 'craze,' the same that sends those with a more liberal allowance to the matinees."[48] For many women, movies might become a "woman's space" experienced within the heterosocial context of commercial recreation. Being a fan and adulating stars mediated heterosocial relations that were more direct, and often problematic, in the dance halls and amusement parks.

PROJECTING HETEROSOCIAL CULTURE

If the nickelodeon theaters affirmed a sense of both community and glamour, the content of the movies and its impact on working-class audiences are more difficult to interpret. In a period when thousands of one-reel films were produced, and only impressionistic descriptions of movie-goers are available, the relationship between film and audience is open to question. It is difficult to know what images and ideas the working-class audiences responded to, and how that response differed by gender, ethnicity, and age. An Italian mother and an Irish American saleswoman might have been influenced by very different films, or even experienced the same film quite differently; a "vamp" film, for example, could offend some women, fascinate others.

Several scholars have seen a close connection between the immigrant working-class audiences and the early movies, which were filled with ordinary people and everyday street scenes. Film historian Lewis Jacobs claims, for example, that, before 1908, film comedies always featured a "common man or woman" as the protagonist and sympathized with the poor against the wealthy because "the audience and filmmakers alike were of this class."[49] Others have argued that although the setting of these films were the tenements and the streets, few of their images were direct reflections of labor, family life, and politics among the laboring masses. Indeed, many films with working-class themes were conceptualized as glimpses of "how the other half lives," assuming an audience unfamiliar with immigrant ghettos and tenement quarters. A Biograph advertisement for the film "The Song of the Shirt" proclaimed, for example, that "several of the scenes are decidedly interesting in the fact that they were actually taken in the thickly settled Hebrew quarters of New York City."[50] Moreover, many early films were made in France by Gaumont and Pathé, which caused one journalist to note that "thousands of dwellers along the Bowery are learning to roar at French buffoonery, and the gendarme is growing as familiar to them as the 'copper on the beat.' "[51] This suggests not so much a direct correspondence between the content of early movies and their audience as rather a more mediated response that played with familiar social relationships.

An examination of the content of the earliest movies suggests that their images were filtered through the traditions of the cheap theater. The routines common in variety and popular melodrama formed the kernel of many movies in the years from 1898 to 1910, when they were exhibited primarily to a working-class audience.

Many were simply filmed versions of vaudeville turns, replete with stock characters, ritualized routines, and painted backdrops. A few films even positioned the movie camera in the seats of a vaudeville theater, so that the film-goer had the sensation of being in an audience viewing a variety skit. While movie-makers quickly learned to manipulate the new technology to create special effects and trick sequences and to develop narratives through cutting and arranging a series of shots, thematically they drew upon the familiar territory of the cheap theater.[52]

The reliance on theatrical traditions is evident in the early films that depicted the social relations between the sexes, a popular theme present in about one-third of the movie comedies made between 1898 and 1910.[53] Particularly before 1905, many films duplicated the salacious sexual imagery and risque humor common in working-class variety. Photographs of women disrobing, glimpses of ankles and limbs, prolonged embraces, and kissing were not unusual. "A Busy Day at the Corset Models'," for example, showed women in undergarments and various states of undress, while "Soubrettes in a Bachelor's Flat" featured a man carousing with three scantily clad chorines, who don Salvation Army costumes when the apartment is raided by the police. Such films were originally projected in peep shows and kinetoscopes in the male world of the penny arcade.[54]

Production of risque films declined as the kinetoscope gave way to the nickelodeon and movies developed a female audience. Still, sexuality transformed into flirtation and suggestiveness continued to dominate the plots of film comedies. The "peeping tom" was a common device that accentuated the position of the audience as voyeur through the film medium. In "The Boarding House Bathroom," for example, two male boarders peer through a keyhole to catch a glimpse of a comely young woman. In another film, "It's a Shame to Take the Money," a boy shines the shoes of a woman who pulls her skirts up above the ankles. The boy, believing that was payment enough, refuses her proffered money. Finally a policeman, who had been watching the proceedings behind a wall, comes out and congratulates the boy.[55]

Sexual intrigue formed the basis of numerous comedies, many of which derived directly from the popular stage. Familiar stories of

the maid pursued by the master of the house, or the cook romancing
the local milkman, appeared again and again. Just as common, however, were films depicting encounters between the sexes in the context of the modern city. These employed the situations of everyday
urban life, heightening the expression of social familiarity and sexual
innuendo. As in "The Veiled Beauty," many film producers used the
beaches and amusement parks of Coney Island as a location for unrestrained fun and humor. Other films were set in businesses where
women and men came into close physical contact, such as doctors'
offices, shoe stores, dancing academies, beauty parlors, and man-
icurists' shops. A 1905 film, for example, entitled "The Broadway
Massage Parlor," depicts a mother and daughter at a physical culture
gymnasium. When the daughter goes off to have a facial, the masseur makes advances to her; the mother rushes in and scolds her
daughter, while the masseur's wife beats him on the head.[56]

Similarly, women's search for employment carried sexual connotations, which movie-makers quickly exploited. Although audiences were dominated by blue-collar workers, films about factory
employment were less common than those involving office romance. This theme received a particularly interesting treatment in a
1904 movie, "The Story the Biograph Told," in which the sexual
snares of women's wage-earning combined with a commentary on
the nature of the movies. The film opens in a business office, where
a man is explaining the operation of a movie camera to an office boy.
The boss and an attractive female secretary then enter his office and
begin embracing, while, unbeknownst to them, the boy cranks the
camera. The scene shifts to a theater, where the boss and his wife
are watching a movie, when inexplicably the intimate office encoun-
ter is thrown on the screen. The next day, the incensed wife
marches into the office, discharges the secretary, and replaces her
with a man.[57] While stressing the dangers of the heterosocial business world, the film unconsciously comments on the movies' ability
to place people in compromising situations for the amusement of an
audience. Like Tilyou's Steeplechase Park, the early movies mar-
keted titillation, voyeurism, and vicarious sexuality in the context of
an "Americanized" culture. Although their endings often asserted
the immorality of such behavior, their action assaulted the conventions of respectability. As Mack Sennett, a master of film comedy,

put it, "I especially liked the reduction of authority to absurdity, the notion that sex could be funny, and the bold insults hurled at Pretension."[58]

Many early films also delighted in street-smart women who could repel sexual advances, defend themselves in dangerous situations, and devise ingenious strategies to attain their goals. A popular genre of movies about "mashers," for example, often depicted quick-witted women outfoxing male harassers. In the 1908 Vitagraph film "Mashing the Masher," two women conspire with their brothers to punish a man who has been sexually harassing them. They arrange a meeting on a street corner, the expectant masher arrives, a load of rubbish is dumped on his head, and "the masher thus is mashed." "The Broker's Athletic Typewriter" more graphically celebrates the modern working girl. In this film, a stenographer who has been pursued by her lascivious boss picks him up and throws him about the office, aided by trick photography.[59]

Women who enjoyed high living were not seriously condemned in many early film comedies, and some displayed a subculture of women—chorus girls, burlesque queens, and soubrettes—who freely smoked and drank, wore lavish clothing, and lived in opulent surroundings. While films depicting the joys of conspicuous consumption and sexual abandon became popular in the late 1910's and 1920's, particularly in the extravaganzas of Cecil B. DeMille, similar themes were developed, although less ostentatiously, in the earliest movies. Even ordinary women were not censured for their interest in dating, men friends, and pleasure. In "Oh, Those Eyes!," a Biograph film of 1912, a father attempts to stifle his daughter's flirtatiousness by conspiring with two of her suitors. They fight a duel and pretend to die, but the flirt remains blasé and unrepentant.[60]

The early movie-makers seem to have been quite aware of the cultural and class divisions marking the terrain of popular amusement, and they consciously ranged themselves against middle-class morality and manners. While the Victorian woman was idealized and celebrated in the famous films of D. W. Griffith, she received a more ambiguous treatment in the mass of films cranked out for the working-class audience. Many films delighted in poking fun at the earnest efforts of moral reformers, temperance advocates, and other uplifters. A one-reeler entitled "Committee on Art," for example, depicts a man gazing longingly at several risque burlesque posters, when the local squad of do-gooders arrive and pin blouses and skirts on the offending manikins.[61]

At the same time, movie producers mocked self-styled "New Women" who advocated political equality and the blurring of gender roles. Dress reform, for example, was attacked in "The Newest Woman," which pointed out the unnaturalness of the female bloomer costume by comparing it to effeminate male dress. Another film, presaging the "companionate marriage" schemes of the 1920's, followed a man's trial marriages to a number of women, each of which ended in some form of domestic violence; as the Biograph advertisement crowed, "All the world is laughing at the humorous possibilities involved in the scheme of 'Trial Marriages' recently proposed by a prominent young New York society matron." In the face of the suffrage movement, movie producers wondered "Will It Ever Come to This?" and replied by reaffirming female domesticity.[62]

Thus the early movies responded primarily with humor to the challenges turn-of-the-century feminism posed to the patriarchal order. Many of them affirmed a heterosocial culture that incorporated some aspects of the "New Woman" without subverting the institutions upholding male power and control. Movie-makers delighted in the young woman capable of navigating her way through urban territory and sexual pitfalls, and who found pleasure in men's company and commercial amusements, not reformers' schemes and feminist utopias. Linking personal freedom with the culture of consumption and heterosociality, these films undercut feminist demands, not simply through direct criticism and humor, but by refashioning the socially appropriate behavior and norms that governed gender relations. Visually and thematically, these films constructed a notion of modern American womanhood that reaffirmed the flamboyant cultural style popular among many young American-born working women and, as Elizabeth Ewen suggests, created new aspirations among the foreign-born.[63]

REGULATING GENDER RELATIONS IN THE MOVIES

As the nickelodeons achieved unparalleled popularity among the masses, they came under attack from public officials, clergy, and reformers, who assailed the condition of the theaters and the content of the shows. Quickly the early movies became a terrain of cultural and political conflict. Movie-makers and exhibitors, themselves working-class but with upward aspirations, clashed with various representatives of the middle class, the elite, and the state. One aspect of the public discourse surrounding the motion pictures concerned the images of sexuality and their potential effects on impressionable youth. The interaction of these groups after 1907, played out in the movement for censorship, recast the movies' earlier projection of a heterosocial culture.

By 1907, the burgeoning numbers of storefront theaters in New York had begun to attract public notice. In that year, several nickelodeon owners were arrested and charged with violating the Sunday closing laws, showing indecent pictures, imperilling the morals of youth, and creating public disturbances. In December, Mayor George McClellan responded to violations of the city's blue laws by closing all places of amusement on Sunday. The Protestant clergy, while decrying Sunday amusements in general, particularly attacked the movie houses. "The cent and five-cent theatres, in particular, should be closed," proposed Rev. Charles Goodell. "There are far too many of them, and children on their way to Sunday school are lured and dragged into them."[64] A massive uproar ensued, crossing class lines. German organizations and the Central Federated Union protested, movie exhibitors sought injunctions, and citizens packed the city council chambers while it debated the issue. Joining in the protest, German women "cheered as vociferously as the men at the attacks on the new Sunday observance ruling."[65] During hearings, many observed that the attacks on cheap theaters and Sunday entertainment were directed primarily at the working class.

The following year, city officials and clergy again battled the storefront theaters. After a balcony collapsed in an overcrowded Rivington Street nickelodeon, the mayor revoked all licenses and held another round of hearings. Defensive movie exhibitors agreed to improve the physical and moral conditions of the theaters. By 1910, an examination of movie shows indicated that the "proprietors display a commendable desire to keep order and to have the proprieties observed. Many of them direct attention against rowdyism, profanity, and smoking." The investigator concluded, "There is an evident desire to secure the patronage of the better people of the neighborhood."[66]

Threatened with official government intervention, movie manufacturers agreed to submit their films to a board of civic leaders and reformers, who would excise unacceptable scenes. The Board of Censorship of Motion Pictures, later called the National Board of Review, was established in 1909 and became the leading agency reviewing motion pictures for the American public. The National Board fought continuing demands of many officials and reformers for stricter censorship while moderating the movie-makers' often lurid efforts to appeal to popular taste. Calling movies a "novel, entrancing and far-reaching form of expression, a purveyor of ideas and symbols and secrets," the National Board recognized that film was a form of communication unlike any other, able to convey to the masses information that previously had been available only to the privileged. While it considered many subjects for censorship, including violence, drugs, and crime, many decisions involved the sexual and social relations between women and men. In regulating gender relations in the movies, the National Board attacked images it defined as immoral, but gave free rein to most "matters of taste," even when they assaulted middle-class sensibilities.[67]

In defining immorality, the National Board drew the line at what it considered suggestive behavior and heightened sensuality in the movies—"the details of immoral sex relations; over-passionate love scenes; stimulating close dancing; unnecessary bedroom scenes in negligee; excessively low-cut gowns; undue or suggestive display of the person." It advised against using homosexual characters or extramarital relationships as a basis for humor and warned that "all loose, suggestive comedy 'business' between the sexes should be removed."[68] The National Board's reviewers accepted flirtatious and sensual comedy scenes if there were no indecent intentions or if they were necessary to the plot. One reviewer, when questioned about "common handling" between the sexes, distinguished between suggestive behavior "apt to arouse unclean thoughts" and "funny horseplay, as Charley Chaplin." The latter, he noted, "is an essential and keeps more young folks from the saloon and dance hall than its possible harm."[69] In controversial subjects such as white slavery, the "social evil," and birth control, the National Board insisted that the films be educational and moralistic, rather than entertaining. The producers of "House of Bondage," a white slave film, eliminated scenes in a brothel and argued that "all suggestiveness such as kissing, embracing, and carousing has been done away with," but the National Board still condemned the picture as too sensationalistic for the public.[70]

Defending themselves against state censorship and acceding to the changes demanded by the National Board, the movie-makers dreamed of attracting a larger middle-class audience. As Russell Merritt has shown, the desire to gain a "class" audience led exhibitors to build movie palaces in business districts that fringed white-collar shopping areas. Such efforts began in New York as early as 1908, with the construction of the Unique on 14th Street, which seated almost twelve hundred in plush surroundings.[71] The defensive posture of the movie industry toward its working-class audience, and its desire for upward mobility, may be seen in the early trade journals of the movie industry. "With the exhibitor and manufacturer progressing in harmony, who can tell to what a high degree of class the cheap amusement may be advanced?" one journal boasted. Ambivalently, they continued to suggest Bowery-style advertising techniques for the storefront shows, while urging exhibitors to label their theaters with more exalted names: "Why so many 'Vaudettes,' 'Nickolets,' 'Dimes,' and 'Nickelodeons'? Why not 'Empire,' 'Majestic,' 'Grand,' 'Washington,' etc. ?"[72]

The film manufacturers and exhibitors, for their part, pushed and played with the social definition of "acceptable" gender relations under the scrutiny of the National Board. In the initial response to censorship, some movie-makers turned to literary plots and middle-class settings that affirmed Victorian morality for their expanding audience.[73] Others, however, continued to create sensual and titillating images. Polling theater owners, Carl Laemmle, the president of Universal Films, claimed, that "Instead of finding that 95 per cent. favored clean pictures, I discovered that at least half, and maybe 60 per cent., want the pictures to be 'risque.' . . . They found their patrons were more willing to pay money to see an off-color than a decent one." Arguing that "one after another [exhibitor] said that it would be wise to listen to the public demand for vampire pictures," he asserted that Universal was not the "guardian of public morals."[74]

Pressured by demands for censorship and desiring to extend

their audience, movie-makers developed new images of women and men in the 1910's that transcended Victorian morals and manners and were acceptable to middle-class audiences. As film historian Lary May has shown, such popular stars as Mary Pickford and Douglas Fairbanks celebrated wholesome sexuality, personal freedom, athleticism, youth, and romantic companionship, placing these values in the context of an upwardly mobile consumer society. These movie stars, viewed in opulent picture palaces, helped to legitimate a heterosocial and expressive culture for an eager middle-class audience in search of new models of behavior. Working-class women too, Elizabeth Ewen has argued, discovered in the movies of the late 1910's and 1920's a dream world of American pleasures, consumption, and romance, a world in which immigrant and familial traditions had little place.[75]

Yet these envisionings were not entirely new to many working-class women, although their opulence and elite pretensions were. The screen stars and filmmakers of the 1910's reformulated cultural patterns that were familiar to the earliest viewers of the movies. Comedians like Mack Sennett and Charlie Chaplin drew upon the early one-reelers' celebration of suggestiveness, physicality, urban sexual encounters, and romance, which often turned Victorian morality into absurdity. Even Mary Pickford, the most famous actress of her day, linked herself culturally to the independent working woman. "I think I admire most in the world the girls who earn their own living," she observed. "I am proud to be one of them."[76] As the movies developed a middle-class audience, they transformed the cultural traditions of cheap theater and nickelodeons, which had played with the sexual expressiveness and heterosocial practices of "Americanized" working-class youth, into a new ethos of romantic companionship and mass consumption.

CHAPTER SEVEN

REFORMING WORKING WOMEN'S RECREATION

While entrepreneurs avidly promoted working women's presence in commercial recreation, middle-class reformers assailed the noisy familiarity and tawdry glitter of dance halls and resorts. "Let us see the amusement exploiter just as he is," warned one middle-class spokesman. "With him the love of fun in the human heart is a cold matter of dollars and cents. He buys youth's freshness of feeling in return for sundry ticklings of sensation, and blights its glad spontaneities with his itching palm."[1] Cheap amusements threatened to inundate New York, appealing to the "low" instincts of the masses, debasing womanly virtues, segregating youth from the family, and fostering a dangerously expressive culture. Reformers imbued the everyday pleasures of working women with a moral reading that linked cheap amusements to promiscuous sexuality and heterosocial relations. The image of the flashily–dressed working woman, joking and flirting with men, spieling late into the night, enjoying a new-found sense of social freedom, resonated uncomfortably within the middle-class public.

This was a period of ferment for middle-class Americans, when new ideas about womanhood, sexuality, and leisure were actively being debated. By the late nineteenth century, the roles of bourgeois women had extended far beyond the home, to include philanthropy and reform, political activity, and professional work. This "New Woman" questioned the "natural" division of women and men's lives into separate spheres of social activity. Still, Victorian values guided most middle-class women in affirming the virtues of chastity and decorum among single women and the primacy of motherhood and domesticity after marriage. The heterosocial culture and expressive sexuality enjoyed by working-class youth, and its commercial exploitation by amusement entrepreneurs, posed an affront and challenge to middle-class reformers. By regulating commercial amusements and creating attractive alternatives, reformers hoped that the transformation of leisure would uplift and purify the social relations between the sexes.

Cultural conflicts developed, however, as middle-class ideals of womanhood met the flamboyant working-class version of the "New Woman." Opposing views of leisure, linked to differing models of what constituted appropriate female behavior, arose along class lines as well as within them. While recreation reformers intended to limit and redefine working women's social behavior, their intentions were not easily realized. Their efforts often met with unenthusiastic responses; indifference and hostility led them to adjust their programs in light of working women's interests. In this process of social interaction, reformers' attitudes about leisure and womanhood were reformulated to accommodate—albeit grudgingly—a heterosocial and expressive commercial culture.[2]

GILDED AGE REFORM

Working women's recreation became defined as a social problem in the Gilded Age, when feminists and reformers turned their attention to the plight of the working girl in the city. Urbanization and industrialization propelled young women into the nation's urban centers alone and unprotected, observed these middle-class advocates. In response, they created a network of institutions to safeguard and aid working women, including boardinghouses, employment agencies, protective unions, and travellers' aid stations. A growing concern among women reformers was the lack of wholesome leisure activities. "The street claims hundreds, the cheap dance halls, theaters and concerts offer attractions to hundreds more," observed Grace Hoadley Dodge, a leader in recreation reform, "while many sit at home in morbid despondency, feeling forsaken, lonely, sad."[3]

Gilded Age reform agencies tackled the problem of working women's recreation with enthusiasm, devising a vast array of activities and organizations. One of the oldest institutions for urban women, the Young Women's Christian Association, offered educational classes, a free lending library, concerts, and entertainments to self-supporting women, in addition to lodging and meals. Church organizations addressed the need for leisure by establishing clubs. The Girls' Friendly Society, a church-based group with over seven hundred members in Manhattan in the early 1890's, provided religious instruction, classes in cooking and sewing, and talks on hygiene. Its secular counterpart, the working girls' clubs, not only offered classes, entertainments, and rooms for sociability but extended insurance coverage and employment referrals to its members. Other reformers, mindful of the high rates of tuberculosis and other diseases among overburdened working women, founded fresh air funds and vacation societies that sent working women to country houses for a week or two of rest and healthful recreation.[4]

The reformers who made working women's recreation a social issue drew upon a complex set of Victorian ideals and assumptions. Their gender and class position served as lenses through which they alternatively perceived working women as unwilling female victims *and* as enthusiastic members of the promiscuous lower orders. In their view, working women were subject to the same tendencies toward rowdiness that afflicted their fathers and brothers. Just as working men dissipated their time and incomes in saloons and pool halls, women enjoyed a social life in public halls and the streets, where, the YWCA observed, "young girls . . . in this unconventional out-of-door life, are so apt to grow noisy and bold." Reshaping working-class cultural practices through rational recreation seemed a solution to the behavioral problems of women as well as men; well-regulated leisure, educational entertainment, and opportunities for orderly sociability would teach standards of womanly deportment and respectability, raising women as a class. The statement of purpose issued by the Girls' Friendly Society exemplifies the middle-class concern with regulating working-class behavior, with its call to "encourage purity of life, dutifulness to parents, faithfulness to employers and thrift."[5]

At the same time, these reformers were themselves primarily women and viewed rational recreation from a female—and, at times, feminist—perspective forged in the experience of "women's sphere" in the nineteenth century. By the 1880's, women had pushed a gender-based ideology of domesticity, moral guardianship, and sisterhood from the realm of home and family into the public arena. Protecting womanhood and the home became public and political issues, which seemed magnified with urban growth.[6] Reformers and journalists often perceived New York as a center of vice, its traps set to ensnare young women into lives of sin. By the 1880's, the growing visibility of working women heightened feminist concern, and investigations of female labor paid close attention to the relationship between low wages and immorality. From this perspective, urban women were "weary and restless, honest, hardworking girls, but pleasure-loving, and needing nobler impulses for their safety," who, without protection, could be easily victimized.[7]

To safeguard young women in the city, reformers created recreational spaces for working women that were patterned after familiar middle-class models, the home and the women's club. In essence, they extended women's sphere into the theatening urban environment. The programs of the Young Women's Christian Association, for example, embodied the ideal of the home as a haven of security and comfort. Acknowledging working women's need for diversion, the YWCA's leaders asserted: "What can the Christian Association do? It can build them a home—not a boarding-house—with cheerful warmth, baths, public parlors, a library with stimulating books for leisure, morning and evening worship." The "Y" could be a "House Beautiful" where young women could find the familial relationships otherwise unavailable to them in the impersonal city.[8] The domestic ideal also permeated the Working Girls' Vacation Society, which sent young women to a dozen country houses in rural New York and Connecticut during the summer months. Each cottage was supervised by a matron, who encouraged the girls to form a close filial relationship with her. "'Just like a mother to us' is a favorite expression of this feeling," they reported with pride.[9]

While employing images of the home and maternal protection as models for urban women's sociability, reformers were even more strongly influenced by another aspect of nineteenth-century women's culture, sisterhood. In their view, working women were too often victimized by employers and other men and needed places to find womanly support, mutual aid, and practical advice. They believed that working women would respond to the shared experience of gender despite class and ethnic differences. In a period when the

club movement dominated middle-class women's extra-domestic activities, notions of cooperation and sisterhood became central ideals
of recreation reform.[10] Although many philanthropic organizations
of the period simply patronized working-class people, the notion of
sisterhood made some reformers aware of class-based resentment.
The Harlem YWCA, for example, felt that bringing young ladies of
leisure and working women together for evening entertainments
would have positive effects on both groups: "It was thought that the
best results could be accomplished by aiding all classes to band
themselves together for mutual help in their social, physical, business, intellectual and spiritual interests." Working-class representatives were appointed to help in planning entertainment programs,
and the leadership made personal appeals to women in factories and
shops to join the Association.[11]

Reformers hoped that YWCA's, vacation societies, and clubs
would be spaces for working women where ideals of womanhood,
purity, domesticity, and sisterhood might flourish in an otherwise
harsh and coarse urban environment. Their confidence in these ideals was undermined, however, by the nagging suspicion that young
working-class women preferred exciting amusements to quiet,
homey evenings around the hearth. The Harlem YWCA acknowledged that "the Association must provide attractions which should
give the pleasure-loving girl all the brightness and entertainment
possible." Supplying such entertainment, however, potentially con-
tradicted their commitment to female self-help and an inclusive sisterhood. The quandary is apparent in the International Board's advice to local Y's on winning the working girls' support. "Meet them
on the common ground of earnest Christian womanhood, share
heartily with them in their amusements and let them fully realize
that you not only need their help but value it," they asserted, before
adding somewhat hesitantly, "—Let them sometimes bring their
men friends."[12]

As reformers developed forms of recreation affirming middle-
class female culture, they faced the problem of attracting working-
class women whose lives were shaped by very different cultural assumptions. For many of them, recreation meant street life, dance
halls, cheap theaters, and excursions, amusements that mingled the
sexes without the presence of elders or chaperones and permitted

them a sense of autonomy and excitement. Such women met the recreation programs with apathy, suspicion, and resistance, challenging reformers' assumptions and forcing the redefinition of their programs.

THE WORKING GIRLS' CLUBS

The working girls' clubs exemplify the recreation reform movement and the cultural conflicts it engendered. The moving spirit behind the clubs was Grace Hoadley Dodge, a wealthy young philanthropist and reformer. As a Sunday school teacher in one of the city's evangelical churches, Dodge sought a means of educating and uplifting the young working women in the parish. In 1884, she established a series of practical talks for women who labored in nearby silk factories, hoping to combine companionship with sisterly advice. Soon thereafter, the 38th Street Working Girls' Society was organized, and other clubs quickly developed in the 1880's and early 1890's. For twenty-five cents each month, working women had access to club rooms, a library, classes, entertainments, and a physician's services. The New York clubs, along with those in other cities, banded together in 1885 to form the Association of Working Girls' Societies, which managed a mutual benefit society, published the journal *Far and Near,* and held annual conventions. By 1894, nineteen working girls' clubs with 2,200 members had been established in New York City alone.[13]

While working-class women comprised the membership of the clubs, leadership positions were generally filled by middle- and upper-class women, who sought to apply the prevailing ideology of women's sphere and the goals of rational recreation to working women's lives. In many ways, the working girls' societies imitated the larger club movement, which by the 1880's involved thousands of middle-class women. As one observer noted, their "meetings are such as any woman's club would hold, except that they occur in the evening."[14] Like women's clubs, they stressed the solidarity and advancement of women, individual self-improvement, service to others, and the benefits of social intercourse. At the same time, the class differences between the working "girls" and middle-class "ladies" lent new meanings and emphases to these ideals.

Self-support, for example, became a primary goal of the working girls' clubs, formalized in their by-laws. Lillian Betts observed that "strenuous effort has always been made in some clubs to make them self-supporting; they seem almost to live for that purpose." Reformers initially sought to prevent the clubs from holding fairs and entertainments to raise money, viewing them as forms of philanthropy, but they later acquiesced, acknowledging that most members could not pay the dues necessary to make the clubs self-sustaining. Indeed, wealthy leaders often stepped in with timely gifts, rent payments, and provisions. Although few clubs achieved the ideal, self-support remained an important symbol. Not only did it strengthen moral fiber and inculcate thrift in working girls, it also affirmed sisterhood by rejecting the philanthropic relationship between the "haves" and "have nots."[15]

A similar concern for cross-class sisterhood emerges in the club leaders' understanding of work and self-help. Clubs sponsored an employment bureau, mutual aid society, and vocational training, but they were not viewed primarily as economic organizations. Reformers' conception of work had more to do with a critique of women's roles in society than with the specific economic and social problems of wage-earning. Like many feminists, they viewed gainful employment as a way for women to avoid the economic dependency that forced them into the marriage market. "Every girl, rich or poor, in our opinion, ought to be educated for some trade or profession, which will give her a place and standing of her own independent of marriage," observed *Far and Near*. "Then let her marry if she chooses."[16] Moreover, club leaders were unwilling to differentiate between paid labor and voluntarism, blurring the distinction between labor that was necessary for survival and work as a matter of choice. Grace Dodge, for example, asserted that she was a worker whose wages had been paid beforehand by her inheritance of wealth. "We women, younger and older, from every form of occupation, can meet on a common ground of sisterhood," one report claimed.[17]

Although the reformers affirmed self-support and cooperation among women as workers, they were cautious about exceeding the boundaries of the "natural" division of labor. Dodge, for example, affirmed that the club movement "shows the true advancement of women not desirous for men's work or place, but remaining where circumstances have placed them, and only anxious to make the best of those circumstances by developing and enlarging the powers God has given them."[18] Indeed, club activities were often directed at teaching women's household and familial roles to working girls, who were perceived to be woefully unprepared for them. Customary working-class housewifery, immigrant traditions, and tenement house conditions offered poor examples of domestic life; it was little wonder that working-class daughters preferred the excitement of the streets to the execution of household tasks. The clubs would help working women through the period of adolescence, training them for the future: "One aim of the first society was that by association together, wives, mothers and homemakers should be developed, [and] that the tone of womanhood be raised."[19] Club leaders argued that such training not only helped the individual working woman but contributed to the overall improvement of working-class life.

Toward this end, clubs instituted cooking and sewing classes, while *Far and Near* ran regular columns on household hints, inexpensive cookery, and sewing the latest fashions on a tight budget. This emphasis is also reflected in the weekly "practical talks" Dodge gave to the 38th Street Working Girls' Society, one of the most popular activities sponsored by the club. In the 1891–1892 season, most discussions centered on household management, the nature of womanhood and familial roles, manners, health, and social behavior, with only a few talks focusing upon women's role in the workforce.[20]

Linked to the effort to domesticate working women came an attack on the culture of working-class youth. The literature of the clubs assailed the ill manners and suggestive behavior that seemed to erupt wherever working-class women and men met. Short stories in *Far and Near* warned of the dangers of unchaperoned buggy rides and nighttime picnics, and editorials urged that young girls not "be anxious to acquire personal popularity in the work room, if the price of it be the sacrifice of purity of thought."[21] Gossiping, flirting with men, using slang, chewing gum, reading "trashy story papers," and wearing ostentatious dress were all customs to be eradicated.

To reformers like Dodge, such practices led to unseemly and

often dangerous relations between the sexes. Working women, she asserted, treated courtship and marriage too lightly in their heedless pursuit of men, dates, and exciting entertainment. She censured working girls' preoccupation with men outside of a familial context. "Thoughts of marriage are constantly in their minds, and meeting with men and boys considered the great excitement of their life," Dodge complained, "while the duties of wifehood and motherhood are utterly unknown to them." In talks on "men friends," "how to get a husband," and "purity," she appealed to working women to set their eyes solemnly on those higher ideals.[22]

Dodge particularly attacked the freer sexual mores and apparent promiscuity of working-class youth, urging young women to follow explicit standards of chastity and decorum. In detail, she drew the line between proper and immoral behavior:

> It is not wrong to have men friends, nor wrong to have pleasant times with them. What is wrong is the trying to attract the attention of strangers, the allowing of too great intimacies, the joking and "carrying on" which girls think fun, the being out late at night with a man, the going with them to places where you should feel blushes at the sights before you.

She particularly decried sexual intimacy among engaged couples, noting that "to keep a man's love you must keep his respect. . . . Until you are married you must not behave as if you were." Chance acquaintances with men, treating, and other interactions that placed women in positions of vulnerability were to be avoided. "It is dangerous as well as wrong to allow a man to give you money or presents of value, to accept invitations from one you do not know all about, to put yourselves in any way in a man's power," she warned.[23]

WORKING WOMEN'S RESPONSE

Disturbed by the clubs' small membership, leaders often voiced their concern about their failure to reach working women. "What have we as individuals done during the past year to bring other women, struggling with the same limitations, burdened by the same wants, needing the same aids?" one asked. "Do we feel all this, and yet leave that great army of sisters outside our doors?"[24] Even more pressing than the indifference of most working women, however, was the response of the membership to female-centered reform and middle-class leadership.

The working-class reaction was complex, reflecting the variety of cultural backgrounds and social experiences of the members. From Grace Dodge's account of the 38th Street Society, working women came from several occupations: "A large majority work in carpet and silk factories, others at corsets, cigarettes, and trimmings; a percentage are in stores and dressmaking establishments; others are telegraph operators or stenographers; a few are teachers." While Dodge was eager to provide nonsectarian clubs for all working women, in practice the clubs attracted mainly American-born women, a minority in the predominantly immigrant female labor force.[25] Such women may have been open to the Anglo-American ideals of the reformers in a way that foreign-born women, following specific national and religious customs, were not.

From the beginning, class antagonisms between "ladies" and "working girls" plagued the clubs. Working women's suspicions of do-gooders' intentions threatened the very first meeting of the 38th Street Society. Seeking to avoid middle-class condescension, Dodge advised club leaders to be businesslike, consult the working women, and "in all respects [treat] the girls as personal friends and acquaintances." Nevertheless, interclass tensions frequently arose; as journalist Helen Campbell reported, "more than for most women, was there mutual distrust and suspicion."[26] Small reminders of class differences were pervasive. One club by-law, for example, advised prospective members that their occupations would be recorded so that "the officers of the clubs may be informed of the moral character of the members." Club activities slowed or ceased in the summer months—the time when working women, laid off in the slack season, could most use them—because officers left the hot city for vacation resorts.[27]

Working-class members complained that the leadership was not always responsive or accessible to them. In the Progressive Club, members moved to establish an advisory council, two-thirds of which would be comprised of working women. Emma Illwitzer, a working girl, observed that her sister wage-earners "are more apt to hear the ideas and opinions of the different members expressed freely during the month than the President ever could." Some women felt awkward about speaking out, "and in that way some good ideas are lost, [and] many misunderstandings, which if spoken over might have been righted, are left unexplained." Mary Brady of the Steadfast Club agreed, stating that the presence of working women on her club's council had made a significant difference: "These six are working girls, having so much in common with the majority of club members, that they are placed in a position to know the common needs, and decide on remedies."[28]

Club members also ridiculed middle-class generalities about work and sisterhood, abstractions that working-class daily life often mocked. The Ivy Club, for example, criticized *Far and Near* for printing "too much that is petty about work, especially woman's work, too much that is sentimental." Deriding reformers' tendency to build up wage-earning as a giant step in the emancipation of women, they observed that the "trend of the times is to overpraise everything women do, and business women trained in business habits object to this as false and silly."[29] Working women's anger over class differences surfaced particularly in discussions of a proposal that club members wear identifying badges or insignia. Three out of four disliked the idea: "Why should we want to tell everyone who rides in the horse-car with us that we are working-girls and that we spend our evenings in a club-room? Are not those two things our own affair and nobody's business?" Another replied: "I did not think of suggesting anything that would advertise our position as working girls; indeed, that is quite unnecessary, as our status is as quickly recognized in public as that of the woman of wealth."[30]

Despite their shared aversion to middle-class patronage, working-class members were not unified in their response to the clubs' programs or reformers' messages. Rather, they formed cliques around particular subcultures and life styles linked to schooling, type of work, and ethnicity. Tensions erupted in the clubs between more and less educated women, between clerical workers and factory girls. Lillian Betts, for example, cites the case of one group splintering off from the main club:

The need of the second club had grown out of the refusal of the girls who earned five to nine dollars a week in various employments to associate with a number of girls working in a tobacco factory, and earning on an average three dollars and a half per week. This last named were rough in speech and manner, and far from stylish in dress—the standard of the elder club.[31]

Such differences among club members reflected the larger social and cultural distinctions prevalent among working-class women.

Cliques formed around two competing cultural styles, those who labelled themselves serious, self-reliant workers and those who identified with leisure pursuits and pleasure. The former responded favorably to reformers' call for self-improvement, wholesome recreation, and propriety. Respectability was a recurrent refrain among these members, who discussed with concern their popular image. Objecting to journalistic portrayals of working women as low and vulgar, they challenged writers to depict women from the working girls' clubs, friendly societies, and temperance unions. M. C. Mountain of the Ivy Club, for example, asserted that "New York working-girls are proverbially intelligent, moral, and contented." Another indignantly observed that "we are as proud of our honor, we are as careful of our reputation" as middle-class women. Some club members turned against those who failed to come up to these standards. Working women would never be socially accepted by the leisured class, opined one writer, "as long as it can be said with any truth . . . that their voices are loud, that their manners are careless and often rough, that their grammar is doubtful."[32] Using slang and chewing gum appeared to be the most heinous offenses, and cliques in some clubs enforced rules against them.

Unlike the middle-class leadership, however, some club members connected the ideals of womanhood, domesticity, and respectability to a specific working-class ideology of cooperation and the dignity of labor, an ideology most thoroughly articulated in the organized labor movement of the 1880's.[33] Some began to argue for an alliance between the clubs and labor organizations, claiming that trade unionism was the logical outcome of ideals of cooperation and self-improvement. In gripping language, Lizzie Burke of the Far and Near Society urged the clubs to

encourage girls to organize "Trade Clubs" of their respective calling, which would be of lasting benefit in aiding to ameliorate the
condition of girls poorly paid and help release them from the
grasp of the grinding "capitalists" whose object is almost to own
them body and soul. . . . In conclusion, I hold that it is in strict
compliance with the rules and usages of the Working Girls Clubs
to foster such organization and assist in promoting the same.[34]

Class-conscious working women scorned reformers whose solutions
to industrial problems lay in didactic lessons and harmless amusements. By the 1890's, a growing political and economic awareness
led some women to abandon the clubs for trade unions and labor
associations, such as the Working Women's Society.[35]

Fearful of class conflict, reformers initially resisted these criticisms. According to one reporter, "In many of the clubs, at that
time, it was found that conversation about trade matters was not
allowed." Club leaders explicitly rejected Lizzie Burke's proposal,
arguing that "labor questions, like politics and religion, must be left
to each member to settle for herself, and our organizations exist for
the improvement of the individual, not to deal with conditions of
work and wages."[36] By 1893, however, the leadership began to respond to members' concerns. *Far and Near* in that year started to
print articles on economic issues and the benefits of organization.
Clubs were beneficial to working women as a class, reformers now
argued, because they supplied training in organizational techniques, helped women advance into higher professions, and habitu-
ated them to a better standard of living.[37]

While some members pushed the clubs toward class-conscious
trade unionism, others rejected the conception of educational recreation that guided the clubs' program. One working woman, for example, noted the declining interest in the clubs and wondered, "Is
it not because, as our name implies, we are *working girls* and
though desirous of mental, physical and spiritual culture, we *most*
need *pleasant recreation?*" One club petitioned *Far and Near* to
print more love stories and less serious fare.[38] More closely tied to
the popular youth culture, these women envisioned the working
girls' societies as social clubs oriented toward pleasure and relaxed
sociability.

Reformers learned that they resisted the pleasure-seekers' demands at their peril, as they "discover[ed] that the success of a club depends, more than upon central position, pleasant rooms, or any external circumstance, upon its power of supplying what the members want."[39] The history of the Girls' Progressive Society typifies reformers' accommodation to their members' social interests. Initially, they followed the advice of the New York Association of Working Girls' Societies to restrict "any effort toward luxury or show" in the club rooms, spending available funds only for educational purposes. They made their rooms as homelike as possible and initiated a variety of instructional classes. Then "during all the month of January we waited for that tremendous influx of new members which we had dreamed of," but to their disappointment, they failed to attract much notice among working women. The club subsequently cancelled a number of classes and instituted Wednesday night receptions, featuring music and refreshments, a successful move that attracted the crowds they desired.[40] By the mid-1890's, most clubs had begun to subordinate didactic talks and classes to a whirlwind of social activities. Fancy dress balls, evening receptions, fairs, ice cream and card parties, theatrical entertainments, and bowling came into vogue. The club season even extended into summer, with picnics, trolley rides, and excursions offered to members.[41]

The accommodation to working women's culture was most pronounced in the reformers' changing attitude toward men and dancing in club life. As early as 1888, a small new society called "Our Club" wrote that "the monthly meetings when young men friends of the girls are invited are perhaps the most enjoyable of all." This innovation was gradually accepted by the clubs in order to attract new female members. In 1899, the 38th Street Society was heralding "the coming of a large number of young men to the monthly entertainments," while another large association, the Riverside Club, invited men to the club rooms two evenings a month. By 1900, most clubs had endorsed the presence of men at entertainments and receptions.[42] Similarly, dancing slowly gained acceptance among club leaders, who preferred to have working women waltz in the club rooms than in the city's public halls. In 1891, facing a "demand on the part of members to learn dancing," the Endeavor Club's leaders agreed to a "dancing drill," which presumably was not as corrupting as commercial dance lessons: "We finally compromised on a drill in which dancing steps should be introduced incidentally and healthfully, in the course of all sorts of marches and exercises." Other clubs permitted members to dance together after meetings or at entertainments. By 1900, as men became part of club life, leaders consented to mixed-sex couple dancing, which quickly became "the really popular thing" among members.[43]

Despite these changes, membership in the clubs dropped dramatically. Many of the oldest and largest clubs of 1890 had lost half or more of their members by 1900. Overall membership in the Manhattan societies declined to 1,267 by 1902, and several clubs disbanded altogether. Grace Dodge resigned as director of the New York Association of Working Girls' Societies in 1896, turning to other reform work. Significantly, she had come to believe that economic problems were the most pressing issues facing working women and that she was unqualified to solve them.[44]

The reasons for this declining interest were manifold. The clubs had never appealed to the vast majority of female wage-earners, who were immigrants or daughters of immigrants; with the great influx of foreign-born families into New York from 1880 to 1920, the clubs' emphasis on the American-born girl was increasingly misplaced. Moreover, clubs competed with many other activities for the attention of working-class women by the turn of the century. While relatively few women were unionized at this time, the Working Women's Society, trade unions, and, by 1906, the Women's Trade Union League offered opportunities for women interested in the labor question. Many more women found the entertainment they craved in the expanding network of commercial amusements available in the metropolis.

Finally, the fabric of middle-class values that had guided the club movement began to unravel. Reformers had sought to extend the middle-class club ideal to working women's social life, affirming a social reality constructed on the basis of gender. These efforts failed in large part because widening class differences could not be transcended in practice. Working women's experience of their sphere was vastly different from that of the middle-class ladies, and they urged reformers to take into account their understanding of gender and class relations. Where reformers sought cross-class sisterhood, didactic recreation, and individual improvement, working women pressed for both heterosocial amusement and greater attention to the problems of labor. Club leaders conceded to these concerns, diluting their woman-centered ideology in the process.

RECREATION REFORM
IN THE PROGRESSIVE ERA

The middle-class experience in working girls' clubs contributed to the redirection of women's recreation reform at the turn of the century. While clubs, friendly societies, YWCA's, and vacation cottages remained active, new reform agencies arose to combat the popular amusements of working women. The Educational Alliance, the People's Institute, settlement houses, and other organizations situated in the city's tenement districts and immigrant ghettos mounted a wholesale attack on the problems of working-class communities, including women's leisure.

In addressing this issue, reform organizations moved away from the Gilded Age programs, criticizing their particularism and emphasis on individual self-help.[45] Two emergent intellectual trends, a stress on environmentalism and a new appreciation of leisure, influenced this generation of reformers. Adopting a more holistic approach, they treated the urban environment itself as the field of reform, directing attention to tenement house laws, playgrounds and parks, public health services, and community centers. The problem of working women's recreation became simply one element in the comprehensive effort to reconstruct community life and save the family. At the same time, leisure and play became central concerns of reformers. Recreation was no longer viewed as idleness, but as a necessary period of renewal and a precious resource. In Belle Israels' words, "Play is not a luxury, but an absolute necessity to the working world of today."[46]

Despite these changes in outlook, reformers after 1900 continued to believe that the primary purpose of recreation reform for working women was to inculcate standards of respectable behavior. Like their predecessors, Progressive reformers perceived a rising tide of promiscuity and immorality in the city. Their panic over white slavery and commercialized prostitution reflects this perception, but organized vice was only one aspect of a larger problem. Social workers mobilized against sexual familiarity, unrestrained heterosocial relationships, and, not least, bad taste. "Everything possible should be done to ennoble the relations between the sexes; to purify the tradition concerning romance through the spread of the great novels; to eliminate cheap kissing games, cheap plays and low dances," they exhorted.[47]

As this admonition suggests, a prime target of Progressive reformers was the growing menace of commercial amusements. As we have seen, investigators infiltrated amusement parks, excursion boats, movie theaters, and dance houses to report on their questionable morality and unhealthy conditions. The threat that commercial amusements posed was closely related, in their view, to the breakdown of the family in industrial society. Just as industrialization had forced family members to seek work away from the home, so commercialization split apart the family in its leisure hours. Each family member sought recreation in different places outside the home, the father going to saloons, adolescent daughters and sons attending dance halls, children flocking to the streets, with only the mother staying at home. Nor could the family in its crowded tenement home provide a wholesome place of recreation or the chaperonage necessary for working-class youth. Since the biological family could no longer provide safe recreation for its daughters, argued settlement leader Mary Simkhovitch, "the community itself must become the foster father and mother."[48]

Reformers lobbied vigorously for the regulation of commercialized recreation through legislation and cooperative agreements with amusement entrepreneurs. Seeing regulation by the state as a substitute for personal chaperonage, Belle Israels fought to limit the sale of liquor and to enforce standards of cleanliness in public dance halls. Others urged legislation to establish chaperones at all amusement resorts. The New York Public Recreation Commission, for example, recommended that "a woman should be present at all places of public amusement where young girls congregate, such as dance halls, cabaret restaurants, motion picture shows, dancing academies, theatres, etc."[49] Community organizations pressured amusement owners to provide a more wholesome environment for single women. The East Side Neighborhood Association convinced "a number of the moving picture proprietors [to] set aside certain seats in their show places for girls who were unescorted." Other groups lobbied to have lights turned up in the nickelodeons during movies to prevent sexual harassment and seduction.[50]

Reformers coupled these restrictive measures with efforts to create positive alternatives outside the commercial nexus. The "neighborhood ideal" would substitute for the familial control that commercialization had destroyed. Social and educational clubs formed the core of settlement work, and by 1910, forty-one settlements sponsored 160 clubs for girls and young women. These were seen as necessary additions to tenement home life. "It is not possible to hold up before East Siders the Anglo-Saxon home ideal," observed a University Settlement report. "When homes have become nothing but eating and sleeping places then clubrooms must make up the difference between this and the ideal."[51] Hoping to teach young women how to protect themselves from the temptations of the city, settlement club work included sex education. "There is one armour-plate that the girl who goes out into the dance hall should have and must have," Belle Israels asserted. "She must have the armour-plate of sensible, wholesome education in matters of sex."[52]

In order to counteract the influence of saloons and dance halls, reformers developed social centers to provide a focal point for neighborhood life, bring family groups together, and allow people to create their own activities. The People's Institute, for example, converted several public schools into neighborhood centers with dancing, athletics, and entertainment for the entire family. Lillian Wald spearheaded an effort to create noncommercial meeting places, with the development of Clinton Hall in 1906. Wald's Henry Street Settlement also sponsored festivals and pageants to express the character of the neighborhood and its people. Believing that cheap amusements were popular only because the city provided few alternatives, reformers initiated such organizations as the Metropolitan Debating Society, Educational Dramatic League, and People's Music League.[53]

Perceiving sexual and social dangers to women in New York's commercial amusements, reformers responded with a multifaceted program for working-class recreation. These efforts were designed to provide working-class youth with family-oriented, wholesome recreation, an alternative to the age-segregated, promiscuous amusements provided commercially. Through education, regulation, and noncommercial forms of amusement, Progressives hoped to counteract the city's dance halls, cheap theaters, and street life and to revitalize the family and community. Unlike the early working girls' clubs, most of these activities assumed the participation of both women and men, with reformers carefully negotiating their social interaction.

The difficulties involved in creating alternative forms of mixed-sex leisure are apparent in the reformers' treatment of dancing in settlement houses and community centers. More than other popular amusements, dancing seemed to link recreation and women's morality, serving as a potent symbol of heterosexual and heterosocial relationships. While Israels and others sought to regulate commercial halls, social workers pondered dancing in their clubs and entertainments. Many associated any form of mixed dancing with promiscuity and barred it; one survey of schools and social service agencies found that "mixed dancing by school-children of the adolescent age has been allowed only in a few places and under considerable restriction." Others, like People's Institute leader John Collier, saw folk dancing as a wholesome alternative to the coarse dances of the public halls and an art form that would strengthen ethnic and generational ties.[54]

More often, settlements accepted dancing cautiously, aware that "this feature might excite the objection of a few conscientious people." Regulated and chaperoned dances, they argued, would improve manners and behavior and, most important, would "offset the vicious influence of the commercialized dance hall."[55] While fearing the explosive potential of mixed-sex activities, reformers found that they could attract working women only by providing opportunities to dance and socialize with men: "One club leader, who found that the girls were leaving the club early, in order to meet boys and walk home with them, has solved the difficulty by inviting the boys in to dance for the last half-hour of the club meeting." University Settlement did not permit mixed clubs, but, agreeing with female members that "fun loses it savor unless it includes boys," sponsored numerous dances and socials.[56] Proper supervision, controlled attendance, and sedate music, reformers hoped, would give dances a respectable atmosphere. Community centers went so far as to select appropriate participants, excluding disorderly youths, gangs, and smokers; as one report noted, "We do not want to invite in at this time those groups which raise new problems."[57]

Despite their best efforts, reformers often failed to entice working-class youth to the well-regulated dance of the settlement or neighborhood school. In P.S. 63, where the People's Institute had established a social center, "we have run two dances, buying decorations, extra lighting and fitting facilities and better music. The dances have not proved a success. The attendance amounted to almost nothing." As in the working-girls' clubs, different cultural styles among working women led to diverse responses; while some women believed that settlement dances were "high toned," many more felt they were "slow" and not as appealing as those run in the large public halls.[58]

At the other extreme, reformers often could not prevent their dances from assuming the character of those in commercial halls. Settlements and social centers often reported rowdy behavior and suggestive movements on the dance floor. University Settlement found it necessary to appoint a floor committee to supervise their dances and "instill a desire for decorum and order among 300 young people on pleasure bent." When ragtime blared in another community center at P.S. 104, reformers reported "disorderly conduct during the last two dances. Miss Daley blames the type of music as cause."[59]

Although reformers agreed that social agencies should bring girls and boys together before they met on street corners and dance halls, their efforts to ensure a purified notion of sexual relations were at times overwhelmed by the customary behavior of working-class youth. In 1905, for example, the People's Club developed some unnamed, dangerous "tendencies to frivolous social pleasure," which seem to have included loose sexual behavior. Social workers apparently intervened, reporting that "the home spirit, so characteristic of the Club in its best days, is well re-established, and the life of intimacy between the members of both sexes leads frequently to its natural results in engagement and marriage."[60]

Similarly, in P.S. 63's community center, the cultural style of working-class youth challenged reformers' ideals and programs. The center had been established as a working model of the "neighborhood ideal," sponsoring dances, sociables, and athletic activities in the 1910's to provide community-controlled, wholesome recreation. By 1919, however, the center had come under the scrutiny of the Committee of Fourteen, whose business was investigating prostitution and vice. The investigator's damning report made a mockery of the reformers' vision. At P.S. 63, he appraised one of the chaperoned dances:

> I visited this school, where a dance was going on. About fifty young couples were dancing, among them boys and girls in age of 12 or 14 years. Most of them didnt behaved [sic], they were using vile language, smoking cigarettes and shimmying while dancing. . . . It is a rendezvous for young men and young girls, who come here purposely to pick each other up.[61]

Aiming to reshape women's recreation and regulate gender relations, reformers at best waged a holding action against the onslaught of commercial culture and heterosocial forms of behavior. Despite numerous efforts, settlement leaders and social workers failed to reach most of their potential working-class constituency. The People's Institute estimated that only one percent of the populace used the parks, playgrounds, settlements, and social centers that reformers had established. Increasingly, they accommodated to the widespread popularity of commercial amusements, sponsoring trips to Luna Park, offering reduced prices for theater and concert tickets, and supporting motion pictures as a wholesome substitute for the saloon. Indeed, some even found themselves seduced by commercialized entertainment; one group of civic leaders, visiting a nickelodeon show, "came to be shocked, but, after the first disappointment was over, they remained to enjoy."[62]

Working women's recreation was only one small aspect of social reform in these years, but it dramatizes a larger cultural process taking place in American cities whereby interclass dynamics helped to redefine the relationship between gender and leisure. In the 1880's and 1890's, reformers sought to extend their notion of women's culture to working women's social life, but they failed to realize their vision, eventually compromising with working-class women who preferred mixed-sex amusement to self-sufficient sisterhood. These young women pioneered new forms of public female behavior, which the dominant culture ultimately incorporated and popularized. As a new generation of reformers struggled to combat commercialized pleasures, other segments of the urban middle class increasingly embraced new "manners and morals" in emergent bourgeois social spaces, the city's cabarets, dance palaces, and movie houses. They too began to seek sensual and exciting leisure pursuits and heterosocial interactions, associating it with a sense of twentieth-century modernity.

For the middle class, women's leisure in the Victorian era had been associated with education, uplift, and sisterly bonds; by the 1920's, it was decisively linked to social freedom, freer sexuality, and mixed-sex fun. Reformers were seen as hopelessly out-of-date by the younger generation, their criticism of heterosocial commercial culture irrelevant. Most feminists today would similarly reject their moralistic assumptions and family-oriented solutions. But the leaders of working-girls' clubs, settlement houses, and other reform agencies understood some of the liabilities of the modern culture for women, its potential for exploitation, as well as its alluring freedoms and pleasures. As Mary Simkhovitch warned, "The young men of the big cities today are not gallantly paying the way of these girls for nothing."[63]

CONCLUSION

When the working day is done, oh! girls just want to have fun.[1]

The reformers' response to working girls' style represents one facet of a larger cultural transformation occurring between 1880 and 1920. Competing conceptions of gender informed much of the cultural ferment of these years, as numerous voices questioned the inviolability of women's traditional sphere. Public attention turned to the "New Woman," who relished personal autonomy and activity in the public arena and challenged the boundaries of domesticity and female self-sacrifice. This emergent sensibility among middle-class women extended from political life to leisure time. Women's massive mobilization for suffrage and temperance, as well as their visibility in radical politics, signified a new scale of participation in public life. Fervid debates over the "new morality" brought the scrutiny of women's sphere into the realm of private life. Greenwich Village feminists, for example, zealously advocated women's sexual satisfaction, personal freedom, and equality in marriage.[2] The bursting of old barriers infectiously appealed to other middle-class women who were less politicized. Dancing sensual dances, attending cabarets and nightclubs, living as "bachelor girls" in apartment houses, these women expressed a new-found sense of freedom and possibility.

At the same time, middle-class men's roles also underwent challenge and redefinition. The Victorian ethic that bound success to hard work and thrift grew more distant from many men's daily experiences. The development of large, impersonal corporations in an increasingly bureaucratic society undermined traditional notions of masculine individuality and conquest. So did the restlessness of men's wives and daughters. Seeking new ways of understanding manliness, some middle-class men became feminists, arguing that women's emancipation meant equality and self-fulfillment for both sexes. Many more, however, turned to leisure activities and consumer goods, which promised the excitement, gratification, and self-expression often denied in the workplace. White-collar jobs could be forgotten in the masculine rituals of football and body-building or in the exotic delights of an urban nightclub.[3]

In the nineteenth century, as a distinct middle class developed in American society, the emergent class found ways to distinguish itself culturally from working-class immigrants, Afro-Americans, and the idle rich. The bourgeois world view counterposed such values as sobriety and domesticity against the dissipation and promiscuity of those higher and lower in social rank. By the early twentieth century, however, these groups—by virtue of their very "otherness"—offered sensuality, colorful adventure, and expressiveness to segments of the urban middle class. While some New Yorkers looked on with disapproval, others found working women who "put on style" an amusing, fashionable, and admirable part of the cultural landscape. What had been seen as rowdy girls' deviant behavior in the mid-nineteenth century was evaluated more ambiguously by the early 1900's. Flamboyant fashion, assertive sexuality, and close social interaction between the sexes held their appeal by being not quite respectable.

An important catalyst in this cultural process was the intensive commercialization of leisure, which defined recreation as a commodity, created new audiences, and profited by the selling of heterosocial culture. Within the working-class community, leisure entrepreneurs consciously encouraged the participation of women in mixed-sex amusements, altering traditional patterns of sociability. Promoters organized dances and excursions on a mass scale, hampering neighborly chaperonage and familial control. Outside the tenement districts, huge dance palaces and large amusement parks beckoned young women who desired spaces for social experimentation, personal freedom, and unsupervised fun. Movies, initially located in immigrant neighborhoods, attracted large numbers of wives and mothers as well as single women, decisively breaking down the segmentation of working-class recreation. All of these commercial amusements transmitted and mediated heterosocial culture to working-class women and men, although in different ways and to different audiences.

Much of this leisure culture made its way into the entertainment of the middle class. Entrepreneurs and promoters scoured the city's "low" dance halls and variety theaters for songs and dance steps and observed street culture for new fads and fashions.[4] Introducing novelties into nightclubs, amusement parks, and the movies, they transformed them into safe, controllable activities that could be sold to all classes. George Tilyou purified the raucous sexuality of the "old" Coney Island by organizing patrons' behavior to produce innocent intermingling and harmless laughter. Dance idols Irene and Vernon Castle toned down tough dancing for high-class cabarets, while movie-makers elevated potentially promiscuous interaction to healthy athleticism and girlish freedom, embodied in such screen stars as Douglas Fairbanks and Mary Pickford.[5] Tamed for the middle class, heterosocial culture promised self-fulfillment for women through consumerism and an ideology of companionate romance and marriage.

This cultural formulation, transmitted in the movies, advertising, advice books, and popular magazines of the 1920's and beyond, obscured the tensions and contradictions lingering below the surface of working women's leisure. Young working women had defined a style that in some ways subverted the traditional bases of their dependency—as dutiful daughters in the patriarchal immigrant family and as submissive workers in a capitalist economy. At the same time, this style continued to be pursued in a context of economic and sexual dependency, where pleasure could blur into vulnerability and peril. Expressing the aspiration for selfhood and fulfillment, it did not attempt to transform the web of gender and class relations in which working women were situated.

Moreover, the leisure pursuits of single working-class women often ceased with marriage or motherhood. Within working-class families, low income, lack of community services and labor-saving technology, and the traditional burdens of housework and child care continued to constrain wives' leisure time after 1920. The growing numbers of working wives, slowly increasing before World War II and dramatically rising thereafter, normalized a "double day" that allowed women little time for leisure. Although the movies, and later radio and television, offered married women wider options for leisure activities, working-class recreation remained quite segregated by gender, as well as age and marital status. Sociological studies of working-class family life suggest the persistence of separate worlds for women and men until the 1970's. At that time, Lillian Rubin observes, the feminist movement and women's greater economic independence spurred many working-class wives to demand greater sharing and companionship within marriage.[6]

Finally, the commercial culture led women to tie self-fulfillment to consumerism. This may have diverted working women from their class interests or heightened expectations of the "good life" in such a way as to encourage collective action and unionization.[7] The dominant vision of consumer individualism and heterosocial companionship did not, however, encourage a feminist consciousness among working-class women. Unaccompanied by substantive changes in the allocation of power, work, and resources by gender, that culture served to foreclose women's options.

The desire of women for self-determined pleasure, sexuality, and autonomy, haltingly expressed by working women at the turn of the century, continues to be a compelling issue several generations later. It remains so in a society whose sophisticated engines of culture rapidly commodify the expression of those outside the mainstream, draining it of its dissonance and challenge in the process. That working women "just want to have fun" may thus be taken as a trivial claim, easily achieved in the world of leisure, or as a profoundly liberating—and unfulfilled—feminist demand.

NOTES

Introduction

1. Ruth S. True, *The Neglected Girl* (New York, 1914), p. 58.

2. Tape I-132 (side A), New York City Immigrant Labor History Collection of the City College Oral History Project, Robert F. Wagner Archives, Tamiment Institute Library, New York University. (Interviewees' names used in my study are fictitious to protect their anonymity; researchers who wish to verify quotations should refer to tape numbers.)

3. Tape I-3 (transcript), Immigrant Labor History Collection.

4. E. P. Thompson, "Time, Work-Discipline and Industrial Capitalism," *Past and Present* 38 (1967): 56–97; Herbert Gutman, *Work, Culture, and Society in Industrializing America* (New York, 1977).

5. See the excellent studies by Roy Rosenzweig, *Eight Hours for What We Will: Workers and Leisure in an Industrial City, 1870–1920* (Cambridge, Eng., 1983); Francis G. Couvares, *The Remaking of Pittsburgh: Class and Culture in an Industrializing City, 1877–1919* (Albany, N.Y., 1984); John T. Cumbler, *Working-Class Community in Industrial America: Work, Leisure, and Struggle in Two Industrial Cities, 1880–1930* (Westport, Conn., 1979); Susan E. Hirsch, *Roots of the American Working Class: The Industrialization of Crafts in Newark, 1800–1860* (Philadelphia, 1978).

6. See, for example, Leslie Woodcock Tentler, *Wage-Earning Women: Industrial Work and Family Life in the United States, 1900–1930* (New York, 1979).

7. John Higham, "The Reorientation of American Culture in the 1890's," in *The Origins of Modern Consciousness*, ed. John Weiss (Detroit, 1965).

8. The literature on women's sphere in the nineteenth century is vast. Among the most significant works are: Nancy F. Cott, *The Bonds of Womanhood* (New Haven, Conn., 1977); Cott, "Passionlessness: An Interpretation of Victorian American Ideology, 1790–1850," *Signs* 4 (Winter 1978): 219–236; Kathryn Kish Sklar, *Catharine Beecher: A Study in American Domesticity* (New Haven, Conn., 1973); Carroll Smith-Rosenberg, "Beauty, the Beast and the Militant Woman: A Case Study in Sex Roles and Social Stress in Jacksonian America," *American Quarterly* 23 (Oct. 1971): 562–584; Smith-Rosenberg, "The Female World of Love and Ritual: Relations Between Women in Nineteenth Century America," *Signs* 1 (Autumn 1975): 1–29.

9. These changes are discussed in Sheila M. Rothman, *Woman's Proper Place: A History of Changing Ideals and Practices, 1870 to the Present* (New York, 1978); Rosalind Rosenberg, *Beyond Separate Spheres: The Intellectual Roots of Modern Feminism* (New Haven, Conn., 1982); Barbara J. Harris, *Beyond Her Sphere: Women and the Professions in American History* (Westport, Conn., 1978); James R. McGovern, "The American Woman's Pre-World War I Freedom in Manners and Morals," *Journal of American History* 55 (Sept. 1968): 315–333.

10. On leisure and new relations between the sexes, see Lewis A. Erenberg, *Steppin' Out: New York Nightlife and the Transformation of American Culture, 1890–1930* (Westport, Conn., 1981); Lary May, *Screening Out the Past: The Birth of Mass Culture and the Motion Picture Industry* (New York, 1980); John Kasson, *Amusing the Million: Coney Island at the Turn of the Century* (New York, 1978). Sexual ideology is discussed in Christina Simmons, "'Living Happily Ever After in Heterosexual Matehood': Fear of Lesbianism in the Ideology of Companionate Marriage," *Frontiers* 4, no. 3 (Fall 1979): 54–59; Simmons, "'Marriage in the Modern Manner': Sexual Radicalism and Reform in America, 1914–1941" (Ph.D. diss., Brown University, 1982). Heterosocial culture in the 1920's is discussed in Paula S. Fass, *The Damned and the Beautiful: American Youth in the 1920's* (New York, 1977); Kenneth A. Yellis, "Prosperity's Child: Some Thoughts on the Flapper," *American Quarterly* 21 (Spring 1969): 44–63; Robert and Helen Lynd, *Middletown: A Study in Contemporary American Culture* (1929; rpt. New York, 1956). On the new consumerism, see Stuart Ewen, *Captains of Consciousness: Advertising and the Social Roots of the Consumer Culture* (New York, 1976).

11. Works that assume a "trickle down" model include Fass, *The Damned and the Beautiful*; Christopher Lasch, *The New Radicalism in America, 1889–1963: The Intellectual as Social Type* (New York, 1965); Henry F. May, *The End of American Innocence* (Chicago, 1959); Erenberg,

Steppin' Out. See Paul Boyer, *Urban Masses and Moral Order in America, 1820–1920* (Cambridge, Mass., 1978), for an example of the "social control" model; Stanley Aronowitz, *False Promises: The Shaping of American Working Class Consciousness* (New York, 1973), for "cultural hegemony."

12. Raymond Williams, *Marxism and Literature* (Oxford, 1977); Gareth Stedman Jones, "Class Expression versus Social Control? A Critique of Recent Trends in the Social History of 'Leisure,'" *History Workshop* 4 (Autumn 1977): 163–170; Stephen Hardy and Alan G. Ingham, "Games, Structures and Agency: Historians on the American Play Movement," *Journal of Social History* 17 (Winter 1983): 285–301; Francis G. Couvares, "The Triumph of Commerce: Class Culture and Mass Culture in Pittsburgh," in *Working–Class America,* ed. Michael H. Frisch and Daniel J. Walkowitz (Urbana, Ill., 1983): 123–152; Roy Rosenzweig, "Middle Class Parks and Working Class Play: The Struggle Over Recreational Space in Worcester, Massachusetts, 1870–1910," *Radical History Review* 21 (Fall 1979): 37–48. I have found particularly useful Stuart Hall and Tony Jefferson, eds., *Resistance Through Rituals: Youth Subcultures in Post-War Britain* (London, 1976).

Chapter One

1. See David C. Hammack's overview in *Power and Society: Greater New York at the Turn of the Century* (New York, 1982), pp. 59–108. The classic work on New York's poor is Jacob Riis, *How the Other Half Lives* (1890; rpt. New York, 1971). For evocative descriptions of New York in these years, see Bayrd Still, *Mirror for Gotham* (New York, 1956), pp. 205–299; Henry James, *The American Scene* (New York, 1907). For a spatial and visual sense of the city, see I. N. Phelps Stokes, *The Iconography of Manhattan Island, 1498–1909* (New York, 1915–1928); John A. Kouwenhoven, *The Columbia Historical Portrait of New York* (Garden City, N.Y., 1953).

2. Robert Coit Chapin, *The Standard of Living Among Workingmen's Families in New York City* (New York, 1909), p. 55; Louise Bolard More, *Wage-Earners' Budgets: A Study of Standards and Costs of Living in New York City* (New York, 1907); National Industrial Conference Board, *Family Budgets of American Wage-Earners: A Critical Analysis* (Research Report no. 41; New York, 1921). See also Frank Hatch Streightoff, *The Standard of Living Among the Industrial People of America* (Boston, 1911). Housing conditions are described in Tenement House Committee of 1894, *Report* (Albany, N.Y., 1895), p. 423; Tenement House Department of the City of New York, *First Report, Jan. 1, 1902–July 1, 1903,* 2 vols. (New York, 1903).

3. U.S. Senate, *Cost of Living in American Towns: Report of an Inquiry by the Board of Trade of London* (S. 22, 62d Cong., 1st sess.; Washington, D.C., 1911), p. 6.

4. Hammack, *Power and Society*, pp. 90, 324; Irving Howe, *World of Our Fathers* (New York, 1976), pp. 119–147.

5. Chapin, *Standard of Living*, pp. 210, 212.

6. More, *Wage-Earners' Budgets*, pp. 97–98.

7. New York State Factory Investigating Commission, *Fourth Report Transmitted to Legislature, Feb. 15, 1915* (S. Doc. no. 43; Albany, N.Y., 1915), vol. 4, p. 1787; U.S. Department of Labor, *How American Buying Habits Change* (Washington, D.C., [1959]), p. 42.

8. Samuel Chotzinoff, *A Lost Paradise* (New York, 1955), p. 70; Thomas Jesse Jones, *Sociology of a New York City Block* (Studies in History, Economics and Public Law, vol. 21, no. 2; New York, 1904), pp. 7, 89; Frederick A. King, "Influences in Street Life," in University Settlement Society of New York, *Report* (New York, 1900), pp. 29–32; "Places of Interest on the Lower East Side," box 19, General Subjects—Community Councils, Lillian D. Wald Collection, Rare Book and Manuscript Library, Columbia University Library, New York; tape IV-12 (side B), New York City Immigrant Labor History Collection of the City College Oral History Project, Robert F. Wagner Archives, Tamiment Institute Library, New York University.

9. John W. Martin, "Social Life in the Street," in University Settlement Society of New York, *Report* (New York, 1899), p. 22; Tenement House Department of the City of New York, *First Report*, vol. 1, p. 140.

10. Chotzinoff, *Lost Paradise*, pp. 174, 69–70; Chapin, *Standard of Living*, p. 212.

11. Katharine Anthony, *Mothers Who Must Earn* (New York, 1914), p. 189; Raymond V. Ingersoll, "The Tenth Ward Home," in University Settlement Society of New York, *Report* (New York, 1899), p. 221; Chotzinoff, *Lost Paradise*, p. 81.

12. Robert W. DeForest and Lawrence Veiller, eds., *The Tenement House Problem*, vol. 1 (New York, 1903), p. 392; Ruth S. True, *The Neglected Girl* (New York, 1914), pp. 64–66; Jones, *New York City Block*, p. 110.

13. Lillian W. Betts, "The Italian in New York," *University Settlement Studies* 1, nos. 3–4 (1905–1906): 94; Jones, *New York City Block*, pp. 31–34, 38–39.

14. DeForest and Veiller, eds., *Tenement House Problem*, vol. 1, p. 392.

15. George E. Bevans, *How Workingmen Spend Their Spare Time* (New York, 1913), pp. 31, 45–49, 61; Susan Levine, "Labor's True Woman: Domesticity and Equal Rights in the Knights of Labor," *Journal of American History* 70 (Sept. 1983): 323–339; Ann Schofield, "Rebel Girls and Union

Maids: The Woman Question in the Journals of the AFL and IWW, 1905–1920," *Feminist Studies* 9 (Summer 1983): 335–358.

16. Elsa G. Herzfeld, *Family Monographs: The History of Twenty-four Families Living in the Middle West Side of New York City* (New York, 1905), p. 50; New York State Legislature, Special Committee of the Assembly Appointed to Investigate the Condition of Female Labor in the City of New York, *Report and Testimony* (Albany, N.Y., 1896), vol. 2, p. 1730.

17. Tape I-104 (transcript), Immigrant Labor History Collection.

18. New York Factory Investigating Commission, *Fourth Report*, vol. 4, pp. 1798, 1802, 1786 (quotations), 1797–1808.

19. In the following analysis, I have benefited greatly from recent historical studies of workingmen's culture, especially Roy Rosenzweig, *Eight Hours for What We Will: Workers and Leisure in an Industrial City, 1870–1920* (Cambridge, Eng., 1983); Francis G. Couvares, *The Remaking of Pittsburgh: Class and Culture in an Industrializing City, 1877–1919* (Albany, N.Y., 1984); Jon M. Kingsdale, "The 'Poor Man's Club': Social Functions of the Urban Working Class Saloon," *American Quarterly* 25 (Oct. 1973): 472–489; John T. Cumbler, *Working-Class Community in Industrial America: Work, Leisure, and Struggle in Two Industrial Cities, 1880–1930* (Westport, Conn., 1979); John Alt, "Beyond Class: The Decline of Labor and Leisure," *Telos* 28 (Summer 1976): 55–80; Gareth Stedman Jones, "Working–Class Culture and Working-Class Politics in London, 1870–1900: Notes on the Remaking of a Working Class," *Journal of Social History* 7 (Summer 1974): 460–508.

20. J. G. Phelps Stokes, "Hartley House and Social Reform," New York *Times*, 27 June 1897, Illustrated Magazine, p. 4; U.S. Bureau of Labor, *The Slums of Baltimore, Chicago, New York, and Philadelphia* (H.R. 257, 53d Cong., 2d sess.; Washington, D.C., 1894), p. 14; Federation of Churches and Christian Workers in New York City, *Second Sociological Canvass: The 19th Assembly District* (New York, June 1897); Federation of Churches and Christian Workers in New York City, *Third Sociological Canvass: The 21st Assembly District* (New York, 1898); Jones, *New York City Block*, p. 47.

21. Bevans, *Workingmen*, pp. 81, 20–21. Bevans' study also found that 51 percent of the workingmen reported drinking liquor at noon; 14.6 percent drank before work (pp. 57–59). See Alt, "Beyond Class."

22. Raymond C. Spaulding, "Saloons of the District," in University Settlement Society of New York, *Report* (New York, 1899), p. 35.

23. Lillian D. Wald, *The House on Henry Street* (1915; rpt. New York, 1971), p. 275; Tape II-38 (side A), Immigrant Labor History Collection.

24. "Investigation of Steamship Ticket Brokers" (1908), n. pag., box 23, Immigration, New York State Commission of Immigration, Wald Collection, Columbia University.

25. Church of the Holy Communion, New York, Workingmen's Club, *Constitution and By-Laws* (New York, 1892), pp. 3–4; Chapin, *Standard of Living,* p. 211.

26. More, *Wage-Earners' Budgets,* p. 44.

27. On Italian benefit societies, see Mabel Hurd Willett, *The Employment of Women in the Clothing Trades* (Studies in History, Economics and Public Law, vol. 16, no. 2; New York, 1902), pp. 131–132. German societies are discussed in Stanley Nadel, "Kleindeutschland: New York City's Germans, 1845–1880" (Ph.D. diss., Columbia University, 1981), pp. 228–235; Bohemian societies in New York State Bureau of Labor Statistics, *Eighteenth Annual Report* (Albany, N.Y., 1900), pp. 310, 312.

28. Belle L. Mead, "The Social Pleasures of East Side Jews" (M.A. thesis, Columbia University, 1904), p. 7; Kehillah of New York City, ed., *The Jewish Communal Register of New York City 1917–1918* (New York, 1918), pp. 732–733, 865; Richard H. Lane, "East Side Benefit Societies," in University Settlement Society of New York, *Report* (New York, 1899), 27–28; Paul Abelson to the Members of the Organization Committee, 7 Dec. 1901, p. 4, box 18, Civic Club, Wald Collection, Columbia University. See also Judith E. Smith's discussion in "Our Own Kind: Family and Community Networks in Providence," in *A Heritage of Her Own,* ed. Nancy F. Cott and Elizabeth H. Pleck (New York, 1979), pp. 393–411.

29. Investigator's Report, Magyar Hall, 1487 First Avenue, 27 May 1919, Records of the Committee of Fourteen, Rare Books and Manuscripts Division, New York Public Library, Astor, Lenox and Tilden Foundations (hereafter cited as COF).

30. U.S. Industrial Commission, *Report of the Industrial Commission on the Relations and Conditions of Capital and Labor Employed in Manufacturing and General Business,* vol. 14 (Washington, D.C., 1901), p. 80; Michael M. Davis, Jr., *The Exploitation of Pleasure: A Study of Commercial Recreations in New York City* (New York, n.d.), pp. 19–20. On the barriers these practices placed on women's participation in unions, see Heidi Hartmann, "Capitalism, Patriarchy and Job Segregation by Sex," in *Women and the Workplace,* ed. Martha Blaxall and Barbara Reagan (Chicago, 1976), pp. 137–170.

31. Investigator's Report, Cornerford Brothers, 301 Eighth Avenue, 14 May 1917, COF. On the affirmation of masculinity in workingmen's leisure, see Francis Couvares, *Remaking of Pittsburgh,* pp. 56–57.

32. Investigator's Report, Odd Fellow's Hall, 67 St. Marks Place, 26 May 1917, COF. See also Investigator's Reports, Wm. Colville, 2849 Eighth Ave., 25 May 1917, and F. Dindl, 234 Eighth Ave., 14 May 1917, COF.

33. Investigator's Report, Geo. Casey's, 251 E. 39th St., 27 June 1917, COF (original spelling).

34. Albert Kennedy, "The Saloon in Retrospect and Prospect," p. 5, Collateral Papers, Prohibition, Papers of Lillian Wald, Rare Books and Manuscripts Division, New York Public Library, Astor, Lenox and Tilden Foundations; John Collier and Edward M. Barrows, *The City Where Crime Is Play* (New York, Jan. 1914), pp. 19-20. For an excellent analysis of treating and mutuality, see Rosenzweig, *Eight Hours for What We Will*, pp. 59-61.

35. Investigator's Reports, Sport Cafe, 414 Eighth Ave., 15 May 1917, and Exchange, 1652 Madison Avenue, 12 Jan. 1917, COF.

36. George J. Kneeland, *Commercialized Prostitution in New York City* (New York, 1913), pp. 53-54. See also Ruth Rosen, *The Lost Sisterhood: Prostitution in America, 1900–1918* (Baltimore and London, 1982), pp. 83–84; Judith R. Walkowitz, *Prostitution and Victorian Society: Women, Class and the State* (Cambridge, Eng., 1980), p. 23.

37. Investigator's Report, Staunton and Dunleary, 144 Eighth Ave., 12 May 1917, COF. See also Investigator's Reports, Frisco Cafe, 402 Eighth Ave., 21 March 1917, and 15 May 1917, COF.

38. More, *Wage-Earners' Budgets*, p. 12.

39. New York Factory Investigating Commission, *Fourth Report*, vol. 4, p. 1667.

40. The relationship between men's work rhythms and leisure are discussed in E. P. Thompson, "Time, Work-Discipline and Industrial Capitalism," *Past and Present* 38 (1967): 56–97; Herbert G. Gutman, *Work, Culture, and Society in Industrializing America* (New York, 1977), pp. 3–78; Alt, "Beyond Class."

41. Tape II-30 (side B), Immigrant Labor History Collection; Susan J. Kleinberg, "Technology and Women's Work: The Lives of Working-Class Women in Pittsburgh, 1870–1900," *Labor History* 17 (Winter 1976): 58–72.

42. Paul Abelson, "The East Side Home," in University Settlement Society of New York, *Report* (New York, 1897), p. 29.

43. More, *Wage-Earners' Budgets*, p. 138. See also Herzfeld, *Family Monographs*, p. 14; Jones, *New York City Block*, p. 30.

44. DeForest and Veiller, eds., *Tenement House Problem*, vol. 1, p. 430.

45. Tape II-30 (side B), Immigrant Labor History Collection. For a superb discussion of women's work in household gatherings and maintaining kin ties, see Micaela di Leonardo, *The Varieties of Ethnic Experience: Kinship, Class, and Gender Among California Italian-Americans* (Ithaca, N.Y., 1984), pp. 191–229.

46. Herzfeld, *Family Monographs*, p. 50; Bevans, *Workingmen*, pp. 75–76; More, *Wage-Earners' Budgets*, pp. 87, 97–98, 101.

47. More, *Wage-Earners' Budgets*, p. 133; Chapin, *Standard of Living*, p. 134.

48. More, *Wage-Earners' Budgets*, p. 142. On gender differences and conflict over access to resources, see Ellen Ross, "'Fierce Questions and Taunts': Married Life in Working-Class London, 1870–1914," *Feminist Studies* 8 (Fall 1982): 575–602; Laura Oren, "The Welfare of Women in Laboring Families: England, 1860–1950," in *Clio's Consciousness Raised: New Perspectives on the History of Women*, ed. Mary S. Hartman and Lois W. Banner (New York, 1974), pp. 226–244. See also Jean Lipman-Blumen, "Toward a Homosocial Theory of Sex Roles: An Explanation of the Sex Segregation of Social Institutions," in *Women and the Workplace*, ed. Blaxall and Reagan, pp. 15–32.

49. More, *Wage-Earners' Budgets*, p. 138.

50. U.S. Bureau of Labor, *Working Women in Large Cities: Fourth Annual Report of the Commissioner of Labor, 1888* (Washington, D.C., 1889), p. 20; More, *Wage-Earners' Budgets*, p. 132; Margaret Byington, *Homestead: The Households of a Mill Town* (1910; rpt. Pittsburgh, 1974), p. 55. See also Lizabeth Cohen's excellent analysis in "Embellishing a Life of Labor: An Interpretation of the Material Culture of American Working-Class Homes," *Journal of American Culture* 3 (Winter 1980): 752–775.

51. Chapin, *Standard of Living*, p. 210; U.S. Industrial Commission, *Report of the Industrial Commission on the Relations and Conditions of Capital and Labor Employed in Manufacturing and General Business*, vol. 7 (Washington, D.C., 1901), p. 177; Jones, *New York City Block*, p. 44.

52. Mary Clare de Graffenreid, "Need of Better Homes for Wage-Earners," *Forum* 21 (May 1896): 311; Herzfeld, *Family Monographs*, p. 14; William T. Elsing, "Life in New York Tenement Houses as Seen by a City Missionary," *Scribner's* 11 (June 1892): 703.

53. DeForest and Veiller, eds., *Tenement House Problem*, vol. 1, p. 414; Lillian W. Betts, *The Leaven in a Great City* (New York, 1902), p. 164.

54. Tapes II-10, II-11, Immigrant Labor History Collection.

55. Rosenzweig, *Eight Hours for What We Will*.

56. Jones, *New York City Block*, pp. 100, 108–109; Tenement House Committee of 1894, *Report*, p. 218. The importance of informal networks among female kin and neighbors in working-class communities has been stressed by Smith in "Our Own Kind."

57. Herzfeld, *Family Monographs*, pp. 59, 58.

58. New York *Tribune*, 12 July 1903, Illustrated Supplement, pp. 5–6, and 17 July 1902, p. 7; tapes II-10 (side A), II-31 (side B), II-2, Immigrant Labor History Collection.

59. Herzfeld, *Family Monographs*, p. 23; Jones, *New York City Block*, p. 115.

60. Kehillah, *Jewish Communal Register*, p. 109; tape I-116 (side B), Immigrant Labor History Collection.

61. Lane, "East Side Benefit Societies," pp. 27–28.

62. Kennedy, "Saloon in Retrospect," p. 4; Helen Campbell et al., *Darkness and Daylight, or Lights and Shadows of New York Life* (Hartford, Conn., 1897), p. 233.

63. Tape II-38 (side A), Immigrant Labor History Collection.

64. Betts, *Leaven*, p. 258; Kennedy, "Saloon in Retrospect," p. 2.

65. Transcript K-3, p. 17, Immigrant Labor History Collection. Chapin, *Standard of Living*, pp. 133–134, implicitly suggests this division when he notes that his informants provided a complete report on liquor drunk at home, but were reticent about non-household expenditures for drink.

66. New York Factory Investigating Commission, *Fourth Report*, vol. 1, p. 783.

67. Investigator's Reports, Jack's Cafe, 539 Ninth Ave., 12 January 1917, and Ihrigs Cafe, 772 Eighth Ave., 17 May 1917, COF. See also Investigator's Reports, Mock's Restaurant, 740/742 Eighth Ave., 17 May 1917; Volks Hotel, 661 Eighth Ave., 16 May 1917; Cavanagh's Cafe, 2802 Eighth Ave., 17 Feb. 1917; Ch. Oltmann's Hotel, 572/574 Eighth Ave., 16 May 1917, COF.

68. Investigator's Report, Eiseman's Cafe, 2428 Eighth Avenue, 16 Feb. 1917, COF. See also Investigator's Reports, Bradley and Sullivan, 261 Eighth Ave., 27 Jan. 1917, and Morrissey's Cafe, 138 E. 110th St., 4 June 1917, COF.

69. Investigator's Report, The Pippin, 2433 Second Ave., 26 Jan. 1917, COF; DeForest and Veiller, eds., *Tenement House Problem*, vol. 1, p. 397. See also Investigator's Reports, Novelli's Cafe, 2295 First Ave., 24 Feb. 1917, and Geo. Casey's, 27 June 1917, COF.

70. DeForest and Veiller, eds., *Tenement House Problem*, vol. 2, p. 27.

71. On the additive nature of working-class culture, see Peter Bailey, "Will the Real Bill Banks Please Stand Up? Towards a Role Analysis of Mid-Victorian Working-Class Respectability," *Journal of Social History* 12 (Spring 1979): 342; Gutman, *Work, Culture, and Society in Industrializing America*.

72. See, for example, Smith, "Our Own Kind"; Virginia Yans-McLaughlin, *Family and Community: Italian Immigrants in Buffalo, 1880–1930* (Ithaca, N.Y., 1977); Tarara K. Hareven, "The Laborers of Manchester, New Hampshire, 1912–1922: The Role of Family and Ethnicity in Adjustment to Industrial Life," *Labor History* 16 (Spring 1975): 249–265.

73. Campbell et al., *Darkness and Daylight*, pt. 2, p. 469; James McCabe, *Lights and Shadows of New York Life* (Philadelphia, 1872), pp. 550–553; Mathew Hale Smith, *Sunshine and Shadow in New York* (Hartford, Conn., 1869), p. 216–217; Hutchins Hapgood, *Types from City Streets* (New York, 1910), p. 117.

74. New York *Tribune,* 17 July 1902, p. 7; 14 Sept. 1902, p. 4; Jones, *New York City Block,* p. 47; Wald, *House on Henry Street,* p. 252; U.S. Senate, *Cost of Living in American Towns,* p. 7.

75. Bevans, *Workingmen,* pp. 39, 80.

76. Chapin, *Standard of Living,* pp. 210, 213, 247; More, *Wage-Earners' Budgets,* pp. 102–104. See also John Modell, "Patterns of Consumption, Acculturation, and Family Income Strategies in Late Nineteenth-Century America," in *Family and Population in Nineteenth Century America,* ed. Tamara K. Hareven and Maris A. Vinovskis (Princeton, 1978).

77. John H. Mariano, *The Second Generation of Italians in New York City* (Boston, 1921), p. 92. On immigrants' income and social mobility, see Thomas Kessner, *The Golden Door: Italian and Jewish Immigrant Mobility in New York City, 1880–1915* (New York, 1977).

78. U.S. Industrial Commission, *Report,* vol. 14, p. 126.

79. New York Bureau of Labor Statistics, *Eighteenth Annual Report* (1900), p. 293; tape I-132 (side B), Immigrant Labor History Collection; Mead, "Social Pleasures," pp. 27–28; Wald, *House on Henry Street,* p. 219; New York *Tribune,* 30 June 1901, Illustrated Supplement.

80. "The Social Side of Synagogue Life," in University Settlement Society of New York, *Report* (New York, 1899), p. 29; Mead, "Social Pleasures," p. 25.

81. U.S. Industrial Commission, *Report,* vol. 14, p. 128; Henry Moskowitz, "A Study of the East Side Chedar," in University Settlement Society of New York, *Report* (New York, 1898), p. 25.

82. Kellogg Durland and Louis Sessa, "The Italian Invasion of the Ghetto," *University Settlement Studies* 1, nos. 3–4 (1905–1906): 113–114.

83. Anthony, *Mothers Who Must Earn,* p. 189.

84. Bevans, *Workingmen,* p. 39.

Chapter Two

1. [Siegel-Cooper Department Store], *Thought and Work,* Dec. 1904, p. 15; "A Salesgirl's Story," *Independent* 54 (31 July 1902): 1821; Harry B. Taplin, "Training for Store Efficiency," 17 March 1915, p. 2, Box 118, Welfare Department Subject File, National Civic Federation Papers, Rare Books and Manuscripts Division, New York Public Library, Astor, Lenox and Tilden Foundations.

2. U.S. Bureau of the Census, *Statistics of Women at Work* (Washington, D.C., 1907), pp. 270–271, 148–151; New York State Factory Investigating Commission, *Fourth Report Transmitted to Legislature, Feb. 15, 1915* (S.

Doc. no. 43; Albany, N.Y., 1915), vol. 1, p. 37, and vol. 4, p. 1478–1489. See also U.S. Bureau of the Census, *Women in Gainful Occupations, 1870–1920*, by Joseph A. Hill (Washington, D.C., 1929). Women's role in the labor force is surveyed in Leslie Woodcock Tentler, *Wage-Earning Women: Industrial Work and Family Life in the United States, 1900–1930* (New York, 1979); Alice Kessler-Harris, *Out to Work* (New York, 1982); Susan Estabrook Kennedy, *If All We Did Was to Weep at Home: A History of White Working-Class Women in America* (Bloomington, Ind., 1979); Miriam Cohen, "Italian-American Women in New York City, 1900–1950: Work and School," in *Class, Sex, and the Woman Worker,* ed. Milton Cantor and Bruce Laurie (Westport, Conn., 1977), pp. 120–143.

3. David C. Hammack, *Power and Society: Greater New York at the Turn of the Century* (New York, 1982), pp. 31–58; Sean Wilentz, *Chants Democratic: New York City and the Rise of the American Working Class, 1788–1850* (New York, 1984), especially pp. 107–142; Bayrd Still, *Mirror for Gotham* (New York, 1956).

4. Mary Christine Stansell, "Women of the Laboring Poor in New York City, 1820–1860" (Ph.D. diss., Yale University, 1979); Amy Srebnick, "True Womanhood and Hard Times: Women and Early New York Industrialization, 1840–1860" (Ph.D. diss., State University of New York at Stony Brook, 1979); Carol Groneman, " 'She Earns as a Child, She Pays as a Man': Women Workers in a Mid-Nineteenth-Century New York City Community," in *Class, Sex, and the Woman Worker,* ed. Cantor and Laurie, pp. 83–100; U.S. Senate, *Report on the Condition of Woman and Child Wage-Earners in the United States, Vol. 9: History of Women in Industry in the United States* (S. 645, 61st Cong., 2d sess.; Washington, D.C. 1910), pp. 115–155.

5. U.S. Bureau of the Census, *Statistics of the Population at the Tenth Census, 1880*, vol. 1 (Washington, D.C., 1883), p. 892; U.S. Bureau of the Census, *Social Statistics of Cities, 1880* (Washington, D.C., 1883), pp. 594–596; Christine Stansell, "The Origins of the Sweatshop: Women and Early Industrialization in New York City," in *Working-Class America,* ed. Michael H. Frisch and Daniel J. Walkowitz (Urbana, Ill., 1983), pp. 78–103.

6. Mary Van Kleeck, *Artificial Flower-Makers* (New York, 1913), p. 235. On the prevalence of homework in New York, see Thomas Kessner, *The Golden Door: Italian and Jewish Immigrant Mobility in New York City, 1880–1915* (New York, 1977), pp. 72–77; Mabel Hurd Willett, *The Employment of Women in the Clothing Trades* (Studies in History, Economics and Public Law, vol. 16, no. 2; New York, 1902), pp. 102, 108; New York State Legislature, Special Committee of the Assembly Appointed to Investigate the Condition of Female Labor in the City of New York, *Report and*

Testimony (Albany, N.Y., 1896), vol. 1, pp. 17–19, and vol. 2, pp. 1024–1025. See also John Modell and Tamara K. Hareven, "Urbanization and the Malleable Household: An Examination of Boarding and Lodging in American Families," *Journal of Marriage and the Family* 35 (Aug. 1973): 467–479; Joan M. Jensen, "Cloth, Butter and Boarders: Women's Household Production for the Market," *Review of Radical Political Economics* 12, no. 2 (Summer 1980): 14–24; Margaret F. Byington, *Homestead: The Households of a Mill Town* (1910; rpt. Pittsburgh, 1974), pp. 138–157.

7. Stansell, "Women of the Laboring Poor," pp. 105–108, 204.

8. *Ibid.*, pp. 139–159; David M. Katzman, *Seven Days a Week: Women and Domestic Service in Industrializing America* (Urbana, Ill., 1981).

9. Stansell, "Women of the Laboring Poor," p. 73; James McCabe, *Lights and Shadows of New York Life* (Philadelphia, 1872), p. 822.

10. Percentage changes in women's employment are derived from U.S. Bureau of the Census, *Tenth Census, 1880*, vol. 1, p. 892; U.S. Bureau of the Census, *Statistics of Women at Work*, pp. 270–271; U.S. Bureau of the Census, *Women in Gainful Occupations*, pp. 204, 206. The demand for women clerical workers is discussed in Margery Davies, *Woman's Place Is at the Typewriter: Office Work and Office Workers, 1870–1930* (Philadelphia, 1982). New York's economy in the early twentieth century is discussed in Hammack, *Power and Society*, pp. 39–51.

11. See note 10, and Susan Porter Benson, " 'The Customers Ain't God': The Work Culture of Department-Store Saleswomen, 1890–1940," in *Working-Class America*, ed. Frisch and Walkowitz, pp. 185–211.

12. John Commons quoted in U.S. Senate, *Woman and Child Wage-Earners*, vol. 9, p. 143; see also Willett, *Women in the Clothing Trades*. Women's industrial jobs underwent extensive examination by New York reformers and social workers; see especially Annie M. MacLean, *Wage-Earning Women* (New York, 1910); Louise C. Odencrantz, *Italian Women in Industry: A Study of Conditions in New York City* (New York, 1919); Mary Van Kleeck, *Artificial Flower-Makers*; Van Kleeck, *A Seasonal Industry: A Study of the Millinery Trade in New York* (New York, 1917); Van Kleeck, *Women in the Bookbinding Trade* (New York, 1913).

13. Elsa G. Herzfeld, *Family Monographs: The History of Twenty-four Families Living in the Middle West Side of New York City* (New York, 1905), p. 12; Katharine Anthony, *Mothers Who Must Earn* (New York, 1914), pp. 49, 59, 62.

14. Kessner, *Golden Door*, pp. 71–99.

15. Helen S. Campbell, *Prisoners of Poverty: Women Wage-Earners, Their Trades and Their Lives* (1887; rpt. Westport, Conn., 1970), p. 148; Gail Laughlin, "Domestic Service," in U.S. Industrial Commission, *Report*

of the Industrial Commission on the Relations and Conditions of Capital and Labor Employed in Manufacturing and General Business, vol. 14 (Washington, D.C., 1901), pp. 758, 756–757. See also Katzman, *Seven Days a Week*, pp. 236–243.

16. Special Committee to Investigate Female Labor, *Report and Testimony*, vol. 2, pp. 989–990, 994, 1083; Van Kleeck, *Women in the Bookbinding Trade*, p. 173.

17. New York State Bureau of Labor Statistics, *Third Annual Report* (Albany, N.Y., 1885), pp. 32–59, 169, and *Fourteenth Annual Report* (Albany, N.Y., 1896), pp. 918–919.

18. Alice P. Barrows, "The Training of Millinery Workers," in *Proceedings of the Academy of Political Science in the City of New York*, vol. 1 (Oct. 1910): 43–44. Testimony on irregular working hours by reformers and working women is extensive; see in particular New York Bureau of Labor Statistics, "Unorganized Workingwomen," *Fourteenth Annual Report* (1896); New York State Factory Investigating Commission, *Preliminary Report Transmitted to Legislature, March 1, 1912* (Albany, N.Y., 1912), vol. 1, p. 296, and *Fourth Report*, vol. 2, pp. 252, 516–517, 592–595; and studies cited in note 12.

19. Tapes I-116 (side A) and II-30 (side B), New York City Immigrant Labor History Collection of the City College Oral History Project, Robert F. Wagner Archives, Tamiment Institute Library, New York University.

20. Consumer's League of New York City, *Behind the Scenes in a Restaurant: A Study of 1017 Women Restaurant Employees* (n.p., 1916), p. 15; Willett, *Women in the Clothing Trades*, p. 74; Sue Ainslie Clark and Edith Wyatt, *Making Both Ends Meet: The Income and Outlay of New York Working Girls* (New York, 1911), p. 190.

21. Cf. New York Bureau of Labor Statistics, *Third Annual Report* (1885), pp. 32–59, and New York Factory Investigating Commission, *Fourth Report*, vol. 2, pp. 424–425, 209–210, 320; Edward Ewing Pratt, *Industrial Causes of Congestion of Population in New York City* (Studies in History, Economics and Public Law, vol. 43, no. 1; New York, 1911), p. 124. The growing acceptance of the half-holiday may be followed in New York State Bureau of Labor Statistics, *Fifth Annual Report* (Albany, N.Y., 1887), p. 555; New York State Bureau of Labor Statistics, *Eighth Annual Report* (Albany, N.Y., 1890), pt. 1, p. 448; New York Bureau of Labor Statistics, *Fourteenth Annual Report* (1896), p. 935; New York Factory Investigating Commission, *Fourth Report*, vol. 2, p. 88.

22. Elizabeth Faulkner Baker, *Protective Labor Legislation* (Studies in History, Economics and Public Law, vol. 116, no. 2; New York, 1925), pp. 113–114, 133–138.

23. Mary Van Kleeck, "Working Hours of Women in Factories," *Charities and the Commons* 17 (6 Oct. 1906): 13; Baker, *Protective Labor Legislation*, pp. 151, 309–313. For an example of employers' maneuvers around the law, see Van Kleeck, *Women in the Bookbinding Trade*, pp. 134, 144–145. Oral testimony of working women confirms large employers' observance of the law, particularly with respect to minors; see, for example, tape II-30 (side A), Immigrant Labor History Collection.

24. Van Kleeck, *Women in the Bookbinding Trade*, pp. 177–181. On unionization in the garment industry, see Nancy Schrom Dye, *As Equals and as Sisters: Feminism, the Labor Movement and the Women's Trade Union League of New York* (Columbia, Mo. and London, 1980); Meredith Tax, *The Rising of the Women* (New York, 1980), pp. 205–240.

25. "Making Ends Meet on the Minimum Wage," *Life and Labor* 3 (Oct. 1913): 302. See also tape I-105, Immigrant Labor History Collection.

26. Kessler-Harris, *Out to Work*, pp. 180–202; Baker, *Protective Labor Legislation*, p. 331; New York Factory Investigating Commission, *Fourth Report*, vol. 2, pp. 123; New York State Department of Labor, *Hours and Earnings of Women in Five Industries* (Special Bulletin no. 121; Albany, N.Y., Nov. 1923), p. 13; Willett, *Women in Clothing Trades*, p. 74; New York Bureau of Labor Statistics, *Third Annual Report* (1885), p. 169; New York Special Committee to Investigate Female Labor, *Report and Testimony*, vol. 1, pp. 60, 86–87; Irving Howe, *World of Our Fathers* (New York, 1976), p. 82.

27. Daniel T. Rodgers, *The Work Ethic in Industrial America, 1850–1920* (Chicago and London, 1974); Alice Kessler-Harris, *Out to Work*, pp. 200–201; Florence Kelley, "Right to Leisure," *Charities* 14 (2 Sept. 1905): 1055–1062.

28. Tapes I-51 (side B) and I-21 (transcript), Immigrant Labor History Collection; New York Department of Labor, *Women in Five Industries*, p. 13.

29. New York Factory Investigating Commission, *Fourth Report*, vol. 4, pp. 1577–1578; Frances R. Donovan, *The Woman Who Waits* (1920; rpt. New York, 1974), p. 50. For an elaboration of this argument, see Tentler, *Wage-Earning Women*.

30. Pathbreaking studies of work cultures include David Montgomery, *Workers' Control in America* (Cambridge, Eng., 1979); Susan Porter Benson, "The Customers Ain't God"; Barbara Melosh, *'The Physicians' Hand': Work Culture and Conflict in American Nursing* (Philadelphia, 1982). See also Karen Brodkin Sacks and Dorothy Remy, eds., *My Troubles Are Going to Have Trouble with Me* (New Brunswick, N.J., 1984), pp. 193–263.

31. Benson, "The Customers Ain't God"; Mary Bularzik, "Sexual Ha-

rassment at the Workplace, Historical Notes," in *Workers' Struggles, Past and Present*, ed. James Green (Philadelphia, 1983), pp. 117–135; Amy E. Tanner, "Glimpses at the Mind of a Waitress," *American Journal of Sociology* 13 (July 1907): 50; Van Kleeck, *Women in the Bookbinding Trade*, p. 83.

32. Mary Gay Humphreys, "The New York Working Girl," *Scribner's* 20 (Oct. 1896): 505; tape II-30, Immigrant Labor History Collection.

33. Dorothy Richardson, *The Long Day: The Story of a New York Working Girl* (1905) in *Women at Work*, ed. William L. O'Neill (New York, 1972), pp. 105–106. Although colored by middle-class moralisms, Dorothy Richardson's autobiographical novel gives a particularly rich portrait of young, unskilled female wage-earners' interactions in the workplace.

34. Taplin, "Training for Store Efficiency," p. 2; MacLean, *Wage-Earning Women*, p. 35; Bessie and Marie Van Vorst, *The Woman Who Toils* (New York, 1903), p. 25.

35. Conference on Welfare Work at Chicago Commons, Minutes of Seventh Meeting, 15 May 1906, p. 3, Box 121, Welfare Conferences, National Civic Federation Papers.

36. New York Factory Investigating Commission, *Fourth Report*, vol. 4, p. 1588; Anthony, *Mothers Who Must Earn*, p. 51.

37. Department Store Study, *Civic Federation Review*, galley 20B, box 116, Department Store Subject File, National Civic Federation Papers; Clark and Wyatt, *Making Both Ends Meet*, p. 184; Richardson, *Long Day*, pp. 96–97.

38. Lillian W. Betts, "Tenement-House Life and Recreation," *Outlook* 61 (11 Feb. 1899): 365.

39. Tapes I-51 (side B) and I-132 (side A), Immigrant Labor History Collection.

40. *Thought and Work*, Dec. 1903, p. 9; Jan. 1904, pp. 10, 15; and Jan. 1905, pp. 1, 3; Department Store Study, draft typescript, p. 38, box 116, Department Store Subject File, National Civic Federation Papers.

41. Tanner, "Glimpses," p. 52; Clark and Wyatt, *Making Both Ends Meet*, pp. 187–188; see also Richardson, *Long Day*, pp. 94–95.

42. Tape I-59 (side A), Immigrant Labor History Collection.

43. *Thought and Work*, June 1903, p. 7; Sept. 1904, p. 5; Jan. 1904, pp. 10, 15; 15 April 1904, p. 6; Nov. 1904, p. 5; April 1905, p. 11; and Jan. 1905, p. 11.

44. *Thought and Work*, Feb. 1905, p. 1.

45. Donovan, *Woman Who Waits*, pp. 20, 26, 80–81; Clark and Wyatt, *Making Both Ends Meet*, p. 188.

46. Committee of Fourteen in New York City, *Department Store Investi-*

gation: Report of the Sub-committee (New York, 1915), p. 10. See also Committee of Fourteen in New York City, *Annual Report* (New York, 1914), p. 40.

47. "Report of the Commission on Social Morality from the Christian Standpoint, Made to the Fourth Biennial Convention of the Young Women's Christian Associations of the U.S.A., 1913," Pamphlets on Marriage and Family Relations, Archives of the National Board of the Young Women's Christian Association of the U.S.A., New York City; Committee of Fourteen, *Department Store Investigation*, p. 10. Cf. Sharon Hartman Strom, "Italian American Women and Their Daughters in Rhode Island: The Adolescence of Two Generations, 1900–1950," in *The Italian Immigrant Woman in North America*, ed. Betty Boyd Caroli et al. (Toronto, 1978), p. 194, in which one informant explained: "You found out about sex through the shop where you worked. The mother don't tell you nothing. The married women would put us wise."

48. New York State Bureau of Labor Statistics, *Second Annual Report* (Albany, N.Y., 1884), pp. 153, 158. Examples of sexual harassment abound; see, New York Bureau of Labor Statistics, *Third Annual Report* (1885), pp. 150–151; Clara E. Laughlin, *The Work-a-Day Girl: A Study of Some Present-day Conditions* (New York, 1913), p. 112; Richardson, *Long Day*, p. 260; U.S. Industrial Commission, *Report of the Industrial Commission on the Relations and Conditions of Capital and Labor Employed in Manufacturing and General Business*, vol. 7 (Washington, D.C., 1901), pp. 389–390. See also Bularzik, "Sexual Harassment."

49. Committee of Fourteen in New York City, *Department Store Investigation*, p. 10; U.S. Industrial Commission, *Report*, vol. 7, p. 59.

50. Wage differentials in New York City according to sex may be seen in U.S. Bureau of the Census, *Report on Manufacturing Industries in the U.S. at the Eleventh Census* (Washington, D.C., 1895), pp. 390–407, 708–710; New York Factory Investigating Commission, *Fourth Report*, vol. 4, pp. 1507–1511, 1081, and vol. 1, pp. 35–36. Estimates for the living wage of self-supporting girls varied; see, for example, Clark and Wyatt, *Making Both Ends Meet*, p. 8.

51. The exact percentage of women living alone varies in different reports. U.S. Senate, *Report on the Condition of Woman and Child Wage-Earners in the United States, Vol. 5: Wage-Earning Women in Stores and Factories* (S. 645, 61st Cong., 2d sess.; Washington, D.C., 1910), p. 15, indicates that 87 percent of factory workers and 92 percent of retail clerks lived at home. Cf. New York Factory Investigating Commission, *Fourth Report*, vol. 5, p. 2561, which stated that 85 percent of women wage-earners lived with families, friends, or relatives. For testimony on women's in-

ability to live alone on low wages, see New York Bureau of Labor Statistics, *Fourteenth Annual Report* (1896), pp. 913–945. For a fictional account of the controversy surrounding a young woman who chooses to live alone, see Anzia Yezierska, *Bread Givers* (1925; rpt. New York, 1975).

52. New York Factory Investigating Commission, *Fourth Report*, vol. 4, p. 1685. For an excellent discussion of the survival strategies of self-supporting women, see Joanne J. Meyerowitz, "Holding Their Own: Working Women Apart from Family in Chicago, 1880–1930" (Ph.D. diss., Stanford University, 1983).

53. Odencrantz, *Italian Women in Industry*, p. 235; Lillian D. Wald, *The House on Henry Street* (1915; rpt. New York, 1971), p. 211; New York Factory Investigating Commission, *Fourth Report*, vol. 4, pp. 1675–1692; Clark and Wyatt, *Making Both Ends Meet*, p. 10.

54. Clark and Wyatt, *Making Both Ends Meet*, pp. 97, 103–104, 108.

55. Ruth S. True, *The Neglected Girl* (New York, 1914), p. 59; New York Factory Investigating Commission, *Fourth Report*, vol. 4, pp. 1512–1513; tape II-30 (side A), Immigrant Labor History Collection.

56. "Salesgirl's Story," p. 1818; New York Factory Investigating Commission, *Fourth Report*, vol. 4, p. 1576, 1585; Clark and Wyatt, *Making Both Ends Meet*, p. 189.

57. New York Factory Investigating Commission, *Fourth Report*, vol. 4, pp. 1698, 1678 (quotations), 1577, 1675–1678, 1695–1714.

58. Tape I-132, Immigrant Labor History Collection.

59. New York Factory Investigating Commission, *Fourth Report*, vol. 4, pp. 1685–1686.

60. New York Factory Investigating Commission, *Fourth Report*, vol. 5, p. 2809; U.S. Industrial Commission, *Report*, vol. 7, p. 59; Laughlin, *Work-a-Day Girl*, pp. 60–61; "Salesgirl's Story," p. 1821; Clark and Wyatt, *Making Both Ends Meet*, p. 28.

61. Consumer's League, *Behind the Scenes*, p. 24; Donovan, *Woman Who Waits*, p. 42.

Chapter Three

1. See, e.g., Paula S. Fass, *The Damned and the Beautiful: American Youth in the 1920's* (New York, 1977).

2. George E. Bevans, *How Workingmen Spend Their Spare Time* (New York, 1913), pp. 27, 31, 33, 35; University Settlement Society of New York, *Report* (New York, 1896), pp. 10–11. On young men's organizations in the

Victorian era, see Joseph F. Kett, *Rites of Passage: Adolescence in America, 1790 to the Present* (New York, 1977), pp. 87–93.

3. Christine Stansell, "Women, Children and the Uses of the Streets: Class and Gender Conflict in New York City, 1850–1860," *Feminist Studies* 8 (Summer 1982): 309–335. Other uses of the street are discussed in Susan G. Davis, "The Popular Uses of Public Spaces in Philadelphia, 1800–1850," paper presented at American Studies Association Biennial Meeting, Philadelphia, 1983; Charles Leinenweber, "Socialists in the Streets: The New York Socialist Party in Working Class Neighborhoods, 1908–1918," *Science and Society* 41 (Summer 1977): 152–177.

4. [Russell Sage Foundation,] *Boyhood and Lawlessness* (New York, 1914); John Collier and Edward M. Barrows, *The City Where Crime Is Play* (New York, Jan. 1914); Samuel Chotzinoff, *A Lost Paradise* (New York, 1955), pp. 85–88; Martin E. Dann, "'Little Citizens': Working Class and Immigrant Childhood in New York City, 1890–1915" (Ph.D. diss., City University of New York, 1978); Frederick A. King, "Influences in Street Life," in University Settlement Society of New York, *Report* (New York, 1900), pp. 29–32.

5. Irving Howe and Kenneth Libo, *How We Lived: A Documentary History of Immigrant Jews in America* (New York, 1979), p. 54.

6. Collier and Barrows, *City Where Crime Is Play*, p. 20; John W. Martin, "Social Life in the Street," in University Settlement Society of New York, *Report* (New York, 1899), p. 23; King, "Street Life," p. 29.

7. Percy Stickney Grant, "Children's Street Games," *Survey* 23 (13 Nov. 1909): 235; Cary Goodman, *Choosing Sides: Playground and Street Life on the Lower East Side* (New York, 1979).

8. Tape IV-12 (side B), New York City Immigrant Labor History Collection of the City College Oral History Project, Robert F. Wagner Archives, Tamiment Institute Library, New York University; also [Russell Sage Foundation,] *Boyhood and Lawlessness*, pp. 155–156; Ruth S. True, *The Neglected Girl* (New York, 1914), pp. 62–63. See also Paul Corrigan, "Doing Nothing," in *Resistance Through Rituals: Youth Subcultures in Post-War Britain*, ed. Stuart Hall and Tony Jefferson (London, 1976), pp. 103–105.

9. True, *Neglected Girl*, pp. 66–67; Transcript K-3, p. 13, Immigrant Labor History Collection; King, "Street Life," p. 32.

10. *Civic Journal* 1, no. 1 (9 Oct. 1909): 5; Herbert Asbury, *The Gangs of New York* (1927; rpt. New York, 1970), pp. 268–269; J. G. Phelps Stokes, "Hartley House and Social Reform," New York *Times*, 27 June 1897, Illustrated Magazine, p. 4; Benjamin Reich, "A New Social Center: The Candy Store as a Social Influence," in University Settlement Society of New York, *Report* (1899), p. 32; Michael M. Davis, Jr., *The Exploitation of Pleasure: A Study of Commercial Recreations in New York City* (New York, n.d.), p. 9;

Martin, "Social Life in the Street," p. 23; John H. Mariano, *The Second Generation of Italians in New York City* (Boston, 1921), pp. 140-141.

11. *University Settlement Studies* 2, no. 2 (1906): 20.

12. Tape I-51 (side B), Immigrant Labor History Collection; Kehillah of New York City, ed., *The Jewish Communal Register of New York City, 1917–1918* (New York, 1918).

13. "Mutual Aid Associations," New York State Factory Investigating Commission, *Fourth Report Transmitted to Legislature, Feb. 15, 1915* (S. Doc. no. 43; Albany, N.Y., 1915), vol. 2, pp. 170–174, and vol. 4, p. 1572; "A Salesgirl's Story," *Independent* 54 (July 1902): 1819.

14. New York State Legislature, Special Committee of the Assembly Appointed to Investigate the Condition of Female Labor in the City of New York, *Report and Testimony* (Albany, N.Y., 1896), vol. 1, p. 85.

15. Tapes I-1 (transcript) and I-117 (side B), Immigrant Labor History Collection; Asbury, *Gangs*, p. 269; Belle L. Mead, "The Social Pleasures of East Side Jews," (M.A. thesis, Columbia University, 1904), p. 6; *University Settlement Studies* 2, no. 2 (1906): 20; New York State Bureau of Labor Statistics, *Eighteenth Annual Report* (Albany, N.Y., 1900), p. 294.

16. Tape I-117 (side B), Immigrant Labor History Collection.

17. Tape IV-12 (side A), Immigrant Labor History Collection.

18. Samuel Lewenkrohn, "Schadchen's Luck," *Settlement Journal* 2, no. 2 (Dec. 1905): 1–3. See also *Civic Journal* 1, no. 1 (9 Oct. 1909): 5.

19. Belle Lindner Israels, "The Way of the Girl," *Survey* 22 (3 July 1909): 486.

20. *Thought and Work*, May 1906, p. 8; see also March 1906, p. 8; July 1905, p. 4; and Aug. 1905, p. 11.

21. Martin, "Social Life in the Street," p. 23; King, "Street Life," p. 30. See also New York Bureau of Labor Statistics, *Eighteenth Annual Report*, p. 294; Investigator's Report, Andrew Murphy (saloon), 806 Eighth Ave., 17 May 1917, Records of the Committee of Fourteen, Rare Books and Manuscripts Division, New York Public Library, Astor, Lenox and Tilden Foundations (hereafter cited as COF).

22. Mary Augusta LaSelle, *The Young Woman Worker* (Boston, 1914), pp. 91, 89; Helen S. Campbell, *Prisoners of Poverty: Women Wage-Earners, Their Trades and Their Lives* (1887; rpt. Westport, Conn., 1970), p. 175; Helen Campbell et al., *Darkness and Daylight, or Lights and Shadows of New York Life* (Hartford, Conn., 1897), p. 257.

23. Lillian W. Betts, *The Leaven in a Great City* (New York, 1902), p. 258; see also Jonathan Prude, "The Uniform of Labor: Some Thoughts on the Changing Meaning of Occupational Costume in Nineteenth Century America" (unpublished paper).

24. Sue Ainslie Clark and Edith Wyatt, *Making Book Ends Meet: The*

Income and Outlay of New York Working Girls (New York, 1911), p. 143; New York Factory Investigating Commission, *Fourth Report,* vol. 4, p. 1528.

25. Tape I-132 (side A), Immigrant Labor History Collection. For the male case, see Abraham Cahan, *The Rise of David Levinsky* (1917; rpt. New York, 1960), p. 101.

26. [New York] State Charities Aid Association, Standing Committee on the Elevation of the Poor in Their Homes, *Moral Elevation of Girls: Suggestions Relating to Preventive Work* (New York, 1885), p. 21. See also the conflicts within working girls' clubs, Chapter 7.

27. Mary Gay Humphreys, "The New York Working Girl," *Scribner's* 20 (Oct. 1896): 504, 502–503.

28. Sadie Frowne, "The Story of a Sweatshop Girl," in *Workers Speak: Self Portraits,* ed. Leon Stein and Philip Taft (New York, 1971), p. 118; Clara E. Laughlin, *The Work-a-Day Girl: A Study of Some Present-day Conditions* (New York, 1913), pp. 14, 136. My thinking about style has been shaped by the analyses in Hall and Jefferson, eds., *Resistance Through Rituals.* For a discussion of the changing definitions of beauty, see Lois Banner, *American Beauty* (New York, 1983).

29. Tape II-31 (side A), Immigrant Labor History Collection.

30. Tape I-132 (side A), Immigrant Labor History Collection.

31. "What It Means to Be a Department-Store Girl as Told by the Girl Herself," *Ladies Home Journal* 30 (June 1913): 8. See also "Salesgirl's Story," p. 1821.

32. Jacob A. Riis, "The Children of the Poor," *Scribner's* 11 (May 1892): 551–552; Dorothy Richardson, *The Long Day: The Story of a New York Working Girl* (1905), in *Women at Work,* ed. William L. O'Neill (New York, 1972), p. 97; Rollin L. Hartt, *The People at Play* (Boston, 1909), p. 197.

33. Ruth Rosen, *The Lost Sisterhood: Prostitution in America, 1900–1918* (Baltimore and London, 1982), p. 107.

34. Lillian D. Wald, *The House on Henry Street* (1915; rpt. New York, 1971), p. 190.

35. Howe and Libo, *How We Lived,* p. 132.

36. New York Factory Investigating Commission, *Fourth Report,* vol. 4, p. 1491–1494. For an extended discussion of parent-daughter relations among immigrant families, see Elizabeth Ewen, "Immigrant Women in the Land of Dollars, 1890–1920" (Ph.D. diss., State University of New York at Stony Brook, 1979), pp. 276–377.

37. New York Factory Investigating Commission, *Fourth Report,* vol. 5, p. 2650.

38. U.S. Bureau of Labor, *Working Women in Large Cities: Fourth An-*

nual Report of the Commissioner of Labor, 1888 (Washington, D.C., 1889), pp. 340–342; U.S. Senate, *Report on the Condition of Woman and Child Wage-Earners in the United States, Vol. 5: Wage-Earning Women in Stores and Factories* (S. 645, 61st Cong., 2d sess.; Washington, D.C., 1910), p. 15; New York Factory Investigating Commission, *Fourth Report*, vol. 5, p. 2562.

39. Mary Van Kleeck, *Artificial Flower-Makers.* (New York, 1913), p. 235; tape IV-12 (side A), Immigrant Labor History Collection; Louise Bolard More, *Wage-Earners' Budgets: A Study of Standards and Costs of Living in New York City* (New York, 1907), p. 87; Louise C. Odencrantz, *Italian Women in Industry: A Study of Conditions in New York City* (New York, 1919), p. 176.

40. U.S. Bureau of Labor, *Working Women in Large Cities*, pp. 340–342; also Dann, "Little Citizens," pp. 235–236; Riis, "Children of the Poor," p. 552.

41. Mabel Hurd Willett, *The Employment of Women in the Clothing Trades* (Studies in History, Economics and Public Law, vol. 16, no. 2; New York, 1902), pp. 87–88; Clark and Wyatt, *Making Both Ends Meet*, p. 61.

42. Annie M. MacLean, *Wage-Earning Women* (New York, 1910), p. 52.

43. Robert Coit Chapin, *The Standard of Living Among Workingmen's Families in New York City* (New York, 1909), p. 210n; tapes II-10, II-11, and II-30, Immigrant Labor History Collection; see also Virginia Yans-McLaughlin, *Family and Community: Italian Immigrants in Buffalo, 1880–1930* (Ithaca, N.Y., 1977).

44. True, *Neglected Girl*, pp. 54–55.

45. Betts, *Leaven*, pp. 215, 140; Lillian W. Betts, "Tenement-House Life and Recreation," *Outlook* 61 (11 Feb. 1899): 365; Robert A. Woods and Albert J. Kennedy, *Young Working Girls: A Summary of Evidence from Two Thousand Social Workers* (Boston, 1913), p. 61.

46. Tape IV-14 (side B), Immigrant Labor History Collection.

47. Investigator's Report, Excelsior Cafe, 306 Eighth Avenue, 21 Dec. 1916, COF; tapes II-11 (side A), II-2 and II-25, Immigrant Labor History Collection; Wald, *House on Henry Street*, p. 197.

48. Tape II-38 (side A), Immigrant Labor History Collection.

49. Investigator's Report, Lexington Cafe, 150 E. 116th St., 27 Jan. 1917, COF.

50. Chotzinoff, *Lost Paradise*, p. 81. On the new locations of urban courtship, see Belle Lindner Israels, "Diverting a Pastime," *Leslie's Weekly* 113 (27 July 1911): 94; Clark and Wyatt, *Making Both Ends Meet*, p. 21; Betts, "Tenement-House Life," p. 366. Leslie Woodcock Tentler elaborates this argument in *Wage-Earning Women: Industrial Work and Family Life in the*

United States, 1900–1930 (New York, 1979), pp. 110–113. On housing conditions, see Frank Hatch Streightoff, *The Standard of Living Among the Industrial People of America* (Boston, 1911), p. 70; Robert W. DeForest and Lawrence Veiller, eds., *The Tenement House Problem* (New York, 1903), vol. 1, p. 417; Tenement House Department of the City of New York, *First Report, Jan. 1, 1902–July 1, 1903,* (New York, 1903), vol. 1, pp. 132–138.

51. Wald, *House on Henry Street,* p. 197; Frowne, "Sweatshop Girl," p. 118; Woods and Kennedy, *Young Working Girls,* pp. 36–37; Betts, *Leaven,* p. 140.

52. Howe and Libo, *How We Lived,* p. 147; Isaac Metzker, ed., *A Bintel Brief* (New York, 1972), p. 14. The rise of the consumer culture is discussed in Stuart Ewen, *Captains of Consciousness: Advertising and the Social Roots of the Consumer Culture* (New York, 1976); Richard Wightman Fox and T. J. Jackson Lears, eds., *The Culture of Consumption* (New York, 1983).

53. Mead, "Social Pleasures," pp. 7, 27.

54. Esther Packard, *A Study of Living Conditions of Self-Supporting Women in New York City* (New York, 1915), p. 40.

55. Willett, *Women in the Clothing Trades,* pp. 92–93; New York Factory Investigating Commission, *Fourth Report,* vol. 4, pp. 1700–1701, and vol. 5, p. 2653; Odencrantz, *Italian Women in Industry,* p. 218.

56. Odencrantz, *Italian Women in Industry,* p. 222.

57. Packard, *Self-Supporting Women,* pp. 22–23.

58. *Ibid.,* p. 72.

59. *Ibid.,* pp. 78, 59.

60. Mary Gay Humphreys, "Women Bachelors in New York," *Scribner's* 20 (Nov. 1896): 632, 634, 630.

61. Transcript K-3, p. 14, and tape I-109 (transcript), Immigrant Labor History Collection.

62. Packard, *Self-Supporting Women,* pp. 51, 52 (quote), 72, 84–85; U.S. Bureau of Labor, *Boarding Homes and Clubs for Working Women,* by Mary S. Fergusson (Bulletin no. 15; Washington, D.C., 1898), p. 142; Mary K. Maule, "What Is a Shopgirl's Life?" *World's Work* 14 (Sept. 1907): 9314; U.S. Department of Labor, *Working Women in Large Cities,* p. 32; Clark and Wyatt, *Making Both Ends Meet,* p. 21.

63. Mary Van Kleeck, *Women in the Bookbinding Trade* (New York, 1913), p. 152; Consumer's League of New York City, *Behind the Scenes in a Restaurant: A Study of 1017 Women Restaurant Employees* (n.p., 1916), p. 16; Clark and Wyatt, *Making Both Ends Meet,* p. 132.

64. Van Kleeck, *Women in the Bookbinding Trade,* p. 154.

65. "Letter from a Working Girl," in New York State Bureau of Labor Statistics, *Third Annual Report* (Albany, N.Y., 1885), p. 158; Thomas H.

Russell, *The Girl's Fight for a Living* (Chicago, 1913), p. 163; New York Factory Investigating Commission, *Fourth Report*, vol. 4, p. 1700.

Chapter Four

1. Belle Lindner Israels, "The Way of the Girl," *Survey* 22 (3 July 1909): 494; Michael M. Davis, Jr., *The Exploitation of Pleasure: A Study of Commercial Recreations in New York City* (New York, n.d.), p. 15, estimated over one hundred dance halls in Manhattan alone.

2. For women's attendance, see Davis, *Exploitation of Pleasure*, pp. 12–13; John M. Oskison, "Public Halls of the East Side," in University Settlement Society of New York, *Report* (New York, 1899), p. 39; Hutchins Hapgood, *Types from City Streets* (New York, 1910), pp. 134–135; A. S. Gilbert to James G. Wallace, 23 Nov. 1912, p. 5, Box 28, Parks and Playgrounds Correspondence, Lillian D. Wald Collection, Rare Book and Manuscript Library, Columbia University, New York; Helen Campbell et al., *Darkness and Daylight, or Lights and Shadows of New York Life* (Hartford, Conn., 1897), p. 230. On dancing's popularity with men, see George E. Bevans, *How Workingmen Spend Their Spare Time* (New York, 1913), pp. 27, 33; movies and theaters were the only forms of commercial amusement more popular among young men aged seventeen to twenty-four.

3. Oskison, "Public Halls," p. 38.

4. Ruth S. True, *The Neglected Girl* (New York, 1914), p. 72; Oskison, "Public Halls," pp. 39–40.

5. Belle L. Mead, "The Social Pleasures of East Side Jews" (M.A. thesis, Columbia University, 1904),p. 6; Verne M. Bovie, "The Public Dance Halls of the Lower East Side," in University Settlement Society of New York, *Report* (New York, 1901), pp. 31–32.

6. Elsa G. Herzfeld, *Family Monographs: The History of Twenty-four Families Living in the Middle West Side of New York City* (New York, 1905), p. 18; Thomas Jesse Jones, *Sociology of a New York City Block* (Studies in History, Economics and Public Law, vol. 21, no. 2; New York, 1904), p. 45; Israels, "Way of the Girl," p. 494; "Report of Murray Hill Committee on Dance Halls," *Yearbook of the Women's Municipal League*, Nov. 1911, pp. 20–21.

7. See the useful discussion in Anya Peterson Royce, *The Anthropology of Dance* (Bloomington, Ind., 1977), p. 98; Frances Rust, *Dance in Society* (London, 1969).

8. Belle Lindner Israels, "Diverting a Pastime," *Leslie's Weekly* 113 (27

July 1911): 94, 100; George J. Kneeland, *Commercialized Prostitution in New York City* (New York, 1913), p. 56. The range of dance halls emerges particularly in the individual Investigator's Reports, Records of the Committee of Fourteen, Rare Books and Manuscripts Division, New York Public Library, Astor, Lenox and Tilden Foundations (hereafter cited as COF).

9. Bovie, "Public Dance Halls," p. 32; Herzfeld, *Family Monographs*, pp. 17–18; True, *Neglected Girl*, pp. 68–69.

10. Oskison, "Public Halls," p. 39. See also Hapgood, *Types from City Streets*, p. 135; Trinity Church Men's Committee, *A Social Survey of the Washington Street District of New York City* (n.p., Oct. 1914), p. 48.

11. Ruth I. Austin, "Teaching English to Our Foreign Friends, Pt. I: Among the Bohemians," *Life and Labor* 1 (Sept. 1911): 261.

12. Davis, *Exploitation of Pleasure*, p. 15.

13. Oskison, "Public Halls," p. 40.

14. Investigator's Report, Manhattan Casino, 2926 Eighth Avenue, 30 June 1919, COF.

15. Oskison, "Public Halls," pp. 39–40; tapes I-6 (side B) and IV-12 (side A), New York City Immigrant Labor History Collection of the City College Oral History Project, Robert F. Wagner Archives, Tamiment Institute Library, New York University; True, *Neglected Girl*, pp. 68–69.

16. Bovie, "Public Dance Halls," p. 32; "Modern industry has produced . . . ," n.d., p. 8, in Box 7, Community Center Work, People's Institute Collection, Rare Books and Manuscripts Division, New York Public Library, Astor, Lenox and Tilden Foundations; Israels, "Diverting a Pastime," p. 100; Davis, *Exploitation of Pleasure*, pp. 15–16.

17. Mead, "Social Pleasures," p. 6.

18. *Ibid.*

19. Herzfeld, *Family Monographs*, p. 17; Bovie, "Public Dance Halls," pp. 32–33.

20. Gilbert to Wallace, 23 Nov. 1912, p. 6. See also Kneeland, *Commercialized Prostitution*, p. 56.

21. Investigator's Report, Manhattan Casino, 26 May 1917, COF.

22. *Trow Business Directory of New York City* (New York, 1895), pp. 449–450; *Trow Business Directory of New York City* (New York, 1910), pp. 446–447; Oskison, "Public Halls," p. 39.

23. Trinity Church Men's Committee, *Social Survey*, p. 48.

24. Bovie, "Public Dance Halls," p. 32; Oskison, "Public Halls," p. 39. See also Louise de Koven Bowen, *The Public Dance Halls of Chicago* (Chicago, 1917).

25. Israels, "Way of the Girl," p. 496; Davis, *Exploitation of Pleasure*, p. 16.

26. Investigator's Report, Central Casino, 103/107 McCombs Place, 25 Jan. 1917, COF.

27. Maria Ward Lambin, *Report of the Advisory Dance Hall Committee of the Women's City Club and the City Recreation Committee* (New York, 1924), pp. 1, 6–8; "Suggestions of Mrs. Orrin S. Goan," box 120, Recreation, National Civic Federation Papers, Rare Books and Manuscripts Division, New York Public Library, Astor, Lenox and Tilden Foundations.

28. Investigator's Reports, Manhattan Casino, 10 March 1917, and Park View Hotel, 2137/2139 Boston Road, 18 March 1917, COF.

29. Mathew Hale Smith, *Sunshine and Shadow in New York* (Hartford, Conn., 1869), pp. 228, 435–441, 632; William Sanger, *History of Prostitution* (New York, 1869), p. 524.

30. Oskison, "Public Halls," p. 38; Davis, *Exploitation of Pleasure*, pp. 13, 15; Israels, "Way of the Girl," p. 494, and "Diverting a Pastime," p. 94.

31. Tape I-59 (side B), Immigrant Labor History Collection.

32. Tape I-51 (side B), Immigrant Labor History Collection.

33. Hapgood, *Types from City Streets*, pp. 134–135; True, *Neglected Girl*, pp. 69–72; Dorothy Richardson, *The Long Day: The Story of a New York Working Girl* (1905), in *Women at Work*, ed. William L. O'Neill (New York, 1972), pp. 94–95.

34. Herzfeld, *Family Monographs*, p. 18; Lillian W. Betts, *The Leaven in a Great City* (New York, 1902), p. 142.

35. Israels, "Diverting a Pastime," p. 94. On the atmosphere of saloon-dance halls, see Campbell et al., *Darkness and Daylight*, p. 230.

36. Investigator's Report, Excelsior Cafe, 306 Eighth Avenue, 16 Dec. 1916, COF.

37. Ruth Rosen, *The Lost Sisterhood: Prostitution in America, 1900–1918* (Baltimore and London, 1982), pp. 112–136.

38. Investigator's Report, Remey's, 917 Eighth Avenue, 11 Feb. 1917, COF.

39. Investigator's Report, Weimann's, 1422 St. Nicholas Ave., 11 Feb. 1917, COF.

40. Investigator's Report, Remey's, 11 Feb. 1917, COF.

41. Investigator's Report, Jim Coffey's, 2923 Eighth Avenue, 17 Feb. 1917, COF.

42. Investigator's Report, Manhattan Casino, 19 Aug. 1917, COF.

43. Kneeland, *Commercialized Prostitution*, p. 68; Louise De Koven Bowen, "Dance Halls," *Survey* 26 (3 June 1911): 384.

44. "Report of Murray Hill Committee," p. 21; see also Belle Lindner Israels, "The Dance Problem," *Proceedings of the National Conference of Charities and Corrections, 1912* (Fort Wayne, Ind., 1912), p. 144.

45. Herzfeld, *Family Monographs*, p. 18.

46. Julian Ralph, "Coney Island," *Scribner's* 20 (July 1896): 18.

47. [Mrs. Edna Witherspoon], *The Perfect Art of Modern Dancing* (London and New York, 1894), pp. 19–20.

48. Richard Henry Edwards, *Popular Amusements* (New York, 1915); see also Bovie, "Public Dance Halls," p. 33.

49. Bowen, *Public Dance Halls of Chicago*, p. 4; Mathew S. Hughes, *Dancing and the Public Schools* (New York, 1917), p. 20. For a superb analysis of the middle-class dance craze, see Lewis A. Erenberg, *Steppin' Out: New York Nightlife and the Transformation of American Culture, 1890–1930* (Westport, Conn., 1981), pp. 146–175.

50. Edwards, *Popular Amusements*, p. 79; Bowen, *Public Dance Halls of Chicago*, p. 5.

51. Israels, "Dance Problem," p. 144. See also "Turkey Trot and Tango—A Disease or a Remedy?" *Current Opinion* 55 (Sept. 1913): 187.

52. Committee on Amusements and Vacation Resources of Working Girls, two-page circular, box 28, Parks and Playgrounds Correspondence, Wald Collection, Columbia University. See also Julian Street, *Welcome to Our City* (New York, 1913), pp. 9–10; Bovie, "Public Dance Halls," p. 33.

53. Street, *Welcome to Our City*, p. 169.

54. Erenberg, *Steppin' Out*, pp. 146–175; see also James R. McGovern, "The American Woman's Pre-World War I Freedom in Manners and Morals," *Journal of American History* 55 (Sept. 1968): 315–333; Henry F. May, *The End of American Innocence* (Chicago, 1959), pp. 334–347.

55. Vernon and Irene Castle, *Modern Dancing* (New York, 1914), foreword.

56. Frank Leslie Clendenen, *Dance Mad; or the Dances of the Day* (St. Louis, 1914), p. 8; J. S. Hopkins, *The Tango and Other Up-to-Date Dances* (Chicago, 1914), p. 39. See also Troy and Margaret West Kinney, *Social Dancing of Today* (New York, 1914), pp. 2–3.

57. Clendenen, *Dance Mad*, p. 8.

58. Castle and Castle, *Modern Dancing*, foreword.

59. Investigator's Report, Ritz Cabaret, 2114/2118 Seventh Avenue, 9 June 1917, COF.

60. "Welfare Inspector at Society Dance," New York *Times* clipping (n.d.), Subject Papers, Policies Concerning Sex Motion Pictures, 1912, 1913, National Board of Review of Motion Pictures Collection, Rare Books and Manuscripts Division, New York Public Library, Astor, Lenox and Tilden Foundations (my emphasis).

61. Investigator's Report, Parisien, 945 Eighth Avenue, 18 May 1917, p. 2, COF.

62. Investigator's Report, Central Casino, 25 Jan. 1917, COF.

63. Investigator's Report, Park View Hotel, 28 April 1917, COF.

64. Erenberg, *Steppin' Out,* pp. 135–137. On the cultural ideal of companionate relationships, see Christina Simmons, "'Marriage in the Modern Manner': Sexual Radicalism and Reform in America, 1914–1941" (Ph.D. diss., Brown University, 1982), pp. 105–149.

65. Investigator's Report, Princess Cafe, 1203 Broadway, 1 Jan. 1917, COF.

66. Gilbert to Wallace, 23 Nov. 1912, p. 7. See also Investigator's Report, Excelsior Cafe, 21 Dec. 1916, COF; Kneeland, *Commercialized Prostitution,* p. 70.

67. Investigator's Report, Manhattan Casino, 17 Feb. 1917, COF.

68. Israels, "Diverting a Pastime," p. 95. On the waiter's role, see, for example, Investigator's Report, Weimann's, 27 Jan. 1917, COF.

69. Israels, "Dance Problem," p. 141; Investigator's Report, Manhattan Casino, 19 Aug. 1917, COF; True, *Neglected Girl,* pp. 70, 72; Herzfeld, *Family Monographs,* p. 18.

70. Investigator's Report, La Kuenstler Klause, 1490 Third Avenue, 19 Jan. 1917, COF.

71. Hapgood, *Types from City Streets,* pp. 134–135. See also Rollin L. Hartt, *The People at Play* (Boston, 1909), p. 200.

72. True, *Neglected Girl,* p. 70.

73. Israels, "Way of the Girl," p. 489. See also Oskison, "Public Halls," pp. 39–40.

74. Bowen, "Dance Halls," p. 385.

75. True, *Neglected Girl,* pp. 54–55.

76. Bowen, *Public Dance Halls of Chicago,* p. 7; Herzfeld, *Family Monographs,* p. 18; J. G. Phelps Stokes, "Hartley House and Social Reform," New York *Times,* 27 June 1897, Illustrated Magazine, p. 4.

77. Kneeland, *Commercialized Prostitution,* p. 70; Israels, "Diverting a Pastime," p. 100; Juvenile Protective Agency, Chicago, *Our Most Popular Recreation Controlled by the Liquor Interests: A Study of Public Dance Halls* (Chicago, 1911).

78. Israels, "Diverting a Pastime," p. 100.

79. Investigator's Report, Grand Union Hotel, 1815–1817 Park Ave., 15 June 1917, COF.

80. Investigator's Reports, Remey's, 1 Jan. 1917; Princess Cafe, 1 Jan. 1917, COF. See also Investigator's Report, Remey's, 9 March 1917, COF; Frank Streightoff, "Eight Dollars a Week," *Consumer's League Bulletin* 4 (Nov. 1914): 38.

81. "A Salesgirl's Story," *Independent* 54 (July 1902): 1821; Betts,

Leaven, pp. 251–252; Robert A. Woods and Albert J. Kennedy, *Young Working Girls: A Summary of Evidence from Two Thousand Social Workers* (Boston, 1913), pp. 8, 106.

82. New York State Factory Investigating Commission, *Fourth Report Transmitted to Legislature, Feb. 15, 1915* (S. Doc. no. 43; Albany, N.Y., 1915), vol. 4, pp. 1585–1586; Clara E. Laughlin, *The Work-a-Day Girl: A Study of Some Present-day Conditions* (New York, 1913), p. 50.

83. Betts, *Leaven*, pp. 81, 219; True, *Neglected Girl*, p. 69.

84. Woods and Kennedy, *Young Working Girls*, p. 87.

85. *Ibid.*, p. 85.

86. "Memoranda on Vice Problem: IV. Statement of George J. Kneeland," New York Factory Investigating Commission, *Fourth Report*, vol. 1, p. 403; Frances R. Donovan, *The Woman Who Waits* (1920; rpt. New York, 1974), p. 71. See also Committee of Fourteen in New York City, *Annual Report* (New York, 1917), p. 15, and *Annual Report* (New York, 1918), p. 32; Woods and Kennedy, *Young Working Girls*, p. 85. Cf. occasional prostitution, discussed in U.S. Senate, *Report on the Condition of Woman and Child Wage-Earners in the United States, Vol. 15: Relation between Occupation and Criminality in Women* (S. 645, 61st Cong., 2d sess.; Washington, D.C., 1911), p. 83; Laughlin, *Work-a-Day Girl*, pp. 51–52.

87. Investigator's Reports, Manhattan Casino, 17 Feb. 1917; Clare Hotel and Palm Garden/McNamara's, 2150 Eighth Avenue, 12 Jan. 1917; La Kuenstler Klause, 19 Jan. 1917; Bobby More's, 252 W. 31st St., 3 Feb. 1917, COF.

88. Investigator's Reports, Manhattan Casino, 26 May 1917; Clare Hotel and Palm Garden/McNamara's, 12 Jan. 1917, COF; see also Investigator's Reports, Manhattan Casino, 10 March 1917; La Kuentsler Klause, 19 Jan. 1917, COF.

89. Laughlin, *Work-a-Day Girl*, p. 50; Investigator's Report, Remey's, 23 Dec. 1916, COF; Donovan, *The Woman Who Waits*, p. 55.

90. Investigator's Report, Semprinis, 145 West 50th St., 5 Oct. 1918, COF.

91. True, *Neglected Girl*, p. 60.

92. Investigator's Report, Manhattan Casino, 20 May 1917, COF; Betts, *Leaven*, pp. 205–206. See also Investigator's Report, Excelsior Cafe, 23 Dec. 1916, COF; Israels, "Diverting a Pastime," p. 94; Woods and Kennedy, *Young Working Girls*, pp. 8, 35; Hapgood, *Types from City Streets*, p. 131; Herzfeld, *Family Monographs*, p. 18; Richardson, *Long Day*, p. 66 and passim.

93. True, *Neglected Girl*, p. 61.

94. On middle-class female friendships, see Carroll Smith-Rosenberg,

"The Female World of Love and Ritual: Relations Between Women in Nine-teenth Century America," *Signs* 1 (Autumn 1975): 1–29.

Chapter Five

1. Agnes M., "The True Life Story of a Nurse Girl," in *Workers Speak: Self Portraits,* ed. Leon Stein and Philip Taft (New York, 1971), pp. 103–104.

2. *Ibid.,* p. 104.

3. John Kasson, *Amusing the Million: Coney Island at the Turn of the Century* (New York, 1978), p. 8.

4. [Russell Sage Foundation,] *Boyhood and Lawlessness* (New York, 1914), p. 150; Robert Coit Chapin, *The Standard of Living Among Work-ingmen's Families in New York City* (New York, 1909), pp. 210–211.

5. James McCabe, *Lights and Shadows of New York Life* (Philadelphia, 1872), p. 446.

6. Tapes I-1, I-2 (transcript), and IV-13, New York City Immigrant Labor History Collection of the City College Oral History Project, Robert F. Wagner Archives, Tamiment Institute Library, New York University; New York State Factory Investigating Commission, *Fourth Report Transmitted to Legislature, Feb. 15, 1915* (S. Doc. no. 43; Albany, N.Y., 1915), vol. 4, pp. 1795–1798.

7. Chapin, *Standard of Living,* p. 211.

8. Samuel Chotzinoff, *A Lost Paradise* (New York, 1955), pp. 159–160; Lillian W. Betts, *The Leaven in a Great City* (New York, 1902), pp. 8–9, 58; Hutchins Hapgood, *Types from City Streets* (New York, 1910), p. 62.

9. Timothy Healy to G[ertrude] B[eeks], 24 Aug. 1911, p. 2, box 120, Recreation, National Civic Federation Papers, Rare Books and Manuscripts Division, New York Public Library, Astor, Lenox and Tilden Foundations; see also Mary Gay Humphreys, "The New York Working Girl," *Scribner's* 20 (Oct. 1896): 512–513.

10. McCabe, *Lights and Shadows,* p. 446; New York State Bureau of Labor Statistics, *Eighth Annual Report,* pt. 1 (Albany, N.Y., 1890), pp. 453, 449.

11. William F. Mangels, *The Outdoor Amusement Industry* (New York, 1952), pp. 17–28; Gary Kyriazi, *The Great American Amusement Parks* (Secaucus, N.J., 1976), pp. 15–16; Stanley Nadel, "Kleindeutschland: New York City's Germans, 1845–1880" (Ph.D. diss., Columbia University, 1981), pp. 222–224; George Ellington, *The Women of New York* (New York, 1869), pp. 317–319.

12. Lillian W. Betts, "Tenement-House Life and Recreation," *Outlook* 61 (11 Feb. 1899): 366, and *Leaven,* p. 142; Oliver Pilot and Jo Ransom, *Sodom by the Sea: An Affectionate History of Coney Island* (Garden City, N.Y., 1941), p. 130. For the number of picnic grounds, see *Trow Business Directory of New York City* (New York, 1895).

13. Healy to B[eeks], 24 Aug. 1911, p. 2.

14. J. G. Phelps Stokes, "Hartley House and Social Reform," New York *Times,* 27 June 1897, Illustrated Magazine, p. 4; Belle Lindner Israels, "The Way of the Girl," *Survey* 22 (3 July 1909): 487; Ellington, *Women of New York,* p. 324.

15. Israels, "Way of the Girl," p. 491.

16. Tape IV-12 (side B), Immigrant Labor History Collection.

17. Humphreys, "New York Working Girl," p. 513.

18. Israels, "Way of the Girl," p. 491.

19. Investigator's Reports, Manhattan Casino, 2926 Eighth Avenue, 20 May 1917 and 19 Aug. 1917, Records of the Committee of Fourteen, Rare Books and Manuscripts Division, New York Public Library, Astor, Lenox and Tilden Foundations.

20. For excursion costs, see Brooklyn Daily Eagle, *A Visitor's Guide to the City of New York* (Brooklyn, 1901), pp. 50–51; Richard Henry Edwards, *Popular Amusements* (New York, 1915), pp. 105–106.

21. Tape I-41 (transcript), Immigrant Labor History Collection.

22. Sue Ainslie Clark and Edith Wyatt, *Making Both Ends Meet: The Income and Outlay of New York Working Girls* (New York, 1911), p. 21.

23. Israels, "Way of the Girl," p. 489.

24. *Ibid.,* pp. 492, 491.

25. *Trow Business Directory of New York City* (New York, 1910), p. 744; Mangels, *Outdoor Amusement Industry,* pp. 17–28.

26. Lucy P. Gillman, "Coney Island," *New York History* 36 (July 1955): 261. The development of Coney Island as a summer resort is discussed in Kasson, *Amusing the Million,* pp. 29–36; Gillman, "Coney Island," pp. 255–290; Robert Snow and David Wright, "Coney Island: A Case Study in Popular Culture and Technical Change," *Journal of Popular Culture* 9 (Spring 1976): 960–975; Pilot and Ransom, *Sodom by the Sea;* Edo McCullough, *Good Old Coney Island: A Sentimental Journey into the Past* (New York, 1957); Kyriazi, *Great American Amusement Parks,* pp. 17–97.

27. Snow and Wright, "Coney Island," p. 964; see also Julian Ralph, "Coney Island," *Scribner's* 20 (July 1896): 9; Pilot and Ransom, *Sodom by the Sea,* pp. 57–92.

28. Kyriazi, *Great American Amusement Parks,* p. 30.

29. McCullough, *Good Old Coney Island,* pp. 32–33. For pictorial evi-

dence of working-class excursions, see *Views of Coney Island* (Portland, Me., 1906, 1907).

30. New York *Tribune*, 30 June 1901, p. 1; Gillman, "Coney Island," p. 283.

31. *International Woodworker* (Chicago), June 1899, quoted in Gillman, "Coney Island," pp. 273–274; see also Pilot and Ransom, *Sodom by the Sea*, p. 28.

32. Ralph, "Coney Island," pp. 16–18.

33. *History of Coney Island: Lists and Photographs of Main Attractions* (New York, 1904), p. 4. Tilyou and his contributions to Coney Island are discussed in Peter Lyon, "The Master Showman of Coney Island," *American Heritage* 9, no. 4 (June 1958): 14–21, 92–95. On the development of West Brighton and Coney's Bowery, see Pilot and Ransom, *Sodom by the Sea*, pp. 28–32; McCullough, *Good Old Coney Island*, p. 322. Cf. descriptions of Manhattan's Bowery in Helen Campbell et al., *Darkness and Daylight, or Lights and Shadows of New York Life* (Hartford, Conn., 1897), p. 212; "Bowery Amusements," in University Settlement Society of New York, *Report* (New York, 1899).

34. Ralph, "Coney Island," p. 16.

35. Flavel Scott Mines, "A Pilgrimage to Coney Isle," *Harper's Weekly* 35 (12 Sept. 1891): 694; Ralph, "Coney Island," p. 17. On early variety audiences, see Chapter 6 and Pilot and Ransom, *Sodom by the Sea*, pp. 102–103; Joe Laurie, *Vaudeville: From the Honky-Tonk to the Palace* (New York, 1953), pp. 10–16, 2–5.

36. Israels, "Way of the Girl"; Ralph, "Coney Island," p. 18.

37. Beatrice L. Stevenson, "Working Girls' Life at Coney Island," *Yearbook of the Women's Municipal League*, Nov. 1911, p. 19. See also Lindsay Denison, "The Biggest Playground in the World," *Munsey's* 33 (Aug. 1905): 566.

38. Israels, "Way of the Girl," p. 488.

39. *Ibid.*, p. 487.

40. Edwin E. Slosson, "The Amusement Business," *Independent* 57 (21 July 1904): 139.

41. Rollin Lynde Hartt, "The Amusement Park," *Atlantic* 99 (May 1907): 676; Betts, "Tenement-House Life," p. 365.

42. Hartt, "Amusement Park," p. 676; Israels, "Way of the Girl," p. 490.

43. The best analysis of the commercial development of Coney Island is in Kasson, *Amusing the Million*. See also Mangels, *Outdoor Amusement Industry*, pp. 38–44.

44. Hartt, "Amusement Park," p. 677; "The Awakening of Coney Island," *Harper's Weekly* 45 (4 May 1901): 466.

45. Theodore Waters, "New York's New Playground," *Harper's Weekly* 49 (8 July 1905): 976.

46. Albert Bigelow Paine, "The New Coney Island," *Century Magazine* 68 (Aug. 1904): 537–538 and pictures preceding pp. 531 and 535. The magazines themselves often reinforced the notion of a new Coney Island clientele by using artists' drawings that emphasized bourgeois refinement and opulence in the clothing and pose of the figures.

47. Denison, "Biggest Playground," p. 562.

48. Lyon, "Master Showman," p. 15; Israels, "Way of the Girl," p. 488.

49. *Views of Coney Island*, n. pag. See also *History of Coney Island*, p. 10; Kasson, *Amusing the Million*.

50. Paine, "New Coney Island," p. 535.

51. Kasson, *Amusing the Million*, pp. 17–28.

52. *History of Coney Island*, p. 28; *Views of Coney Island*, n. pag. See also Mangels, *Outdoor Amusement Industry*, pp. 42–44, for a listing of Luna's attractions.

53. One souvenir guide claimed, for example: "You may recall the stories in the papers, but without a visit here you will never know how Mount Pelee really looked when it burst forth its death-dealing stream" (*History of Coney Island*, p. 40).

54. *History of Coney Island*, pp. 10–11.

55. Maxim Gorky, "Boredom," *Independent* 63 (8 Aug. 1907): 312.

56. *Ibid.*

57. Kyriazi, *Great American Amusement Parks*, pp. 71–72. See also Pilot and Ransom, *Sodom by the Sea*, p. 172.

58. Israels, "Way of the Girl," p. 488.

59. "Coney Needs Cleansing," New York *Tribune*, 15 July 1901, p. 12. For the police department's response, see "Coney Island Decent Now," New York *Tribune*, 19 July 1901, p. 3. Cf. Paine, "New Coney Island," p. 533.

60. West End Improvement League of Coney Island, *Neglected Coney Island* (New York, [1912]), p. 25; see in particular photographs on pp. 19, 28–29, which show women and men on the beach holding each other around the shoulders or waist, chasing each other, and generally assuming relaxed and joyous postures. See also Pilot and Ransom, *Sodom by the Sea*, pp. 126–127.

61. Brooklyn Daily Eagle, *Visitor's Guide to New York*, p. 38; Edwards, *Popular Amusements*, p. 107.

62. *History of Coney Island*, p. 44; Hartt, "Amusement Park," pp. 676–677. For similar rides and sideshows, see the photographs in *Souvenir of Coney Island* (New York, n.d.).

63. McCullough, *Good Old Coney Island,* p. 311. While largely anecdotal, McCullough's history clearly identifies the alternative conception of amusement that Steeplechase embodied.

64. See *ibid.,* pp. 309–310, for a description of these amusements.

65. *Ibid.,* pp. 311–313.

66. For an excellent description, see Pilot and Ransom, *Sodom by the Sea,* pp. 136–141.

67. *Glimpses of the New Coney Island: America's Most Popular Pleasure Resort* (New York, 1904), n. pag. *History of Coney Island,* p. 36, lists the sixteen attractions. On the three amusement parks' appeal to different audiences, see Pilot and Ransom, *Sodom by the Sea,* p. 157.

68. McCullough, *Good Old Coney Island,* p. 316; Pilot and Ransom, *Sodom by the Sea,* p. 157.

69. On middle-class sexual ideology in the early twentieth century, see Christina Simmons, "'Marriage in the Modern Manner': Sexual Radicalism and Reform in America, 1914–1941" (Ph.D. diss., Brown University, 1982), especially pp. 105–149. Some of the connections between sexuality and a consumption-oriented society are explored in Stuart Ewen, *Captains of Consciousness: Advertising and the Social Roots of the Consumer Culture* (New York, 1976), pp. 177–184; Mary Ryan, *Womanhood in America* (3d ed.; New York, 1983), pp. 217–244.

Chapter Six

1. *Views and Films Index* 2 (26 Oct. 1907).

2. Belle Lindner Israels, "The Dance Problem," *Proceedings of the National Conference of Charities and Corrections, 1912* (Fort Wayne, Ind., 1912), p. 141.

3. On the relationship between popular entertainment and popular attitudes, see H. E. Meller, *Leisure and the Changing City, 1870–1914* (London, 1976), p. 214.

4. Sadie Frowne, "The Story of a Sweatshop Girl," in *Workers Speak: Self Portraits,* ed. Leon Stein and Philip Taft (New York, 1971), p. 118; Robert A. Woods, *The City Wilderness* (Boston, 1898), p. 178; Rollin L. Hartt, *The People at Play* (Boston, 1909), p. 161.

5. James McCabe, *Lights and Shadows of New York Life* (Philadelphia, 1872), p. 481; Helen Campbell et al., *Darkness and Daylight, or Lights and Shadows of New York Life* (Hartford, Conn., 1897), pt. 2, pp. 464.

6. Hartt, *People at Play,* pp. 169, 182; Samuel Chotzinoff, *A Lost Para-*

dise (New York, 1955), p. 95; Campbell et al., *Darkness and Daylight*, pt. 2, pp. 462–465; Belle L. Mead, "The Social Pleasures of East Side Jews" (M.A. thesis, Columbia University, 1904), p. 10.

7. Tape I-59, New York City Immigrant Labor History Collection of the City College Oral History Project, Robert F. Wagner Archives, Tamiment Institute Library, New York University.

8. Jacob Gordin, "The Yiddish Stage," in University Settlement Society of New York, *Report* (New York, 1901), p. 27; F. H. McLean, "Bowery Amusements," in University Settlement Society of New York, *Report* (New York, 1899), p. 17. See also Maxine S. Seller, ed., *Ethnic Theater in the United States* (Westport, Conn., 1983); Irving Howe, *World of Our Fathers* (New York, 1976), pp. 460–496.

9. John Collier and Edward M. Barrows, *The City Where Crime Is Play* (New York, Jan. 1914), p. 41; "Italian Plays for a Nickel," New York *World*, 5 May 1895, p. 25.

10. Parker R. Zellers, "The Cradle of Variety: The Concert Saloon," *Educational Theatre Journal* 20 (Dec. 1968): 578–586, 580 (quote); H. E. Cooper, "Variety, Vaudeville and Virtue," *Dance Magazine* 7 (Dec. 1926): 31–32, 64. For contemporary accounts of Manhattan's concert saloons, see New York City Press, *Vices of a Big City: An Expose of Existing Menaces to Church and Home in New York City* (New York, 1890), p. 7; McCabe, *Lights and Shadows*, p. 594; Herbert Asbury, *The Gangs of New York* (1927; rpt. New York, 1970), p. 182; Mathew Hale Smith, *Sunshine and Shadow in New York* (Hartford, Conn., 1869), p. 371. On music halls in the 1890's, see Campbell et al., *Darkness and Daylight*, pt. 2, pp. 465–466; McLean, "Bowery Amusements," pp. 16–17.

11. Cooper, "Variety," p. 64; Scrapbook of Tony Pastor's Opera House, Theater Arts Collection, Lincoln Center Library of the Performing Arts, New York Public Library.

12. Albert F. McLean, Jr., *American Vaudeville as Ritual* (Louisville, Ky., 1965), p. 69; Edward B. Marks, *They All Sang: From Tony Pastor to Rudy Vallee* (New York, 1934), pp. 112, 128; Carolyn Caffin, *Vaudeville* (New York, 1914), p. 15; Brett Page, *Writing for Vaudeville* (Springfield, Mass., 1915), p. 170; Edwin Milton Royle, "The Vaudeville Theatre," in *Land of Contrasts*, ed. Neil Harris (New York, 1970), p. 183.

13. McLean, "Bowery Amusements," pp. 15, 18.

14. Paul Klapper, "The Yiddish Music Hall," *University Settlement Studies* 2, no. 4 (1905): 20–21; McLean, "Bowery Amusements," p. 17; John Corbin, "How the Other Half Laughs," in *Land of Contrasts*, ed. Harris, p. 166; Michael M. Davis, *The Exploitation of Pleasure: A Study of Commercial Recreations in New York City* (New York, n.d.), p. 30; Collier and Bar-

rows, *City Where Crime Is Play*, p. 41; Lillian D. Wald, *The House on Henry Street* (1915; rpt. New York, 1971), p. 272.

15. Davis, *Exploitation of Pleasure*, pp. 21, 30; Howard Brown Woolston, *A Study of the Population of Manhattanville* (Studies in History, Economics and Public Law, vol. 35, no. 2; New York, 1909), p. 80.

16. Louis, Bolard More, *Wage-Earners' Budgets: A Study of Standards and Costs of Living in New York City* (New York, 1907), p. 142; Davis, *Exploitation of Pleasure*, p. 30; Annie M. MacLean, *Wage-Earning Women* (New York, 1910), p. 72. On women avoiding Bowery concert halls, see McLean, "Bowery Amusements," p. 16.

17. Caffin, *Vaudeville*, p. 16; Royle, "Vaudeville Theater," p. 182.

18. On theater trips and treating, see Belle Lindner Israels, "Diverting a Pastime," *Leslie's Weekly* 113 (27 July 1911): 94; Hutchins Hapgood, *Types from City Streets* (New York, 1910), p. 131. Ticket prices are indicated in Davis, *Exploitation of Pleasure*, p. 25; McLean, "Bowery Amusements," p. 15. For patterns of theater-going, see Robert Coit Chapin, *The Standard of Living Among Workingmen's Families in New York City* (New York, 1909), pp. 211, 213; George E. Bevans, *How Workingmen Spend Their Spare Time* (New York, 1913), pp. 37–43; Chotzinoff, *Lost Paradise*, p. 95; More, *Wage-Earners' Budgets*, p. 142.

19. Thomas Jesse Jones, *Sociology of a New York City Block* (Studies in History, Economics and Public Law, vol. 21, no. 2; New York, 1904), pp. 47, 48; Hapgood, *Types from City Streets*, p. 63; Hartt, *People at Play*, p. 24.

20. Klapper, "Yiddish Music Hall," p. 22; John Collier, "Cheap Amusements," *Survey* 20 (11 April 1908): 74; U.S. Industrial Commission, *Report of the Industrial Commission on the Relations and Conditions of Capital and Labor Employed in Manufacturing and General Business*, vol. 14 (Washington, D.C., 1901), p. 117.

21. Mead, "Social Pleasures," p. 7.

22. Collier, "Cheap Amusements," p. 75. For a discussion of the early movies, see Robert Sklar, *Movie-Made America: A Cultural History of American Movies* (New York, 1976); Lary May, *Screening Out the Past: The Birth of Mass Culture and the Motion Picture Industry* (New York, 1980); Garth Jowett, *Film: The Democratic Art* (Boston, 1976); Lewis Jacobs, *The Rise of the American Film: A Critical History* (1939; rpt. New York, 1968); Daniel J. Czitrom, *Media and the American Mind* (Chapel Hill, N.C., 1982), pp. 30–59. Penny arcades and amusement parlors are discussed in *Moving Picture World* 1 (8 June 1907): 214; Davis, *Exploitation of Pleasure*, p. 10; S. C. Kingsley, "Penny Arcade and the Cheap Theater," *Charities and the Commons* 18 (8 June 1907): 295–297.

23. Office of Commissioner of Accounts, City of New York, *A Report on*

the Condition of Moving Picture Shows in New York, March 22, 1911, pp. 7–8, National Board of Review of Motion Pictures Collection, Rare Books and Manuscripts Division, New York Public Library, Astor, Lenox and Tilden Foundations (hereafter cited as NBRMPC); Davis, *Exploitation of Pleasure,* p. 22; Marks, *They All Sang,* pp. 147–148; Robert Grau, *The Stage in the Twentieth Century* (1912; rpt. New York, 1969), pp. 63–64.

24. Davis, *Exploitation of Pleasure,* pp. 23, 26–28, 30, 35; *Moving Picture World* 1 (5 Oct. 1907): 487; Collier, "Cheap Amusements." See Russell Merritt's excellent discussion of nickelodeons in "Nickelodeon Theaters, 1905–1914: Building an Audience for the Movies," in *The American Film Industry,* ed. Tino Balio (Madison, Wisc., 1976), pp. 59–82, and in "Nickelodeon Theaters," *American Film Institute Report* 4, no. 2 (May 1973): 4–8.

25. J[ohn] C[ollier] to Charles F. Powlison, 9 Nov. 1910, Subjects Correspondence, Children and the Motion Pictures, 1910–1916, NBRMPC; *Nickelodeon* 1 (Feb. 1909): 48, and 1 (Jan. 1909): 8.

26. Bevans, *Workingmen,* pp. 19–22, 31, 37–43, 75. "A Study of Families," in New York State Factory Investigating Commission, *Fourth Report Transmitted to Legislature, Feb. 15, 1915* (S. Doc. no. 43; Albany, N.Y., 1915), vol. 4, p. 1787, indicated that one-third of the poor families studied went to the movies. See also *Moving Picture World* 2 (22 Feb. 1908): 137; 2 (7 March 1908): 181; and 2 (1 Feb. 1908): 77. Recent film historians have debated the social class of early film audiences; see especially Garth S. Jowett, "The First Motion Picture Audiences," *Journal of Popular Film* 3 (1974): 39–54, and Merritt, "Nickelodeon Theaters."

27. Report of the Women's Municipal League and People's Institute, quoted in *Moving Picture World* 2 (22 Feb. 1908): 137.

28. *Moving Picture World* 2 (11 Jan. 1908): 21, and 2 (1 Feb. 1908): 77; *Views and Films Index* 2 (5 Oct. 1907): 3; *Nickelodeon* 1 (Feb. 1909): 33–34; Davis, *Exploitation of Pleasure,* p. 30. See also Elizabeth Ewen's excellent analysis in "City Lights: Immigrant Women and the Rise of the Movies," *Signs* 5, supp. (Spring 1980): S45–S65.

29. *Views and Films Index* 2 (11 May 1907): 3; *Nickelodeon* 1 (Feb. 1909): 33–34.

30. See advertisement for Joseph Levi's announcement slides, *Views and Films Index* 3 (29 Feb. 1908): 5.

31. Commissioner of Accounts, *Report on the Condition of Moving Picture Shows,* p. 12; "People's Institute Motion Picture Show Report" (c. 1909–1910), Box 8, Miscellaneous Papers, Motion Pictures and Vaudeville Shows, Jacob A. Riis Neighborhood Settlement Records, Rare Books and Manuscripts Division, New York Public Library, Astor, Lenox and Tilden

Foundations; *Views and Films Index* 2 (5 Oct. 1907): 3, and 3 (22 Feb. 1908): 5. See also Roy Rosenzweig, *Eight Hours for What We Will: Workers and Leisure in an Industrial City, 1870–1920* (Cambridge, Eng., 1983), pp. 198–204.

32. Lewis E. Palmer, "The World in Motion," *Survey* 22 (5 June 1909): 356.

33. On social interaction in the theaters, see Jowett, *Film*, p. 41; Marks, *They All Sang*, p. 214; *Views and Films Index* 3 (4 Jan. 1908): 5; Davis, *Exploitation of Pleasure*, p. 24. On ethnic vaudeville, see *Settlement Journal*, Jan. 1914, p. 5; Mary Heaton Vorse, "Some Picture Show Audiences," *Outlook* 98 (24 June 1911): 446.

34. Vorse, "Picture Show Audiences," pp. 445.

35. "The Nickelodeon," *Moving Picture World* 1 (4 May 1907): 140.

36. [Russell Sage Foundation,] *Boyhood and Lawlessness* (New York, 1914), pp. 67–68.

37. "People's Institute Motion Picture Show Report," Riis Neighborhood Settlement Records; Collier and Barrows, *City Where Crime Is Play*, p. 32.

38. See, for example, Orrin G. Cocks, "A Saloon Substitute: The Motion Picture Show," c. 1914, p. 2, Subjects Correspondence, Drinking and the Movies, NBRMPC.

39. New York Factory Investigating Commission, *Fourth Report*, vol. 4, p. 1697. See also Esther Packard, *A Study of Living Conditions of Self-Supporting Women in New York City* (New York, 1915), p. 51; Vorse, "Picture Show Audiences," pp. 443, 445; Lucy France Pierce, "The Nickelodeon," *Nickelodeon* 1 (Jan. 1909): 8; "The Nickel Craze in New York," *Views and Films Index* 2 (5 Oct. 1907): 3.

40. Ruth S. True, *The Neglected Girl* (New York, 1914), p. 116; Hartt, *People at Play*, p. 125; Davis, *Exploitation of Pleasure*, pp. 34, 22.

41. Committee of Fourteen in New York City, *Annual Report* (New York, 1914), p. 50; tape I-65 (side B), Immigrant Labor History Collection.

42. Robert A. Woods and Albert J. Kennedy, *Young Working Girls: A Summary of Evidence from Two Thousand Social Workers* (Boston, 1913), p. 114; "Nickel Craze," p. 2; Belle Lindner Israels, "The Way of the Girl," *Survey* 22 (3 July 1909): 490; Franklin H. Sargent to Orrin Cocks, 11 Aug. 1915, Subjects Correspondence, Children and the Motion Pictures, 1910–1916, NBRMPC; Louise De Koven Bowen, *Five and Ten Cent Theatres* (Chicago, 1909, 1911).

43. Cornelia E. Marshall to W. D. McGuire, 12 Jan. 1915, Subjects Correspondence, Children and the Motion Pictures, 1910–1916, NBRMPC; cf. Israels, "Way of the Girl," p. 487.

44. Ewen, "City Lights," S58; Sharon Hartman Strom, "Italian American

Women and Their Daughters in Rhode Island: The Adolescence of Two Generations, 1900–1950," in *The Italian Immigrant Woman in North America,* ed. Betty Boyd Caroli et al. (Toronto, 1978); Louise C. Odencrantz, *Italian Women in Industry: A Study of Conditions in New York City* (New York, 1919), p. 235.

45. True, *Neglected Girl,* p. 72; Woods and Kennedy, *Young Working Girls,* pp. 61, 106.

46. "Interview with Orrin G. Cocks . . . ," typescript (n.d.), p. 3, Subjects Correspondence, Children and Motion Pictures, Related Papers, NBRMPC; Sklar, *Movie-Made America,* p. 40; Jacobs, *Rise of American Film,* p. 89.

47. Untitled speech of John Collier at Yorkville Civic Forum in Hungarian National Hall, New York City, c. 1910–1911, Subjects Papers, People's Institute, NBRMPC.

48. True, *Neglected Girl,* p. 67. By the 1920's, this new woman's space would be fully exploited by mass cultural institutions, which began, for example, to target such magazines as *True Story* and *Photoplay* to a female, predominantly working-class audience. See Christina Simmons, "The Dream World of Confession Magazines, 1920–1940," paper presented at the Fifth Berkshire Conference of Women's Historians, June 1981.

49. Jacobs, *Rise of American Film,* pp. 17, 67, 70–72.

50. Kemp R. Niver, comp., *Biograph Bulletins, 1896–1908* (Los Angeles, 1971), pp. 396, 403; Merritt, "Nickelodeon Theaters."

51. "Nickel Craze," p. 3.

52. Merritt, "Nickelodeon Theaters," p. 6; Jowett, "First Motion Picture Audiences," p. 43.

53. Discussion of the content of early films is based on an examination of advertisements in *Moving Picture World* and *Views and Films Index,* the leading trade journals for the motion pictures, as well as the extensive listing of films in Kemp R. Niver, *Motion Pictures from the Library of Congress Paper Print Collection, 1894–1912* (Berkeley, 1967). This source supplies synopses for over 3,000 films, many of which were never advertised in trade publications or examined by the early film historians. My examination focuses on comedies, the most numerous and popular of the early movies. On their popularity, see *Views and Films Index* 2 (14 Sept. 1907): 3.

54. Niver, *Paper Print Collection,* pp. 20, 92.

55. *Ibid.,* pp. 53, 15.

56. *Ibid.,* pp. 18, 38.

57. *Ibid.,* p. 91. See also "Bobby's Kodak," in Niver, comp., *Biograph Bulletins,* p. 336. Early movies on secretary-employer relations include "The Woman Hater" (1909), p. 112; "The Typewriter" (1902), p. 103; and "She Meets with Wife's Approval" (1902), p. 87, all in Niver, *Paper Print Collection.*

58. Edward Wagenknecht, *The Movies in the Age of Innocence* (Normal, 1962), p. 41.

59. "Mashing the Masher" advertisement, *Views and Films Index* 3 (29 Feb. 1908): 2. Other masher movies include "Old Mashers," *Views and Films Index* 2 (9 Feb. 1907): 9, and "The Gibson Goddess" (1909), in Niver, *Paper Print Collection*, p. 39.

60. Niver, *Paper Print Collection*, p. 73; see also "Troubles of a Flirt," *Views and Films Index* 3 (11 April 1908): 11. For a discussion of DeMille's films, see May, *Screening Out the Past*, pp. 200–236.

61. Niver, *Paper Print Collection*, pp. 24, 109, 57, 56. D. W. Griffith's films are analyzed in May, *Screening Out the Past*, pp. 60–95.

62. Niver, *Biograph Bulletins*, p. 284; *Views and Films Index* 6 (7 Jan. 1911): 9. See also *Views and Films Index* 3 (11 April 1908): 11; Niver, *Paper Print Collection*, pp. 26, 71, 100. See Kay Sloan's fine discussion in "Sexual Warfare in the Silent Cinema: Comedies and Melodramas of Woman Suffragism," *American Quarterly* 33 (Fall 1981): 412–436.

63. Ewen, "City Lights."

64. New York *Times*, 16 Dec. 1907, p. 3; the story unfolds in the *Times* on 6, 7, 8, 9, 18, and 22 Dec. 1907. See also *Moving Picture World* 1 (11 May 1907): 153; and 1 (3 Aug. 1907): 344.

65. New York *Times*, 9 Dec. 1907, p. 2.

66. James P. Warbasse to John Collier, 10 March 1910, Enclosure "Observations," Regional Correspondence, New York, New York City (Manhattan), 1910–1919, NBRMPC. The 1908 movie crisis may be followed in the New York *Times* on 13, 21, 24, 25, 26, and 28 Dec. 1908.

67. "Program for Organization of Moving-Picture Censorship," Subjects Papers, Relating to the Formation and Subsequent History up to 1926 of the NBRMP, 1908–1915, NBRMPC; this collection contains extensive documentation of movie reformers' activities. See also Daniel Czitrom, "The Redemption of Leisure: The National Board of Censorship and the Rise of Motion Pictures in New York City, 1900–1920," paper presented at the American Studies Association Biennial Meeting, Nov. 1983; Kathleen D. McCarthy, "Nickel Vice and Virtue: Movie Censorship in Chicago, 1907–1915," *Journal of Popular Film* 5 (1976): 37–55; Robert Fisher, "Film Censorship and Progressive Reform: The National Board of Censorship of Motion Pictures, 1909–1922," *Journal of Popular Film* 4 (1975): 143–156.

68. Orrin Cocks, "Public Amusements Safeguarded," p. 10; "Policies and Standards" (1916); National Board of Censorship, "Special Bulletin on Motion Picture Comedies" (c. 1912); and Orrin G. Cocks, "The Motion Picture and Moral and Religious Interests," all in Subjects Papers, Relating to the Formation and Subsequent History . . . of the NBRMP, 1908–1915, NBRMPC; "Special Bulletin to Motion Picture Producers," in Subjects

Correspondence, Children and the Motion Pictures, 1910–1916, NBRMPC.

69. "A Questionnaire on Juvenile Standards," (23 November 1915) in Subjects Correspondence, Children and the Motion Pictures, 1910–1916, Related Papers, NBRMPC.

70. "House of Bondage," box 106 (Controversial Films Correspondence), NBRMPC.

71. Merritt, "Nickelodeon Theaters, 1905–1914"; *Moving Picture World* 2 (4 Jan. 1908): 8; Palmer, "World in Motion," p. 356; Davis, *Exploitation of Pleasure,* pp. 33–34; Grau, *Stage in Twentieth Century,* p. 309.

72. *Views and Films Index* 3 (22 Feb. 1908): 11, and 2 (27 July 1907): 4. For the industry's ambivalence, see also *Views and Films Index* 3 (11 Jan. 1908): 5; 3 (22 Feb. 1908): 5; and 2 (12 Oct. 1907): 4.

73. Jacobs, *Rise of American Film,* p. 156.

74. Harlem, New York *Home News,* 3 May 1916, clipping, in Regional Correspondence, New York, New York City (Manhattan), 1910–1919, NBRMPC.

75. May, *Screening Out the Past,* especially pp. 96–146; Ewen, "City Lights."

76. May, *Screening Out the Past,* p. 119.

Chapter Seven

1. Richard Henry Edwards, *Popular Amusements* (New York, 1915), p. 140.

2. My approach in this chapter is to understand reform itself as a social relationship between groups of individuals, not a program or set of ideas imposed on passive or powerless people. Recent scholars have criticized the concept of social control and developed more interactive models of change that acknowledge working-class agency. See especially Stephen Hardy and Alan G. Ingham, "Games, Structures and Agency: Historians on the American Play Movement," *Journal of Social History* 17 (Winter 1983): 285–301; Gareth Stedman Jones, "Class Expression versus Social Control? A Critique of Recent Trends in the Social History of 'Leisure,'" *History Workshop* 4 (Autumn 1977): 163–170; Roy Rosenzweig, "Middle Class Parks and Working Class Play: The Struggle Over Recreational Space in Worcester, Massachusetts, 1870–1910," *Radical History Review* 21 (Fall 1979): 31–48; Francis G. Couvares, "The Triumph of Commerce: Class Culture and Mass Culture in Pittsburgh," in *Working-Class America,* ed. Michael H. Frisch

and Daniel J. Walkowitz (Urbana, Ill., 1983), pp. 123–152; Raymond Williams, *Marxism and Literature* (Oxford, 1977), pp. 108–114.

3. Grace Dodge, "Working Girls' Societies," *Chautauquan* 9 (Jan. 1889): 223. On the Gilded Age response to the urban working woman, see Mari Jo Buhle, "The Nineteenth Century Woman's Movement: Perspectives on Woman's Labor in Industrializing America," Bunting Institute Working Paper, 1979; Lynn Weiner, "From the Working Girl to the Working Mother: The Debate Over Women, Work and Morality in the United States, 1820–1920" (Ph.D. diss., Boston University, 1981), pp. 68–96; Amy Srebnick, "True Womanhood and Hard Times: Women and Early New York Industrialization, 1840–1860" (Ph.D. diss., State University of New York at Stony Brook, 1979), pp. 79–158.

4. Reform organizations and activities in New York City are listed in William Howe Tolman and William I. Hull, *Handbook of Sociological Information with Especial Reference to New York City* (New York, 1894). Further information may be found in Working Girls' Vacation Society of New York, *Annual Reports* (New York, 1885–1915); U.S. Bureau of Labor, *Boarding Homes and Clubs for Working Women*, by Mary S. Fergusson (Bulletin no. 15; Washington, D.C., 1898), pp. 141–196.

5. Young Women's Christian Association of New York City, *Twenty-fourth Annual Report* (New York, 1895), p. 16; New York State Bureau of Labor Statistics, *Eighteenth Annual Report* (Albany, N.Y., 1900), p. 387. On rational recreation, see Peter Bailey, *Leisure and Class in Victorian England: Rational Recreation and the Contest for Control, 1830–1885* (London, 1978).

6. The ideology of women's sphere in the nineteenth century is discussed in Nancy F. Cott, *The Bonds of Womanhood* (New Haven, Conn., 1977). On the application of this ideology to feminist and urban reform efforts, see Carroll Smith-Rosenberg, "Beauty, the Beast and the Militant Woman: A Case Study in Sex Roles and Social Stress in Jacksonian America," *American Quarterly* 23 (Oct. 1971): 562–584; Karen Blair, *The Club Woman as Feminist: True Womanhood Redefined* (New York, 1980); Estelle Freedman, "Separation as Strategy: Female Institution Building and American Feminism, 1870–1930," *Feminist Studies* 5 (Fall, 1979): 512–529; Buhle, "Nineteenth Century Woman's Movement."

7. Young Women's Christian Association of New York City, *Twenty-third Annual Report* (New York, 1894), p. 17. A typical investigation of working woman and morality is Carroll Wright, *The Working Girls of Boston* (1889; rpt. New York, 1969). Sensationalized depictions of New York as a center of sin may be found in James McCabe, *Lights and Shadows of New York Life* (Philadelphia, 1872); Mathew Hale Smith, *Sunshine and Shadow in New*

York (Hartford, Conn., 1869); Helen Campbell et al., *Darkness and Daylight, or Lights and Shadows of New York Life* (Hartford, Conn., 1897).

8. Young Women's Christian Association International Board, *Report* (New York, 1889), p. 23; Harlem Young Women's Christian Association, *Building Souvenir* (n.p., 1897), p. 12; see also Young Women's Christian Association of New York City, *Twenty-second Annual Report* (New York, 1893), p. 16.

9. Working Girls' Vacation Society, *Sixth Annual Report* (1889), p. 6.

10. See Karen Blair, *Club Woman as Feminist,* for a discussion of this ideology and its practice among middle-class women.

11. Harlem YWCA, *Building Souvenir,* p. 17.

12. *Ibid.,* pp. 17–18; Young Women's Christian Association International Board, *Report* (New York, 1887), pp. 44–45.

13. Grace Dodge's involvement with the Working Girls' Clubs is discussed at length in Esther Katz, "Grace Hoadley Dodge: Women and the Emerging Metropolis, 1856–1914" (Ph.D. diss., New York University, 1980), pp. 57–115. The significance of the clubs for women of all classes is discussed in Joanne Reitano, "Working Girls Unite," *American Quarterly* 36 (1984): 112–134. On the activities and membership of the New York clubs, see Tolman and Hull, *Handbook of Sociological Information,* p. 225; New York Association of Working Girls' Societies (hereafter cited as NYAWGS), *Annual Reports* (New York, 1884–1901); *Far and Near* (1891–1894); 38th Street Working Girls' Society, *Circular of the Domestic Circle* (n.p., n.d.).

14. U.S. Bureau of Labor, *The Attitude of Women's Clubs and Associations Toward Social Economics,* by Ellen M. Henrotin (Bulletin no. 23; Washington, D.C. 1899), p. 514. See also Blair, *Club Woman as Feminist,* and Reitano, "Working Girls Unite."

15. Lillian W. Betts, *The Leaven in a Great City* (New York, 1902), p. 145; Dodge, "Working Girls' Societies," p. 224; NYAWGS, *Seventh Annual Report* (1891), pp. 8, 20–21; NYAWGS, *Reasons for Advancing the Principles of Self-Support* (n.p., n.d.), p. 4.

16. *Far and Near* 1 (Dec. 1890): 32. The feminist attack on women's economic dependency is discussed by Sondra R. Herman, "Loving Courtship or the Marriage Market? The Ideal and Its Critics, 1871–1911," in *Our American Sisters,* ed. Jean E. Friedman and William G. Shade (2d ed.; Boston, 1976), pp. 233–252.

17. NYAWGS, *Seventh Annual Report* (1891), p. 5; Robert D. Cross, "Grace Hoadley Dodge," in *Notable American Women, 1607–1905,* ed. Edward T. James (Cambridge, Mass., 1971), p. 490; Dodge, "Working Girls' Societies," p. 224.

18. Dodge, "Working Girls' Societies," p. 225.

19. *Far and Near* 1 (Dec. 1890): 21; NYAWGS, *Sixteenth Annual Report* (1900–1901), p. 9; NYAWGS, *Fourth Annual Report* (1888), p. 3; NYAWGS, *Seventh Annual Report* (1891), p. 24.

20. 38th Street Working Girls' Society, *Tuesday Evening Practical Talks, 1891–92* (leaflet; n.p., n.d.). Grace Dodge, *Bundle of Letters to Busy Girls on Practical Matters* (New York, 1877), is a compilation of typical talks. See also U.S. Bureau of Labor, *Working Women in Large Cities: Fourth Annual Report of the Commissioner of Labor, 1888* (Washington, D.C., 1889), p. 49.

21. See, e.g., *Far and Near* 2 (July 1892): 180; 2 (Aug. 1892): 201; 3 (April 1893): 112; 3 (May 1893): 134; and 3 (June 1893): 158; Dodge, *Bundle of Letters,* pp. 105–106; NYAWGS, *Fifth Annual Report* (1889), p. 5; NYAWGS, *Seventh Annual Report* (1891), p. 18.

22. Dodge, "Working Girls' Societies," p. 223; Dodge, *Bundle of Letters,* p. 37.

23. Dodge, *Bundle of Letters,* pp. 103–104, 39, 33–34. See also *Far and Near* 1 (Sept. 1891): 208.

24. NYAWGS, *Fourth Annual Report* (1888), p. 22.

25. Dodge, "Working Girls' Societies," p. 24. See also U.S. Bureau of Labor, *Working Women in Large Cities,* p. 49.

26. Dodge, "Working Girls' Societies," p. 225; Helen Campbell, "Association in Clubs with Its Bearings on Working-Women," *Arena* 5 (Dec. 1891): 63; Katz, "Grace Hoadley Dodge," pp. 59–60.

27. NYAWGS, *Third Annual Report* (1887), pp. 20, 2–3; NYAWGS, *Fourth Annual Report* (1888), pp. 6–7. See also Alice Kessler-Harris, *Out to Work* (New York, 1982), pp. 93–94; Weiner, "Working Girl to Working Mother," p. 94. Such tensions were common in most cross-class organizations. See, for example, Alice Kessler-Harris, "Organizing the Unorganizable: Three Jewish Women and their Union," *Labor History* 17 (Winter 1976): 5–23; Nancy Schrom Dye, "Creating a Feminist Alliance: Sisterhood and Class Conflict in the New York Women's Trade Union League," *Feminist Studies* 2 (1975): 24–38.

28. *Far and Near* 1 (Nov. 1890): 9, and 1 (Dec. 1890): 25.

29. *Far and Near* 2 (Feb. 1892): 79.

30. *Far and Near* 1 (Jan. 1891): 39, and 1 (Feb. 1891): 58–59. Similar perceptions are discussed in Mary Gay Humphreys, "The New York Working Girl," *Scribner's* 20 (Oct. 1896): 503, 512.

31. Betts, *Leaven,* pp. 147 (quote), 148–158.

32. *Far and Near* 2 (May 1892): 144; 1 (Jan. 1891): 39; 1 (Feb. 1891): 56–57; 2 (Nov. 1891): 15; and 2 (Sept. 1891): 208.

33. Susan Levine, "Labor's True Woman: Domesticity and Equal Rights in the Knights of Labor," *Journal of American History* 70 (Sept. 1983): 323–339; see also Herbert G. Gutman, "Protestantism and the American Labor Movement: The Christian Spirit in the Gilded Age," in Gutman, *Work, Culture, and Society in Industrializing America* (New York, 1977), pp. 79–117.

34. *Far and Near* 2 (Nov. 1891): 16.

35. Humphreys, "New York Working-Girl," pp. 502–513. Rosalyn Baxandall et al., eds., *America's Working Women* (New York, 1976), p. 214, also suggest this movement toward unionism.

36. Humphreys, "New York Working-Girl," p. 506; *Far and Near* 2 (Nov. 1891): 16.

37. See, for example, E. G. Balch, "Working-Girls' Clubs as a Factor in Social Development," *Far and Near* 3 (March 1893): 87–88. Katz, in "Grace Hoadley Dodge," pp. 105–113, discusses in detail the internal debates among club leaders over this issue.

38. *Far and Near* 2 (July 1892): 187, and 2 (Feb. 1892): 79.

39. NYAWGS, *Fifth Annual Report* (1889), p. 5.

40. NYAWGS, *Fourth Annual Report* (1888), pp. 6–8; NYAWGS, *Third Annual Report* (1887), p. 20.

41. See list of entertainments in NYAWGS, *Sixteenth Annual Report* (1900–1901), pp. 21–22.

42. NYAWGS, *Fourth Annual Report* (1888), p. 16; NYAWGS, *Fifteenth Annual Report* (1899–1900), pp. 21–22; NYAWGS, *Sixteenth Annual Report* (1900–1901), p. 21; *Far and Near* 1 (March 1891): 86.

43. NYAWGS, *Seventh Annual Report* (1891), p. 14; NYAWGS, *Sixteenth Annual Report* (1900–1901), p. 21; NYAWGS, *Eighth Annual Report* (1892), p. 23.

44. For the decline in membership, cf. NYAWGS, *Seventh Annual Report* (1891), p. 38, and *Eighteenth Annual Report* (1902–1903), pp. 7–8. For further discussion of the decline and Dodge's resignation, see Katz, "Grace Hoadley Dodge," pp. 108–113, and Cross, "Grace Hoadley Dodge," p. 490.

45. See, for example, Stanton Coit's criticism of working girls' clubs in *Neighbourhood Guilds: An Instrument of Social Reform* (1891; rpt. New York, 1974).

46. Belle Israels, "Regulation of Public Amusement," *Proceedings of the Academy of Political Science in the City of New York* 2 (July 1912): 126. The literature on Progressive era reform affecting working-class communities is vast. A good starting point is Paul Boyer, *Urban Masses and Moral Order in America, 1820–1920* (Cambridge, Mass., 1978); Allen Davis, *Spearheads for Reform: The Social Settlements and the Progressive Movement, 1890–*

1914 (New York, 1967). Boyer discusses environmentalism on pp. 179–180. On emergent middle-class attitudes toward leisure, see Daniel T. Rodgers, *The Work Ethic in Industrial America, 1850–1920* (Chicago and London, 1974).

47. Robert A. Woods and Albert J. Kennedy, *Young Working Girls: A Summary of Evidence from Two Thousand Social Workers* (Boston, 1913), p. 98; see also George J. Kneeland, *Commercialized Prostitution in New York City* (New York, 1913); University Settlement Society of New York, *Report* (New York, 1897), p. 27; Jane Addams, *Spirit of Youth and the City Streets* (New York, 1912). For a subtle analysis of these middle-class concerns, see Don S. Kirschner, "The Ambiguous Legacy: Social Justice and Social Control in the Progressive Era," *Historical Reflections* 2 (Summer 1975): 69–88.

48. Mary Kingsbury Simkhovitch, "A New Social Adjustment," *Proceedings of the Academy of Political Science in the City of New York* 1 (Oct. 1910), pp. 86–87; Lillian D. Wald, *The House on Henry Street* (1915; rpt. New York, 1971), pp. 173–174, 195–96.

49. New York Public Recreation Commission, *Report* (1912–1913), p. 21; Israels, "Regulation of Public Amusements"; Belle Lindner Israels, "Dance Problem," *Proceedings of the National Conference of Charities and Corrections, 1912* (Fort Wayne, Ind., 1912), p. 142.

50. University Settlement Society of New York, *Report* (New York, 1912), p. 41.

51. University Settlement Society of New York, *Report* (New York, 1897), p. 10; University Settlement Society of New York, *Report* (New York, 1894), p. 11. On the number of settlement clubs, see Annie M. MacLean, *Wage-Earning Women* (New York, 1910), p. 38; "Social Settlements," in New York Bureau of Labor Statistics, *Eighteenth Annual Report* (1900), p. 257. Typical club activities are noted in University Settlement Society's *Reports.*

52. Israels, "Dance Problem," p. 144; Wald, *House on Henry Street*, p. 198; University Settlement Society of New York, *Report* (New York, 1913), p. 26; Betts, *Leaven*, p. 253. On the broader social purity and sex education movements, see David J. Pivar, *Purity Crusade* (Westport, Conn., 1973); Christina Simmons, "'Marriage in the Modern Manner': Sexual Radicalism and Reform in America, 1914–1941" (Ph.D. diss., Brown University, 1982).

53. C. S. Childs and John Collier, "Summary of Results to Date of Social Center Experiment of P. S. 63, Manhattan"; "The Redemption of Leisure: A Program Presented by the People's Institute of New York"; "The People's Institute and the Recreational Needs of Greater New York" all in box 7, Committee on Recreation, Printed Matter on the Use of Leisure Time,

People's Institute Collection, Rare Books and Manuscripts Division, New York Public Library, Astor, Lenox and Tilden Foundations; People's Institute, *Seventeenth Annual Report* (New York, 1913–1914), p. 19; Lillian Wald and Social Halls Association, to ——, 11 Sept. 1921, box 29, Lillian D. Wald Collection, Rare Book and Manuscript Library, Columbia University, New York; Wald, *House on Henry Street*, pp. 184–188, 225–227. Kirschner, "Ambiguous Legacy," discusses the "neighborhood ideal."

54. Michael M. Davis, *The Exploitation of Pleasure: A Study of Commercial Recreations in New York City* (New York, n.d.), p. 47; John Collier, "Leisure Time, the Last Problem of Conservation," *Playground* 6 (June 1912): 93–106; New York Public Recreation Commission, *Report* (1912–1913), p. 14.

55. "Social Settlements," in New York Bureau of Labor Statistics, *Eighteenth Annual Report* (1900), p. 265; University Settlement Society of New York, *Report* (New York, 1914), p. 8; New Era Clubs, "The New Era Idea" (n.p., n.d.), box 18, Wald Collection, Columbia University.

56. "H.S.S. on Adolescent Girl" (1913), p. 5, box 94 (Settlements), Wald Collection, Columbia University; University Settlement Society of New York, *Report* (New York, 1912), p. 30.

57. "Memorandum from meeting with Miss Draper," box 7, Community Center Work, People's Institute Collection; *Notes on Community Center Work in School Buildings, Pamphlet No. 1, March 8, 1915*, box 7, Social Center Committee, People's Institute Collection.

58. "Tentative Outline of Work Centering in the Public School Buildings," p. 4, box 7, Committee on Recreation, Printed Matter on the Use of Leisure Time, People's Institute Collection; C. S. Childs, "Proposed Social Center Dance Hall," box 21, Annual Reports, Essays, Reprints and Pamphlets, People's Institute Collection; Woods and Kennedy, *Young Working Girls*, p. 124.

59. University Settlement Society of New York, *Report* (New York, 1912), p. 28; University Settlement Society of New York, *Report* (New York, 1898), p. 50; "P.S. 104, Committee Meeting, April 14," box 7, Committee Center Work and Committee on Recreation, People's Institute Collection.

60. People's Institute, *Eighth Annual Report* (New York, 1905), pp. 10–11.

61. Investigator's Report, P.S. 63, 23 June 1919, Records of the Committee of Fourteen, Rare Books and Manuscripts Division, New York Public Library, Astor, Lenox and Tilden Foundations.

62. Davis, *Exploitation of Pleasure*, p. 34; "The Redemption of Leisure," p. 3, People's Institute Collection; People's Institute, *Twelfth Annual Report* (New York, 1909), p. 26; Lester Francis Scott, "Play-Going for Working

People," clipping from *New Boston* (n.d.), Theater Arts Collection, Lincoln Center Library of the Performing Arts, New York Public Library; Czitrom, "Redemption of Leisure."

63. Simkhovitch, "New Social Adjustment," pp. 86–87.

Conclusion

1. Cyndi Lauper, "Girls Just Want to Have Fun," *She's So Unusual* (Red Sox Music Productions/Portrait Records/CBS Inc., 1983).

2. For the various strands of the women's movement, see Linda Gordon, *Woman's Body, Woman's Right: Birth Control in America* (New York, 1977); June Sochen, *The New Woman in Greenwich Village, 1910–1920* (New York, 1972); Mari Jo Buhle, *Women and American Socialism, 1870–1920* (Urbana, Ill., 1981); William L. O'Neill, *Everyone Was Brave: A History of Feminism in America* (Chicago, 1969).

3. Peter Filene, *Him/Her/Self* (New York, 1974); Elizabeth H. and Joseph H. Pleck, eds., *The American Man* (Englewood Cliffs, N.J., 1980); Ellen Kay Trimberger, "Feminism, Men, and Modern Love: Greenwich Village, 1900–1925," in *Powers of Desire: The Politics of Sexuality,* ed. Ann Snitow et al. (New York, 1983).

4. For a description, see Edward B. Marks, *They All Sang: From Tony Pastor to Rudy Vallee* (New York, 1934).

5. Lewis A. Erenberg, *Steppin' Out: New York Nightlife and the Transformation of American Culture, 1890–1930* (Westport, Conn., 1981); Lary May, *Screening Out the Past: The Birth of Mass Culture and the Motion Picture Industry* (New York, 1980); John Kasson, *Amusing the Million: Coney Island at the Turn of the Century* (New York, 1978).

6. Recent sociological studies of the working-class family include Lee Rainwater et al., *Working-man's Wife* (New York, 1959); Mirra Komarovsky, *Blue-Collar Marriage* (New York, 1967); Lillian Breslow Rubin, *Worlds of Pain: Life in the Working-Class Family* (New York, 1976).

7. The latter possibility is suggested in Roy Rosenzweig, *Eight Hours for What We Will: Workers and Leisure in an Industrial City, 1870–1920* (Cambridge, Eng., 1983), p. 228.

INDEX